Research Series on the Chinese Dream and China's Development Path

Drawing on a large body of empirical studies done over the last two decades, the *Research Series on the Chinese Dream and China's Development Path* seeks to provide its readers with in-depth analyses of the past and present, and forecasts for the future course of China's development. Thanks to the adoption of Socialism with Chinese characteristics, and the implementation of comprehensive reform and opening, China has made tremendous achievements in areas such as political reform, economic development, and social construction, and is making great strides towards the realization of the Chinese dream of national rejuvenation. In addition to presenting a detailed account of many of these achievements, the authors also discuss what lessons other countries can learn from China's experience. This series will be an invaluable companion to every researcher who is trying to gain a deeper understanding of the development model, path and experience unique to China.

More information about this series at http://www.springer.com/series/13571

Yanzhong Wang

Social Security in China: On the Possibility of Equitable Distribution

SSAP

Springer

Yanzhong Wang
The Institute of Ethnology
and Anthropology
Chinese Academy of Social Sciences
Beijing
China

ISSN 2363-6866 ISSN 2363-6874 (electronic)
Research Series on the Chinese Dream and China's Development Path
ISBN 978-981-13-5451-9 ISBN 978-981-10-5643-7 (eBook)
DOI 10.1007/978-981-10-5643-7

Jointly published with Social Sciences Academic Press

The print edition is not for sale in The China Mainland. Customers from The China Mainland please order the print book from: Social Sciences Academic Press.

Printed on acid-free paper

This Springer imprint is published by Springer Nature
The registered company is Springer Nature Singapore Pte Ltd.
The registered company address is: 152 Beach Road, #21-01/04 Gateway East, Singapore 189721, Singapore

Series Preface

Since China's reform and opening began in 1978, the country has come a long way on the path of Socialism with Chinese Characteristics, under the leadership of the Communist Party of China. Over thirty years of reform efforts and sustained spectacular economic growth have turned China into the world's second largest economy, and wrought many profound changes in the Chinese society. These historically significant developments have been garnering increasing attention from scholars, governments and the general public alike around the world since the 1990s, when the newest wave of China studies began to gather steam. Some of the hottest topics have included the so-called "China miracle", "Chinese phenomenon", "Chinese experience", "Chinese path" and the "Chinese model". Home-grown researchers have soon followed suit. Already hugely productive, this vibrant field is putting out a large number of books each year, with Social Sciences Academic Press alone having published hundreds of titles on a wide range of subjects.

Because most of these books have been written and published in Chinese, however, readership has been limited outside China—even amongst many who study China— for whom English is still the lingua franca. This language barrier has been an impediment to efforts by academia, business communities and policy-makers in other countries to form a thorough understanding of contemporary China, of what is distinct about China's past and present may mean not only for her future but also for the future of the world. The need to remove such an impediment is both real and urgent, and the *Research Series on the Chinese Dream and China's Development Path* is my answer to the call.

This series features some of the most notable achievements from the last 20 years by scholars in China in a variety of research topics related to reform and opening. They include both theoretical explorations and empirical studies and cover economy, society, politics, law, culture and ecology, the six areas in which reform and opening policies have had the deepest impact and farthest-reaching consequences for the country. Authors for the series have also tried to articulate their visions of the "Chinese Dream" and how the country can realize it in these fields and beyond.

All of the editors and authors for the *Research Series on the Chinese Dream and China's Development Path* are both long-time students of reform and opening and recognized authorities in their respective academic fields. Their credentials and expertise lend credibility to these books, each of which having been subject to a rigorous peer-review process for inclusion in the series. As part of the Reform and Development Program under the State Administration of Press, Publication, Radio, Film and Television of the People's Republic of China, the series is published by Springer, a Germany-based academic publisher of international repute, and distributed overseas. I am confident that it will help fill a lacuna in studies of China in the era of reform and opening.

Xie Shouguang

Acknowledgements

After a relatively short gestation period, the *Research Series on the Chinese Dream and China's Development Path* has started to bear fruits. We have, first and foremost, the books' authors and editors to thank for making this possible. And it was the hard work by many people at Social Sciences Academic Press and Springer, the two collaborating publishers, that made it a reality. We are deeply grateful to all of them.

Mr. Xie Shouguang, president of Social Sciences Academic Press (SSAP), is the mastermind behind the project. In addition to defining the key missions to be accomplished by it and setting down the basic parameters for the project's execution, as the work has unfolded, Mr. Xie has provided critical input pertaining to its every aspect and at every step of the way. Thanks to the deft coordination by Ms. Li Yanling, all the constantly moving parts of the project, especially those on the SSAP side, are securely held together, and as well synchronized as is feasible for a project of this scale. Ms. Gao Jing, unfailingly diligent and meticulous, makes sure every aspect of each Chinese manuscript meets the highest standards for both publishers, something of critical importance to all subsequent steps in the publishing process. That high-quality if also at times stylistically as well as technically challenging scholarly writing in Chinese has turned into decent, readable English that readers see on these pages is largely thanks to Ms. Liang Fan, who oversees translator recruitment and translation quality control.

Ten other members of the SSAP staff have been intimately involved, primarily in the capacity of in-house editor, in the preparation of the Chinese manuscripts. It is time-consuming work that requires attention to details, and each of them has done this, and is continuing to do this with superb skills. They are, in alphabetical order: Mr. Cai Jihui, Ms. Liu Xiaojun, Mr. Ren Wenwu, Ms. Shi Xiaolin, Ms. Song Yuehua, Mr. Tong Genxing, Ms. Wu Dan, Ms. Yao Dongmei, Ms. Yun Wei and Ms. Zhou Qiong. In addition, Xie Shouguang and Li Yanling have also taken part in this work.

Ms. Song Yuehua is the SSAP in-house editor for the current volume.

Our appreciation is also owed to Ms. Li Yan, Mr. Chai Ning, Ms. Wang Lei and Ms. Xu Yi from Springer's Beijing Representative Office. Their strong support for the SSAP team in various aspects of the project helped to make the latter's work that much easier than it would have otherwise been.

We thank Ms. Chen Xiaoshuang for translating this book. The translation and draft polish process benefited greatly from the consistent and professional coordination service by Beijing Moze International Culture Development Co., Ltd. We thank everyone involved for their hard work.

Last, but certainly not least, it must be mentioned that funding for this project comes from the Ministry of Finance of the People's Republic of China. Our profound gratitude, if we can be forgiven for a bit of apophasis, goes without saying.

Social Sciences Academic Press
Springer

Contents

Prologue: Regulating Income Distribution to Promote Equity and Inclusivity

The Social Security System is a governmental policy tool which could regulate income distribution effectively and promote stability and harmony in a society. As an integral part of the modern system of social governance, the Social Security System plays a prominent role in promoting equality and justice, realizing inclusivity and enhancing solidarity and social cohesion amongst members of society. Therefore, no modern society could afford to disregard the development of Social Security System.

The Role of the Social Security System in Regulating Income Distribution in China

The widening income disparity in China, since the initiation of reform and opening-up, has become a pressing issue that has triggered conflict and debate amongst social circles on the direction of the reform of the Chinese economy. The regulation of income distribution and the narrowing of income disparity between the wealthy and the poor have always been important agendas of the Chinese government under market economy. However, not much impressive results have been achieved. Taxation and the Social Security System are the key institutional arrangements to amend and regulate the income distribution during redistribution in the country. In many countries, compared with taxation, the Social Security System is a more effective way in regulating income distribution. China has seen gradual development of the Social Security System, especially the enlargement of the Social Security Fund in the last decade. The role of the Social Security System in levelling the income disparity in China has begun to be realized.

The Subsistence Allowance System exerts direct influence on the income distribution over a population through the allocation of basic allowances and financial stipends to citizens whose annual income fall below the established poverty line. Through this, the issues of income disparity and poverty are addressed in a systematic and targeted manner. In the early days of the People's Republic of China, the "Five Guarantees System" was established in China for the purpose of providing financial and economic aid to the elderly, the disabled, and children under 16 in the countryside who were incapable of work and whose subsistence was deemed insufficient. In the 1990s, the Subsistence Allowance System was established. As of 2011, 75.825 million urban and rural residents enjoyed subsistence security benefits, in addition to the 5.51 million rural residents that were supported by the "Five Guarantees System" and the 1,93,000 urban residents who had no "source of income, capability of work and/or legal guardian". A total of RMB 144.93 billion was disbursed to support low-income urban and rural residents through social security policies such as the "Five Guarantees System". Accordingly, the income of a beneficiary of the Social Security System increased by RMB 1782 on average, which went directly to improving their standard of living.

A fair and equitable Social Security System plays a significant role in narrowing income disparity. The Social Security System covering pension insurance, medical insurance, work-related injury insurance and unemployment insurance amongst other types of Social Insurance is a risk-sharing mechanism and a deferred compensation system that could be an effective way in tackling income disparity, through the utilization of the law of large numbers. In many countries, the expenditure for Social Insurance like those aforementioned accounted for 1/3 and even 1/2 of fiscal expenditures and 1/5 or even 1/3 of GDP. These levels of fiscal expenditures on Social Insurance have a major impact on income distribution in these countries. According to a survey of beneficiaries conducted in China, income from Social Insurance accounted for 14.5% of the per capita income of the respondents and constituted a significant part in the income of urban and rural beneficiaries and the only source of income for some senior citizens. It has been estimated that Social Insurance income has decreased China's Gini Coefficient by 0.04, suggesting that Social Insurance is playing an active role in bridging the income gap. However, within the system there appears to be significant benefit disparity amongst the beneficiaries and over-high proportion of the fund-accumulation system. This presents counter regulatory to the income distribution. Studies suggest that the intervention of the Pension Insurance System has actually widened the income gap between urban and rural residents. The Housing Fund, Enterprise Annuity, Employee Pension and Medical Insurance have also contributed to the overall income disparity.

Social Welfare ensures that low-income residents can have equal access to public services, which in turn theoretically reduce the income disparity. Social Welfare is therefore not only an integral part of the Social Security System, but also a key part of public services. Apart from the benefits received through the Social Security System by disadvantaged members of society, such as old people, children, women, the disabled and entitled groups, Social Welfare also includes public services enjoyed by the general public as well, such as public education and public health services. Social Welfare guarantees low-income groups equitable access to public services, which means the government purchases public goods for them by utilizing public finance as a means of income transfer. The more comprehensive a country's Social Welfare is, the higher the ability of a government to transfer and regulate the income disparity in a population. Of course, it is important to note that experiences and lessons from other countries with high Social Welfare have demonstrated that lack of proper consideration of economic efficiency and capacity makes Social Welfare considerably unsustainable. In the case of China, Social Welfare remains to be highly insufficient, so enormous efforts are still needed for its development.

Realizing Equity, Inclusivity and Effective Social Governance Through a Bigger Role of the Social Security System

In 2015, the 5th Plenary Session of the 18th CPC Central Committee proposed a new development plan for China's economic growth. The plan stipulates the role of Innovation, Coordination, Green Development, Openness and Inclusivity in driving economic growth for the country. This new development plan proposes a new objective and orientation of the Social Security System in China. The goals of Social Security System are to firstly play a role in building a moderately prosperous society and to act as a safeguard against economic turmoil. Secondly, more efforts were needed to deepen the reform to develop a fairer and more sustainable Social Security System, and let it play the role of promoting equity, inclusivity and social governance.

Firstly, the Social Security System must be able to cover all members of society. The rapid development of industrialization and urbanization has substantially improved the living conditions of humankind. However, there are also people that are left behind and are suffering economic hardships. It happens in any society, even the highly developed ones. These disadvantaged sectors of society are unable to alleviate their hardships without external intervention. Social Welfare is an institutional policy that helps alleviate the problem of these aforementioned sectors. Its role is not only to provide for basic subsistence income, but also to provide residents with a sense of security so as to allow them to participate in a social life without distractions. This is a fundamental condition for a society to realize effective governance.

Secondly, the Social Security System needs to provide support for the government to perform social management and offer public services. As state governance systems continuously improve, the boundary between the government, markets, and the society becomes clearer. In most countries, governments have reduced their functions of governance to macroeconomic regulation, market supervision, social management, and public services. Unlike other types of public services, Social Welfare is a system that is difficult to realize proper self-regulation based on market mechanism. Therefore, in most countries, the Social Security System is a legal institution implemented with government mandate and oversight. In these countries, Social Welfare takes up not only a substantial part of government expenditure, but also the largest amount of manpower and material resources.

Thirdly, as an important measure of macroeconomic regulation, the Social Security System should play an active role in guiding consumption and regulating supply. With economic development, many countries have gradually extended the role of Social Welfare from economic security to a tool to improve the quality of life and the value of human capital of its residents. Social security expenditure is expanding in terms of scale and becomes a policy instrument affecting macroeconomic. In the perspective of the government, Social Welfare is a part of fiscal expenditure (or fiscal expenditure in a broad sense), laying restraints on the government's financial resources. For a society, these expenditures are a part of social consumption, laying restraints on production capacity of a society. In the perspective of individuals, Social Welfare is a part of income affecting their decisions on labour supply decisions and consumption patterns and thus becoming a significant variable for national macroeconomic regulation.

Fourthly, the Social Security System should be utilized as a tool to enhance social solidarity and stability. A feature of a modern society is the promotion of independence and self-determination. As a result, Chinese social traditions based on family kinship and regional allegiances for group reliance are gradually weakening. This individualization of the society is being supported by the Social Security System, where mutual assistance and the distribution of responsibilities are emphasized instead of the traditional Chinese social traditions. Though the public have certain interest in national interests, they care more about issues closely related to their own interest, such as retirement pension, health care and employment. Social Security is not only a major issue for the democratic election of a country, but also a basic system bonding individuals.

Lastly, the Social Security System could also show the advantages of the socialist institution with Chinese features. Against the backdrop of globalization, the competition amongst countries is not only reflected in its productivity, but also at the standard of living and a welfare system. Under transnational capital flows, though excessive welfare may become a negative factor for the competitiveness of a country's labour costs, a sound Social Security System may reflect a profound respect for human capital and constitutes a more competitive factor other than just cheap labour. It could be seen through comparison that highly competitive countries tend to be those who enjoy a mature Social Security System, where people enjoy a better quality of life.

The 13th Five-Year Plan (2016–2020) is going to be a critical period for the goal of building a Moderately Prosperous Society, where the Social Security System will play an important role. According to *Suggestions on Making the 13th Five-Year Plan for Economic and Social Development* issued by the CPC Central Committee, during the 13th Five-Year Plan, a more equitable and sustainable Social Security System should be established. The development of the Social Security System will not only focus on the expansion of coverage and the enlargement of the Welfare Fund, but also priority the refinement of the equitability, sustainability and inclusivity of the Social Security System.

The effective functioning of the Social Security System depends heavily on the improvement of the governance of the system itself. The development of the Social Security System should also include the modernization of its governance, where there should be legal support, government supervision, professionalization and wide social participation. The creation of a legal framework for the Social Security System should be accelerated, so as to allow for the designation of administrative functions and the establishment of professional and independent Social Welfare agencies to provide convenient and efficient welfare services. A multiple evaluation system of the social security should be established, which covers the governments, executive agencies, professional agencies and the society. The Social Security System should also encourage public participation in the supervision and evaluation of the system, and actively conduct satisfaction surveys amongst all of its stakeholders.

More external support and reform motivation are needed for continuous improvement of the Social Security System. We should further step up fiscal input in social security. There should be an established mechanism designed to adjust benefits according to the needs of urban and rural, low- and middle-income groups, as well as central and western regions. We should further improve the institutional design, especially the design of the public service and basic security system, mainly focusing on the needs of middle- and low-income population and poverty-stricken population. National coordination should be pursued to realize an urban employee's basic pension insurance system. Provincial coordination should also be realized for the urban employee's basic medical insurance. Other components of the basic Social Insurance System should also be coordinated and enhanced accordingly.

In the implementation of the Social Security System, proper adjustment of the premium rate of benefit should be established. It is also suggested that the option of having a flexible benefit rates should also be explored. The development plan also proposes increased social coordination and the reduction of the contribution ratio of personal accounts in the system, whilst improving the level of benefits targeting low-income groups through establishing a differentiated benefit adjustment mechanism based on the gradual improvement of overall benefits. Furthermore, it has been proposed that further streamlining of the system's bureaucracy should be placed in order to bring about greater equity and efficiency in the operation of the system. It has also been suggested that more effort needs to be channelled towards the development of the Social Security System with a particular focus on the Social Welfare such as education and health care.

To summarize, the Social Security System is a basic economic system and a modern system of social governance for modern countries. With the promotion of industrialization and democratization, its function and influence will eventually expand to various fields of social and economic management and become an integral part of the state's system of governance. Therefore, it should be given more attention to ensuring that the Social Security System is more equitable and sustainable. Additionally, Social Welfare should be based on China's domestic needs and requirements and not just the replication of foreign systems of Social Welfare. As a vehicle for the promotion of social equity and inclusivity, the Social Security System will play a prominent role in building a modern China.[1]

---

[1]This prologue is based on "Bring into Play the Role of Social Security in Regulating Income Distribution" (*People's Daily*, April 3, 2013), with some additional contents.

Chapter 1
The Development of China's Social Welfare System

It was acknowledged in the 17th CPC National Congress that China should channel substantial effort into constructing projects for improving the livelihood of the people by building a harmonious socialist country, which "ensures that all citizens enjoy the right to education, employment, medical care, elderly care, and housing". These projects cover employment, education, medical care, housing, social security, social welfare and social work, which are all contained within the social welfare system in a broad sense. The social welfare system in this report mainly covers social security affairs such as social assistance, labor insurance, social insurance, medical insurance, and social welfare sponsored mainly by the government. For the purpose of discussing the relationship between the social welfare system and urbanization, this report also covers aspects of the social welfare system in a wider sense such as education and housing.

1.1 The Preliminary Establishment of the Chinese Social Welfare System Framework

The establishment and development of the social welfare system in modern China occurred during two periods before and after reform. However, the beginning of the second period was not exactly equivalent to the year 1978 when the reform of the economic system began. The first period mainly consisted of three stages, namely the establishment of a framework (1949–1956), uneven development (1958–1978) and reconstruction (1978–1985). The first stage was a phase in which China's socialist economic system gradually became established, and large-scale industrial construction was conducted under the planned economic system. The building of economic infrastructure and a relatively stable social environment enabled the recovery and development of cities and accelerated urbanization. In 1949, China only had an urban population of 57.65 million, accounting for 10.164% of the total

Y. Wang, *Social Security in China: On the Possibility of Equitable Distribution*,
Research Series on the Chinese Dream and China's Development Path,
DOI 10.1007/978-981-10-5643-7_1

national population, which rose to 99.49 million and 15.139% respectively in 1957. However, after the establishment of the household registration system upon the promulgation of the "Regulations of the People's Republic of China on Household Registration" in 1958, the spontaneous migration of rural households to cities for employment and living was no longer permitted, which, in addition to the great fluctuation in economic growth during the "Great Leap Forward" and the "Cultural Revolution", seriously constrained the urbanization of the rural population. During the period between 1958 and 1978 the total urban population (not of rural households) increased from 107.21 million to 172.45 million, with a growth of about 65 million people. However, because these people mainly resulted from the natural growth of the urban population, the urbanization rate during the same period experienced weak growth increasing from 16.125% in 1958 to 17.192% in 1978, with a decline in urbanization over certain periods (1963, 1965–1972, and 1974).

Though the seeds of the welfare system of modern society preceded the process of urbanization driven by industrialization, the process of urbanization was undoubtedly one of the key factors leading to the formation and development of the welfare system of modern society. Land and family played the role of an economic and social safeguard in agricultural society with little fluctuation. However, this is impossible for urban residents, who without land or stable employment and with increasingly smaller family sizes, instead, require a more stable and socialized social security and benefit system to address such social risks as illness, old age and unemployment. In fact, the establishment of a socialized social security and benefit system began the very first day the People's Republic of China (PRC) was founded.

The PRC was confronted with several basic problems in its early days: first, the settlement of wounded and disabled soldiers; second, unemployed urban residents who had been seriously affected by an extended period of war and turmoil; and third, a large number of victims of various natural disasters. The "Common Program of the Chinese People's Political Consultative Conference" promulgated in 1949 stated that "dependents of those who have given their lives for the revolution and of members of the revolutionary forces, who are in need, shall receive preferential treatment from the state and from society. The people's government shall make appropriate arrangements for disabled or retired servicemen who participated in the revolutionary war, providing them with means of livelihood or occupations." This provision, in effect, laid a foundation for China to establish a social security system for servicemen centering on veteran benefit and placement in China. As for the large number of unemployed workers in cities, the government relied mainly on the development of production for job placements as well as providing temporary relief to families living in extreme poverty. In 1950, the Government Administration Council introduced the "Instruction on Relieving Unemployed Workers", and the Ministry of Labor introduced the "Interim Measures for Relieving Unemployed Workers", which served as prototypes for a modern unemployment insurance system to be established in China. In 1951, the Government Administration Council promulgated the "Regulations of the People's Republic of China on Labor Insurance", which, after two revisions in 1953 and 1956, comprehensively established a labor insurance system suitable for urban employees. This system, which resolved the main risks and concerns of urban workers, was one of the most fundamental social systems meeting the demands of urbanization, and therefore became the most important of all social security systems established in the early years of the PRC.[1] Besides the labor insurance system established for enterprise employees, the state gradually established systems such as "medical services at state expenses" and "retirement and resignation" for employees in government departments and public institutions. As to victims of natural disasters spread across rural areas, the PRC established guidelines for disaster relief from the very first day it was founded to take up the responsibility for social relief. In December 1949, the Government Administration Council promulgated the "Instruction on Disaster Relief", and established the Central Disaster Relief Committee to handle disaster relief throughout the country. This responsibility was later succeeded by the Ministry of Internal Affairs (currently the Ministry of Civil Affairs) and has continued to the present as long-term work and basic work for China's social relief system. In addition to the social relief system, China established a "five guarantees system" addressing the elderly, disabled and children under 16 in rural areas, incapable of working and whose subsistence is not guaranteed in the "Constitution on Advanced Agricultural Cooperatives" adopted in 1956. During this period, the central government or relevant departments issued a series of regulatory documents addressing problems such as employment benefits, social welfare services, welfare factories and allowances for those living in straitened circumstances. Over several years' of continued effort, the PRC preliminarily established a basic framework for relieving poverty-stricken urban and rural residents as well as victims of natural disasters, focusing on labor insurance for enterprise employees, supplemented by veteran benefits and placements and state guarantees for public employees.

1.2 Uneven Development of China's Social Welfare Services

In the two decades between 1958 and 1978, China's social security and welfare system was constantly developing and expanding along with a zigzag process of socialist economic construction. In view of the construction of the social insurance system, a major development was initiated with the establishment of the employees' retirement pension system. In 1957 and 1958, the State Council introduced the "Interim Regulations on the Retirement Treatment of Workers and Employees" and the "Interim Regulations on the Resignation Treatment of Workers and Employees" to establish a retirement pension system for enterprise employees and workers. However, as large-scale industrialization was at the heart of its inception, old-age

[1]Zheng Gongcheng et al., *China's Social Security System: Change and Evaluation*, China Renmin University Press, 2002, p. 4.

security was not a serious problem. Due to the ups and downs of the political environment and the economic development at the time, certain new characteristics appeared in the construction of the social security system, particularly reflected in the rapid development of health and education.

The development of healthcare security and healthcare services during this period greatly improved the health of all citizens. By using the establishment of the planned economic system for mass mobilization and vigorously developing the patriotic health campaign, China established an urban-rural triple healthcare service network and an urban-rural healthcare security system consisting of the free healthcare system, the labor healthcare system and the cooperative healthcare service. These covered the overwhelming majority of the population. Meanwhile, the government, through planning and budgeting, strictly controlled the conduct of public hospitals. In addition to drug pricing, a mechanism to balance medical care and drugs was established to ensure that the medical service system "provided basic medical services to all people in the country at a low cost".[2] Despite the failure of a backward economy to relieve China from the shortage of medical services and drugs, the development of medical security and health services greatly improved the health of urban and rural residents, and life expectancy rose from 34 years of age in the early days after the PRC was founded to over 60 years of age.

Meanwhile, the development of education services improved people's level of education. Education occupies an important position in the social welfare system. Despite the historical tradition of valuing education in China, literate and educated people often accounted for a very small portion in the total population. In 1949, 80% of the population of China was illiterate, the enrollment rate of elementary schools and junior middle schools was only 20 and 6% respectively, and there were only 117 thousand students in institutes of higher education.[3] The education of the urban and rural population was continuously improved by vigorously developing education services and with the campaign for wiping out illiteracy. In the second national census, those with college education background amounted to 2.8715 million, 2416 times that of 1949; the number of people receiving elementary and secondary education also enjoyed a huge growth. However, the illiterate population above 13 years of age still accounted for 38% of the total population. The educational cause was subjected to a tremendous blow during the "Cultural Revolution", with a significant decline in the quality of higher education, however elementary and secondary education still saw substantial development. According to the third national census in 1982, the ratio of illiterate and semi-illiterate members of the population was reduced from 38.11% in 1964 to 23.15%, while the number of people who received elementary and secondary education rose substantially.

---

[2]Liu, Xiaomei (2009). The Reform of China's Social Security System: Direction and Comments. In Yoshinori Hiroi and ShenJie (Eds.), *The Social Security System in China and Japan: Comparison and Reference* (p. 55). Beijing: China Labor and Social Security Press.

[3]CPC Party Group of the Ministry of Education: People's Education Builds a Solid Foundation for China: Great Achievements in the Development and Reform of Education in New China over Six Decades, *Qiu Shi*, Vol. 19, 2009.

However, the development of the social security and welfare systems during this period was influenced by frequent abrupt changes in the political environment, the economic plan system and economic and social policies. With regards to China's social welfare system, several institutional changes during this period exerted tremendous and far-reaching effects: First, household registration systems were established. To safeguard the implementation of the national industrialization strategy and prevent the free migration of a huge rural population to cities and towns, the state established the household registration system in urban and rural areas in 1958. This classified the population of China into rural and non-rural households. The establishment of the household registration system artificially divided China's social welfare system and labor market into two blocks, urban and rural, resulting in a typical "binary social" system on the basis of the "binary economy" of a developing country. Second, the social security system became unit-based and closed. During the "Cultural Revolution", the economy and social management became locked in turmoil. In 1968, the Ministry of Internal Affairs, which was in charge of social relief and social welfare, was removed, the Labor Union responsible for labor insurance affairs was paralyzed and the labor department became impaired. As a result, the government had difficulties maintaining the effective operation of the social security system. In February 1969, the Ministry of Finance issued "Opinions on the Reform of Several Systems in the Financial Work of State-Owned Enterprises", which provided that the drawing of labor insurance funds all be suspended in state-owned enterprises, and the labor insurance premiums originally spent as labor insurance funds be converted to enterprises' non-operating expenditures. From then on, the social security system was only able to rely on a number of units and organizations for maintenance, "labor insurance was deprived of the coordination mechanism to turn it into an enterprise or unit security system", while the monopoly of such social affairs by urban enterprises and institutions expanded rapidly. As a result, social security, to a very large extent, turned into "a self-enclosed and unit-based system".[4] In connection with the household registration system and the unit security system were the system of commodity price allowance, the system of public housing and the system of unit welfare for urban residents. The commodity price allowance was for urban residents, while public housing and unit welfare were mainly provided to employees in urban state-owned enterprises and institutions. The lack of adequate price flexibility and supply stimulus led to serious shortage of various goods, especially housing. Social relief thus became very limited, only addressing extremely impoverished people "without economic income, labor capacity or supporters" and disaster-stricken people. Third, China at that time believed unemployment did not exist under the socialist system in place and did not admit the presence of unemployment; therefore no unemployment insurance system was established at that time.

---

[4]Zheng Gongcheng et al., *China's Social Security System: Change and Evaluation*, Renmin University of China Press, 2002, p. 7.

1.3 The Recovery, Adjustment and Pilot Reform of China's Social Welfare Services

During this period, the construction of China's social welfare system underwent three phases: the recovery and adjustment stage (1978–1986), the exploratory reform stage (1986–1993) and the pilot reform stage for the combination of social pooling and individual accounts (1993–1997).

(1) The recovery and adjustment of the social security system. The Third Plenary Session of the Eleventh CPC Central Committee held at the end of 1978 marked the start of a new era of reform and opening-up in China. This year is generally taken as the starting point for the reform of the economic system. However, for the social security system, the Third Plenary Session of the Eleventh CPC Central Committee did not mean the beginning of reform, as the system had largely recovered and reconstruction had taken place for some time by then. In 1978, the State Council promulgated the "Interim Measures of the State Council on Assisting Old, Weak, Sick and Disabled Cadres" and the "Interim Measures of the State Council Concerning the Retirement and Resignation of Workers", which restored the provisions on retirement benefits. During the same year, the Ministry of Civil Affairs and the Ministry of Finance re-issued the "Measures on the Management and Use of Pension and Relief Operating Expenses", which led to the recovery of the pension and relief system; in 1979, the pension standard was raised. However, the significant increase of retiring employees led to an increasingly serious conflict between old and new enterprises with uneven burdens caused by the increase in retirement payments and the direct payment by enterprises. To address the imbalance of social security burdens among state-owned enterprises, a pilot reform on social pooling for retirement and resignation payments for employees of state-owned enterprises was conducted in a number of cities and counties in Guangdong, Jiangsu, Fujian and Liaoning provinces in 1984. The scope of pooling was limited mainly to state-owned enterprises in municipal or county first-level administrative areas. In line with the principle of ratifying expenditures according to revenues on a balanced budget with a small surplus, uniform collection and issuance of old-age pensions and the uniform management of employees' old-age support were implemented. To relieve the problem of too rapid an increase of medical expenses, some enterprises conducted pilot reforms on lump-sum payments of medical expenses with regards to labor insurance medical care. In 1985, the "Proposal of the CPC Central Committee on Formulating the Seventh Five-Year Plan for the National Economy and Social Development" clearly put forward, for the first time, the concept of "social security", and gave the umbrella name of social security system to such systems as social insurance, social welfare, social relief and veteran benefits and placement.

(2) The exploratory reform of the social security system. The main developments of the social security system during this period included: the establishment of an unemployment insurance system. With the gradual deepening of the reform of state-owned enterprises, enterprises urgently needed to establish an independent employment mechanism and had to establish a social security system for employees' withdrawal. In 1986, the State Council promulgated the "Interim Regulations on Unemployment Insurance of Employees in State-owned Enterprises", which introduced the labor contract system and the unemployment insurance system in state-owned enterprises. The applicable scope of unemployment insurance was small, as the unemployment insurance system was implemented only among newly recruited contract workers. During the reform of the old-age pension insurance system, the "Interim Regulations on the Implementation of the Labor Contract System among State-owned Enterprises" issued by the State Council in 1986 stated: an enterprise shall submit 15% of the total wages of workers into the labor contract system as an old-age pension fund for contract workers, and such workers shall also submit 3% of their standard wages as old-age pension premiums. This was the introduction of individual premium payments into China's social insurance system. In 1991, the State Council issued the "Decision on the Reform of the Old-age Insurance System of Enterprise Employees", which stated that social pooling for retirement pay be implemented, with a gradual transition from municipal and county pooling to provincial pooling. Meanwhile, the conception of multi-level old-age support was put forward for "gradually integrating basic old-age insurance with enterprises' supplementary old-age insurance and employees' individual savings old-age insurance". Besides local pooling, some industries also attempted to implement pooling in the old-age insurance industry. By 1993, 11 industries had implemented pooling for the old-age insurance industry. To gradually establish a socialized old-age support system in rural areas, the Ministry of Civil Affairs implemented rural social old-age insurance pilot projects in rural areas in 1986, and promulgated the "Basic Plan for Rural Social Old-age Insurance at County Levels (for trial implementation)" in 1992, which marked the inception of the rural social old-age insurance system. With regards to medical security, some cities conducted various forms of reform on the free medical care system and the labor medical system successively. To overcome the difficulty of a single enterprise paying employees' medical expenses, some cities started to implement social pooling for medical expenses of enterprise employees with serious illnesses, and some places implemented social pooling for the medical expenses of retirees, in an attempt to relieve enterprises from the difficulty of paying medical expenses for employees who suffered from serious illness. On the whole, the reform of the social security system at this stage, which was mainly for the purpose of supporting the reform of state-owned enterprises, was only attempted at a local level, without fundamentally affecting the old system for social security.

(3) Pilot reform for the combination of social pooling and individual accounts. In 1993, the Third Plenary Session of the Fourteenth CPC Central Committee, in the "Decision on Several Issues Concerning the Establishment of the Socialist Market Economic System", acknowledged the social security system to be an important part for the construction of China's socialist market economic framework, marking the transition of the reform of China's social security system from supporting the reform of state-owned enterprises to serving the development of a socialist market economic system. The "Decision on Several Issues Concerning the Establishment of the Socialist Market Economic System" also proposed that an employees' basic old-age insurance system and basic medical insurance system by "integrating social pooling and individual accounts" be established according to China's national conditions, for which a diverse number of pilot reform projects were conducted. In 1995, the State Council launched two reform plans for the local development of pilot projects of a new old-age insurance system. Plan I was inclined towards focusing on individual accounts, while Plan II was inclined towards focusing on social pooling. Each place selected different plans for their respective pilot projects. Some places even managed to invent a Plan III and a Plan IV. As a result, such projects were not uniform, provoking great controversy. With regards to the reform of the medical security system, the State Council selected Zhenjiang, Jiangsu Province and Jiujiang, Jiangxi Province for conducting pilot projects in 1994. The two cities successively formulated and implemented a new mode of medical insurance "combining social pooling and individual accounts," this expanded the scope for the implementation of medical social insurance, established a stable fund raising mechanism, enhanced socialization of medical insurance and brought the rapid increase of medical expenses under control.[5] The coverage of pilot projects gradually expanded. During this period, development was achieved in the construction of other social security projects. In 1994, the Ministry of Labor promulgated the "Provisional Measures for Maternity Insurance of Enterprise Employees", which stated that social pooling shall also be implemented for maternity insurance.[6] In 1996, the Ministry of Labor introduced the "Provisional Measures for Work-related Injury Insurance of Enterprise Employees", with which the work-related injury social insurance system was gradually developed. Some cities established the system of minimum subsistence for urban residents, gradually expanding the coverage from "households of the five guarantees system" to all members of society who lived under the "minimum living standard". During this period, the rural social old-age insurance system also saw rapid developments.

[5]Wang Yanzhong, ShenZhiyu and Du Yingfen, The "Double Jiang" Mode in the Reform of the Medical Insurance System, *China Industrial Economics*, Vol. 7, 1999.

[6]Pan Jintang, The Social Security System for Females in China: Evolution and Evaluation, in Zheng Gongcheng et al., *China's Social Security System: Change and Evaluation*, Renmin University of China Press, 2002, p. 281.

1.4 From Unit Security to Social Security: "Three Lines of Security" and "Two Guarantees"

Since the 1990s, China has been confronted with the increasingly serious problem of unemployment, laid-off workers and urban poverty. Alongside the constant rise of urban employment during this period, the number of traditionally employed persons (urban employees) fell continuously. The number of urban employees was reduced from its largest point in 1995 by 44.16 million to its smallest in 2003, (while a small uptrend began in 2004). The major factor attributing to the sharp reduction of the number of urban employees was the laying off of employees in state-owned enterprises and collective enterprises in the course of restructuring the economic system and adjusting the economic structure. In a short period of over ten years, the number of jobholders in state-owned and collective units was reduced by 77.84 million (the number of employees dropped by 75.34 million). This adjustment of the economic and employment structure is the largest of its kind in the history of mankind. The years of 1997 and 1998 after the outbreak of the economic crisis in Asia were the two years which saw the most drastic adjustment of the economic and employment structures in China, during which 32.39 million jobholders in state-owned and collective units were laid-off (including 31.93 million employees). The way in which to address such a severe peak of unemployment became a formidable challenge facing the Chinese government.

China, in the course of restructuring the economic system and adjusting the economic structure, implemented a certain number of reforms on the traditional unit-based security system. From the 1990s onwards, China began to define the reform of the unit security system and gradually developed a socialized social security system. The "Decision on the Reform of the Old-age Pension System of Enterprise Employees" promulgated in 1991 initiated the reform of the old-age insurance system for employees in state-owned enterprises. From 1993 onwards, some cities gradually established a system of minimum subsistence for urban residents with wider coverage and higher guarantee standards than the "Five Guarantees" relief system. In the "Decision on Several Issues Concerning the Establishment of a Socialist Market Economic System", such reform attempts were defined as establishing a multi-level social security system commensurate with the socialist market economic system, including the social insurance system and the social relief system etc. Centering on the above objectives, the Chinese government conducted pilot reforms on the basic old-age insurance system and the basic medical insurance system for urban employees in the early 1990s, and gradually established the unemployment insurance system ("waiting for work" was changed to "unemployed" in 1994, and it was not until 1999 that the unemployment insurance system was officially established), work-related injury insurance, maternity insurance and the system of minimum subsistence for urban residents were established. However, these newly established social security systems, which were small in scale, could hardly address all of the security needs of such large numbers of laid-off employees from state-owned and collective enterprises at one time. For example, of the 5.53 million registered unemployed people and 8.15 million laid-off employees nationwide in 1996, only 3.31 million people could receive unemployment insurance payments and benefits, accounting for only 24% of all laid-off employees in that year; in 1997, only 3.19 million people could receive unemployment insurance payments and benefits, accounting for only 26% of all the laid-off employees in that year. In 1996 and 1997, the urban residents receiving subsistence allowances totaled only 850,000 and 880,000 respectively, far fewer than the population stricken by poverty (totaling about 20 million). As for weak enterprises with difficulties which did not participate in the basic old-age insurance scheme, their retirees could not receive any or the full amount of old-age pension from the basic old-age insurance system. Thus, the unemployment insurance system, the system of minimum subsistence for urban residents, and the basic old-age insurance system for enterprise employees in their preliminary forms could only partly resolve the severe problems of unemployment, urban poverty as well as the timely and full payment of old-age pensions.

These problems were not only related to the basic life and immediate interests of tens of millions of people, but were also directly related to social stability and to the crucial tasks of economic system transformation and economic structure adjustment in the context of an economic crisis in Asia. Special policies had to be implemented over special periods. The "Three Lines of Security" were launched against these backdrops.

The Three Lines of Security mean the following three systems: basic living allowance for laid-off employees of state-owned enterprises, unemployment insurance and the system of minimum subsistence for urban residents, of which the most unique was the basic living allowance for laid-off employees of state-owned enterprises.

"Laid-off employees" was a special term coined in the 1990s in China. Despite the fact that laid-off employees were found in the early 1990s, it was not until 1997 that China started to publish the number of laid-off employees each year successively from 1997. From 1996 to 2000, the total number of laid-off employees was close to 10 million a year, far exceeding the number of registered unemployed persons. The annual amount of laid-off employees from state-owned enterprises, who constituted the bulk of laid-off employees, also exceeded the number of registered unemployed persons. Therefore, the significance of successfully ensuring the subsistence of laid-off employees from state-owned enterprises was no better than the establishment of an independent unemployment security system. This was a transitional measure with Chinese characteristics. To complete the task of downsizing for enhancing efficiency, the state provided several main preferential policies to laid-off employees from state-owned enterprises. Laid-off employees could receive a basic living allowance and their former enterprises were obliged to buy varied kinds of social insurance for them, and in the case that they were re-employed or self-employed they were entitled to certain preferential policies such as tax reduction or exemption. Preferential treatment regarding industrial and commercial registration, and credit preference was also given. The prerequisite for any laid-off employee to receive the above security was that they should enter the re-employment service center, which was a custodian agency for laid-off employees, funded by public finance, enterprises and society (unemployment insurance), including an annual subsidy of about RMB 10 billion from state revenues. According to policy regulations, laid-off employees should sign an agreement upon entering the "center" and could remain at the "center" for a period of three years at most. This was because the labor relationship with their respective enterprises had to be terminated after three years, and those failing to be re-employed would be transferred to unemployment insurance. Thanks to stable funding, the subsistence of laid-off employees was secured, and the number of people with security accounted for about 95% of the total number of laid-off employees in state-owned enterprises. The re-employment service center was not only responsible for the subsistence of laid-off employees from state-owned enterprises but also actively conducted re-employment training and provided job referral services so that 1/3-1/2 of laid-off employees were re-employed.

In the course of establishing a subsistence security system for laid-off employees, China rapidly improved the unemployment insurance system and the system of minimum subsistence for urban residents as top priorities in the establishment of a socialized social security system. In January 1999, the State Council introduced the "Regulations on Unemployment Insurance", which changed "insurance for those awaiting employment" to "unemployment insurance" and "relief payment for those awaiting employment" to "unemployment insurance benefits"; the coverage of unemployment insurance expanded from state-owned enterprises to various urban enterprises and institutions, the proportion of payment of unemployment insurance premiums was raised (the proportion paid by the employer increased from 1% of the total salary to 2%), an individual payment was added (1% of the individual's salary), and the payment standard and terms of unemployment insurance benefits were provided for. The standard of unemployment insurance benefits was lower than the local minimum wage and higher than the minimum subsistence level of local urban residents, and the period in which one could receive payment was no longer than 24 months. The "Interim Regulations on the Collection of Social Insurance Premiums" promulgated at the same time further defined the coverage and payment obligors of unemployment insurance, to ensure the affordability of unemployment benefits. The promulgation and implementation of the "Regulations on Unemployment Insurance" provided institutional and funding security for laid-off employees "leaving the center".

Meanwhile, to settle the problems regarding livelihood of many poverty-stricken urban residents, such as laid-off workers, people waiting for work, and old people with a long period of retirement, in September 1997, the State Council promulgated the "Circular on Establishing the System of Minimum Subsistence for Urban Residents Throughout the Country", which required that this system be established in all cities and county seats nationwide by the end of 1999. On the basis of summarizing the work experience of various places in establishing the minimum subsistence system, the State Council introduced the "Regulations on the Minimum

Subsistence for Urban Residents" in September 1999, which specified the relief principle of the minimum subsistence system, providing full relief to impoverished people "without income, labor capacity or supporters" according to the minimum subsistence standard and making up for the gap between a family's average per capita income and the local minimum subsistence standard for those urban residents with regular income. To effectively address the difficulties faced by impoverished citizens, the state raised the standard of the minimum subsistence level and fiscal support. By March 2000, 3.01 million impoverished urban residents were covered by the minimum subsistence system, including 2.36 million enterprise employees, unemployed and retired persons (accounting for 78% of the total population covered by security).

In order for the three guarantee systems (basic living allowance for laid-off employees of state-owned enterprises, unemployment insurance and minimum subsistence for urban residents) to function effectively, the State Council launched a series of policies and regulations for establishing and improving the social security system from 1997 to 1999. These systems, together with the Three Lines of Security, became important measures for resisting the impact of the Asian economic crisis in 1997, boosting domestic demand and curbing deflation, and supporting the reform of state-owned enterprises. To make sure that the above regulations and measures played an effective role, the government further defined the policy of "Two Guarantees". This guaranteed that laid-off employees from state-owned enterprises entering the re-employment service center could receive their basic living allowance on time and that the center would pay social insurance premiums on their behalf and also guaranteed that the basic old-age pensions for enterprise retirees in the old-age insurance plan be issued on time and in full.

The policy of "Three Lines of Security" and "Two Guarantees" made a great contribution to China's coping successfully with the unemployment and lay-off peak in the mid and late 1990s. In the year 2000, for example, 3.3 million unemployed people in China received unemployment insurance benefits, about 6.5 million laid-off employees of state-owned enterprises received living allowance, and over 3 million poor urban residents enjoyed the minimum subsistence allowance. These people amounted to over 12 million, accounting for about 6% of the total number of urban citizens in employment. Of them, the number of people receiving unemployment insurance benefits and living allowances for laid-off employees was close to 10 million, exceeding the total number of laid-off and unemployed persons in cities by 60%. Thus, the basic living conditions of the above-mentioned poorer members of society was well guaranteed, social stability was maintained, and economic system restructuring and economic structure adjustments were facilitated. This made a positive contribution to China's coping with the difficult situation of a substantial decline in exports and sluggish economic growth in the aftermath of the Asian economic crisis, resulting in the recovery of high-speed growth of China's economy and to China's preparation for its accession to the WTO.

1.5 Gradually Establishing the Basic Framework of a Modern Social Security System

From 1997 onwards, with the construction of the social security system, China accelerated the formulation and implementation of laws and regulations on social insurance, social assistance, social welfare and rural social security, which marked the transition of the social security reform from pilot reforms to institutional construction. With over ten years of work, the basic framework of a modern social security system was preliminarily established.

With regards to old-age insurance, the State Council introduced the "Decision on Establishing a Uniform Basic Old-age Insurance System for Enterprise Employees" in July 1997, which unified the payment ratios of enterprises and individual employees, unified the scale of individual accounts, and unified the measures for the calculation and payment of basic old-age pensions, marking the start of the unification stage of basic old-age insurance for urban enterprise employees in China. In 2005, the policy for insurance participation and the premium payment of urban self-employed individuals and laborers of flexible employment was unified,[7] the method for calculation and payment of basic old-age pensions was reformed, and the pilot scope of fully funding individual accounts which began in Liaoning Province in 2001 was expanded. Meanwhile, the state actively developed enterprise annuity, promoted the reform of social old-age insurance systems in government departments and public institutions as well as in rural areas, and explored the establishment of an old-age insurance system for rural areas, land-requisitioned farmers and rural migrant workers in cities.

In terms of medical security, the State Council promulgated the "Decision on Establishing a Basic Medical Insurance System for Urban Employees" in 1998, which defined the mode of combining social pooling and individual accounts for basic medical insurance and provided that all employees in urban units should partake in basic medical insurance. To cope with the diverse forms of employment, the coverage of basic medical insurance extended to all employed people in cities in 2003 and 2004. To address the medical security problems of urban residents, choosing not to be employed, pilot projects on the basic medical insurance system for urban residents began in 2007. The pilot implementation of new rural co-operative medical care in the second half of 2003 covered 2679 counties (only 50 counties were not covered), and 810.4 million rural residents (accounting for 91% of the total rural population). Meanwhile, the state sponsored the establishment of medical subsidies for civil servants and subsidies for large-sum medical bills, enterprise supplementary medical insurance and urban and rural medical assistance systems.

---

[7]From 2001, pilot projects on substantiating personal accounts started in Liaoning; by the end of 2006, such pilot projects had been conducted in 11 provinces and regions nationwide, and a personal accounts fund of RMB 48.5 billion had been substantiated. See Basic Conditions of Social Insurance in China, *China Labor Insurance News*, November 30, 2007.

In terms of unemployment security, the State Council promulgated the "Regulations on Unemployment Insurance" in 1999, which marked the gradual transition of China's unemployment security system towards a law-based track. The coverage of unemployment insurance began to expand from state-owned enterprises to all urban enterprises and public institutions including state-owned enterprises, private enterprises and other enterprises. The unemployment insurance system, together with the subsistence security system for laid-off employees and the minimum subsistence system for urban residents established at that time, constituted the "three lines of security" for unemployed people in cities, especially the large number of laid-off workers, and played an active role in addressing the laying-off of a large number of redundant employees in state-owned enterprises during the period of system transformation and structural adjustment.

In terms of work-related injury and maternity insurance, the State Council promulgated the "Regulations on Work-related Injury Insurance" in 2003, which established the basic framework of China's work-related injury insurance system by stating that all types of enterprises, institutions and non-profit organizations must establish a work-related injury insurance system for their employees, that the work-related injury insurance premiums shall be paid by employers and the system of combining work-related injury prevention, work-related injury compensation and work-related injury rehabilitation shall be practiced. During the same period, the participation rate continued to rise and coverage of maternity insurance continued to expand. Especially worth mentioning was the establishment and development of the system of minimum subsistence for urban and rural residents. In 1993, Shanghai took the lead in exploring the establishment of a system of minimum subsistence for urban residents. This Shanghai experiment was promoted nationwide by the Ministry of Civil Affairs in 1995. The State Council issued the "Circular on Establishing the System of Minimum Subsistence for Urban Residents Nationwide" in 1997 and the "Regulations on Minimum Subsistence for Urban Residents" in 1999, which provided that urban residents whose per capita family income was lower than the standard of minimum subsistence may apply for minimum subsistence benefits. Meanwhile, to resolve the problems of residents covered by subsistence security in children's education, medical care, housing and heating etc., China gradually established medical aid, educational aid and housing aid systems.[8] In 2006, the State Council revised the "Regulations on the Support of People Covered by the Five Guarantees System" implemented in 1994, which brought the fund for such support into the fiscal budget. In 2007, the State Council decided to establish the system of minimum subsistence in rural areas nationwide and established a new national strategy of poverty reduction in China's rural areas (the original strategy focused on poverty relief by productive development). From 2003 onwards, China promulgated regulations such as the "Measures for the Management of Aid for Vagrants and Beggars in Cities" (2003) and the "Regulations on the Management of

[8] Tang Jun, Urban and Rural Subsistence Allowance System: History, Status Quo and Future, *Red Flag Manuscript*, Vol. 18, 2005.

Public Emergencies", while the disaster emergency coping mechanism and the disaster relief systems have been gradually improved.

The social security management mechanism has been gradually improved. In August 1998, the State Council issued the "Circular on Relative Issues Concerning the Delegation of Provincial and Industrial Pooling of Basic Old-age Insurance for Enterprise Employees to Local Management", which resolved the long-term conflict resulting from the compartmentalization of industrial pooling and local pooling. The Ministry of Labor and Social Security which was established in 1998[9] is responsible for the centralized management of old-age insurance, medical insurance, unemployment insurance, work-related injury insurance and maternity insurance for urban enterprise employees and rural social old-age insurance. In 1999, the State Council promulgated the "Interim Regulations on the Collection and Payment of Social Insurance Premiums", which provided for the scope of collection and payment, management of collection and payment, supervision, inspection and punishment concerning social insurance premiums, thus gradually improving the social insurance system. The level of old-age insurance pooling continued to rise. By the end of 2006, 13 provinces and municipalities had implemented provincial pooling. To address the pressure from fund payments that might follow a future aging population, the state started to establish a national social security fund of strategic reserves from the year 2000, and had accumulated about RMB 500 billion by the end of 2007.

1.6 Developing a Modern Social Welfare System

At the Seventeenth National Congress of the Communist Party of China held in 2007, the report delivered by Hu Jintao on behalf of the CPC Central Committee clearly put forward the objectives of "ensuring that all citizens enjoy the right to education, employment, healthcare and elderly care, and housing", which were taken as basic requirements in the improvement of people's livelihood and the construction of a harmonious society. Compared with past reforms on the social security system, these objectives had richer connotations, which were tantamount to a new conception for the establishment and development of a modern social welfare system. The social security system is only a preventive measure addressing a survival crisis, while the modern social welfare system is more comprehensive, equitable and sustainable, as it is a more proactive security measure and a people-based strategic measure meeting the requirements of the scientific outlook on development and promoting coordinated development of the economy and society. The establishment of a modern social welfare system not only stresses risk

[9]In 2008, the new central government administration combined the Ministry of Personnel and the Ministry of Social Security into the "Ministry of Human Resources and Social Security", for the further unified management of national social security affairs.

prevention but also emphasizes comprehensive security and advocates social co-construction and all-round sharing. Only when a sound education security system is established and compulsory education is not subject to the restriction of family income can the objective of "education for all" be realized for school-age children; only when a sound employment security and unemployment insurance system is established can the objective of "making work pay" be realized; only when a medical security system, an old-age security system, and a housing security system shared by all are established can the objective of "all people enjoying the right to medical care, old-age support and housing" be realized.[10]

Since the Seventeenth CPC National Congress, some new developments have been achieved in the construction of the modern social welfare system upon the existing basic framework of the social security system. First, new steps have been taken in the equalization of the public service system. Compared to an excessive emphasis on "industrialization", "commodification" and "market-orientation" in the fields of social development such as education, health and housing, more emphasis is laid on the equalization of basic public services by realizing indiscriminate nine-year compulsory education in urban and rural areas nationwide, vigorously implementing the fiscal transfer payment system, and improving the capabilities of government departments in less developed regions to provide public services in attempts to provide various equalized basic public services to all of the people in China. Second, the reform of urban-rural household registration systems has deepened, and coordinated urban and rural development was advocated. According to the new national conditions of industrialization and urbanization of China and the new stage of development of the national economy, the development approach of "supporting agriculture with industry and promoting rural development with urban development" has been put forward, with more stress on the support of agriculture and the benefits for farmers so as to promote the more rapid development of the rural social welfare cause. Third, new measures have been adopted in social relief, the construction of rural social security and the reform of medical and health services. Social relief, as a point of progression in coordinating the urban and rural social security systems, was widely developed nationwide in 2007. The next step is to construct a comprehensive relief system. In 2008, the Ministry of Human Resources and Social Security promulgated the "Guiding Opinions on Developing Pilot Projects of New Rural Social Old-age Insurance", and extensively solicited opinions from the general public. In August 2009, the State Council held a working conference on the pilot projects of "national new rural social old-age insurance", which put forward that "new rural insurance" be experimented in 10% of the counties nationwide in 2009 and then the pilot project should be gradually expanded to basically realize full coverage by 2020. Through long periods of multi-party demonstration, China promulgated the implementation plan for the reform of the medical and health system in 2009, which took the improvement of

[10]Wang Mengkui ed., *Establishing a Developing Social Welfare System in China*, China Development Press, 2009.

the medical security system as its key component in the reform plan. By the end of 2009, the number of people covered by basic medical security amounted to 362.95 million; in addition to over 800 million rural residents covered by new rural co-operative medical insurance, nearly 1.2 billion people were covered by the social medical insurance system, accounting for 90% of the national population. Fourth, the construction of the housing security system has accelerated. In light of the problem of the constant rise of prices in commercial residential housing and the small amount and narrow coverage of affordable housing, the Chinese government has stepped up efforts in the construction of low-rent housing while encouraging enterprises to provide dormitories to employees, especially migrant workers. In light of a shrinking market caused by an international financial crisis, the government takes the construction of security housing such as low-rent housing as an important area for expanding investment and mobilizing domestic demand, which plays an important role in solving the housing problem of low-income families.[11]

[11]This chapter is based on some contents of "The Development of the Social Welfare System in China and Its Impact on Urbanization" (*Journal of the Graduate School of the Chinese Academy of Social Sciences*, Vol. 2, 2010) and "Unavoidable 'Three Security Lines' and 'Two Guarantees'" (*China Social Security*, Vol. 11, 2007).

Chapter 2
The Deviation of China's Social Insurance Fund Mode and Its Corrections

The function of the social insurance system as a key part of the modern social security system is reflected in the operation of social insurance funds. The mode of social insurance funds forms the foundation for the social insurance system. To address the pressure of an aging population and to meet the demands of the rapid development of the capital market (especially in international capital flows), along with international momentum for reforming the social security system, intense debates have been triggered on the traditional pay-as-you-go social insurance mode.

2.1 Debates on the Social Insurance Fund Modes

Of the three main worldwide funding modes for social insurance funds (mainly old-age pensions), namely the pay-as-you-go system, the fund accumulation system and the hybrid system or the partial fund accumulation system (see Table 2.1 for their basic characteristics), those which have drawn most attention and provoked controversy are the pay-as-you-go system and the fund accumulation system. Since the successful transition from the pay-as-you-go system to the fund accumulation system in Chile in the 1980s, as well as the rise of the ROI rate of the fund accumulation mode, people have come to prefer the fund accumulation system. It is believed that it is an important pillar for developing the capital market and an effective prescription for overcoming the problems concomitant with an aging population, while helping to increase savings, enhance the fund use rate and promote economic growth.

The main argument is as follows:

(1) the pay-as-you-go system cannot address the heavy burden of an aging population. An aging population, which demands the continuous increase of the social insurance tax rate, may aggravate unemployment and early retirement

Y. Wang, *Social Security in China: On the Possibility of Equitable Distribution*, Research Series on the Chinese Dream and China's Development Path, DOI 10.1007/978-981-10-5643-7_2

Table 2.1 Comparison of the basic modes of social insurance funds

Fund mode	Fund source and management	Advantages	Disadvantages
Pay-as-you-go	Public, tax, and ratification of expenditures according to revenue	Strong re-distribution function (inter-generational diversion and horizontal transfer), and simple management	With great demands from an aging population, the premium rate has to be adjusted frequently
Fund accumulation	Compulsory, private management, and ratification of expenditures according to revenue	Incentive payment and compulsory savings, promoting capital market and economic growth	The fund is susceptible to the impact of the macro-economy and inflation. It has a poor redistribution function. The investment management is complicated
Hybrid mode	Compulsory source, partial ratification of expenditures according to revenue and partial ratification of revenue according to expenditure	Considering both the re-distribution function and the accumulation function	Management is extremely complicated, and function orientation tends to change

and lead to a reduction in permanent savings and investment. The growth of implicit public pension debts is difficult to sustain.

(2) Fund accumulation may promote economic growth. Old-age pensions are an important force in the capital market. In 1996, gross global assets amounted to about USD 42 trillion, of which about 20% (USD 10-12 trillion) were the pension assets of developed countries (Dawei et al. 2000).

(3) The success of the Chilean model. Chile successfully made the transition from the pay-as-you-go system to the fund accumulation system in the early 1980s. In a period of over 10 years, the country not only made up deficits, but also accumulated a fund of over USD 20 billion. As a result, the difficulty in paying pensions was resolved and fiscal and enterprise burdens were alleviated. The personal contribution rate was also lowered and the pension replacement rate was increased, thus providing a large amount of funds for economic construction.

(4) The accumulation mode is conducive to improving the saving rate and stimulating economic growth. Economic growth is a function of savings. Chile and Switzerland, through compulsory savings plans, increased their respective national savings rate. The savings rate in Switzerland increased from a GDP of 6–8.5%, and Chile's also increased to some extent. Some studies hold that a

pension reform could increase the original aggregate savings rate by about 10–30% (James 1998).

(5) The high ROI of investment funds. Generally speaking, in countries with more open fund management, the ROI of investment funds is higher in the capital market, such as in France, Australia, the United Kingdom, the United States, Ireland and Canada, with notably more outstanding performance in English-speaking countries (see Table 2.2).

(6) Since the 1970s, there has been a wave of reforms of the social security system worldwide, with the purpose of seeking a new relationship between national actions and private actions and strengthening individuals' responsibility for themselves and others.

While analyzing the role of the fund accumulation system, we should note that people have varied opinions regarding the fund accumulation mode. In fact, the fund accumulation system is overrated, thus giving rise to the fallacy of "anything from the fund accumulation system must be good."

The reasons are as follows:

(1) Fund accumulation does not necessarily increase the national savings rate. Cases proving that the accumulation system can enhance the savings rate are found only in Switzerland and Chile, of which the ratio of savings to GDP in Chile dropped from 21% in 1980 to 20% in 1989. As compulsory savings only account for a part of gross national savings, the increase of the compulsory savings rate is not tantamount to the increase of the gross savings rate.

(2) The role of the capital market is overrated. The role of the capital market is growing, but at the expense of huge risks. The Asian Financial Crisis that broke out in 1997 was an obvious case which highlights this point. Stiglitz observes that developing countries should not simply imitate the capital market in developed countries but should face reality, that is, it is very likely, if not inevitable, that their domestic capital market may operate rather poorly (Stiglitz 1989).

(3) The management cost of the fund accumulation mode, especially for private pension funds, is quite high, even significantly higher than the public system. The management cost and commission charges of commercial old-age insurance in the United States account for 35% of insurance premiums, the profit loss caused by the management cost of private funds in the United Kingdom amounts to 5.2% each year, and the management cost of private old-age pensions in Chile accounts for 1.5% of the salary base (see Table 2.3). The International Labor Organization has, after conducting a survey, concluded that it is certainly wrong to consider that the expenditure of administering the public sector is higher than that of the private sector.

(4) Insurance fund modes require a large amount of government subsidies, as is the case with Chile and other countries.

(5) Over-emphasis on fund accumulation, though improving fund efficiency to some extent (but not fully, as no adequate evidence is available so far), also

Table 2.2 Investment portfolio and ROI of old-age insurance funds and gross assets in diverse countries (regions)

Country	Item							
	Bond (%)	Stock (%)	Cash (%)	Real estate (%)	Average ROI (%) (1983–1993)	Gross assets by the end of 1993 (USD 1 billion)		
	Domestic	International	Domestic	International				
Australia	35.87	4.00	36.37	12.05	3.83	7.88	12.1	122.2
Belgium	38.31	11.94	13.93	17.41	7.46	10.95	9.0	5.6
Canada	47.93	0.46	26.85	8.61	8.46	7.49	8.3	162.3
Denmark	67.93	0	18.67	0	6.05	6.35	8.2	14.4
France	62.00	5.00	20.00	0	2.00	11.00	13.0	199.7
Germany	65.05	1.59	9.97	0.91	8.38	12.00	6.5	254.2
Hong Kong	2.10	11.03	34.03	49.05	3.99	0	8.1	6.8
Ireland	33.67	7.14	21.43	27.55	3.06	7.15	11.8	13.8
Japan	53.58	9.00	24.18	5.01	5.01	3.22	6.2	1752.7
The Netherlands	60.60	5.81	7.69	11.31	3.40	11.19	7.5	216.2
New Zealand	25.87	11.19	27.97	23.08	2.80	9.09	10.8	7.9
Norway	74.52	4.70	5.91	1.09	8.70	5.08	8.0	30.6
Singapore	97.35	0	0	0	2.65	0	1.8	32.9
Spain	95.00	0	3.02	0	0	1.98	8.8	13.4
Sweden	92.43	0	4.66	0	0.97	1.94	7.2	61.8
Switzerland	59.00	4.00	9.00	2.00	10.00	16.00	3.5	195.3
The United Kingdom	8.96	3.05	56.01	23.01	3.06	5.91	11.5	726.4
The United States	33.05	0.72	48.52	3.61	11.76	2.34	9.5	2908.0

Source World Bank (1998, p. 79), Lianyou (2000, p. 82)

Table 2.3 A Survey of the International Labor Organization (ILO) on expenditure of social security management

Pay-as-you-go pattern		Fund accumulation pattern		Private pension management cost	
Country	Management cost (%)	Country	Management cost (%)	Country	Management cost (%)
France	1.7	Singapore	0.8	The United	35
Germany	1.5	Malaysia	4.5	States	5.2
The United States	0.8	India	5.4	The United Kingdom Chile	1.5

Source Ministry of Finance (1998, p. 248)

weakens the re-distribution function of the social security system, because only individuals possessing more accumulated funds acquire more gains. This also involves the basic problem of value judgment; that is, how to handle the re-distribution function of social security and how to balance the fairness and efficiency of the social security system.

The debate over the pay-as-you-go mode and the fund accumulation mode is still continuing to provoke controversy in theoretical circles, with no substantial conclusion. Different opinions may be formed from viewing the issue from different perspectives. Gruat, an ILO scholar, believes that despite the claim of a crisis in the World Bank's "Averting the Old Age Crisis: Policies to Protect the Old and Promote Growth", the solution to the crisis proposed in this report not only fails to provide a better guarantee for old-age pension benefits, but also presents larger potential risks than the correctly designed and managed fixed benefit system (Gruat 1998). The World Bank report also acknowledges that without a developed capital market and being unable to establish an effective regulatory authority, it is impracticable for many countries to adopt the solution of fixed pay In practice, most countries around the world, including developed countries and covering OECD countries, have practiced or still practice the pay-as-you-go mode, with the basis for old-age insurance still being public old-age insurance run by the government. Currently, only 18 countries with great differences in levels of economic development, low socialization and a small scale of economic aggregate, such as Fiji and Ghana adopt the fund accumulation system (Jiangang 1999). However, in light of the disadvantages of the pay-as-you-go mode and the advantages of the fund accumulation system, and inspired by the successful transition of countries such as Chile to implement the fund accumulation system, the World Bank proposed the multi-pillar mode including the fund accumulation system in the early 1990s, which has exerted a degree of influence upon the reform of the social insurance system of many countries (including China).

2.2 Institutional Deviation of the Hybrid Mode of the Social Insurance Fund in China

(i) Institutional design of "completing the whole task in one stroke"

In the course of establishing a socialist market economy, China should reform its traditional social security system. Unlike the transformation of the social insurance system in countries like Chile, the reform of the social insurance system in China is confronted with two basic tasks: First, in coordination with the socialist market economic system, to establish a socialized social security system and complete the institutional transformation from enterprise (unit) insurance to social insurance. That is an important characteristic quite different from the reforms of the social security system having occurred in any other country. Such a transformation is not within the scope of controversy over the pay-as-you-go or the fund accumulation modes. If the pay-as-you-go practice was adopted in the past, this transformation is to meet the demands of increasingly expanding pay-as-you-go practice. The second task is to establish a multi-pillar system including the fund accumulation system so as to follow the trend of economic development and the reform of social security reforms worldwide. The hybrid system (partial fund accumulation system) combining social pooling and personal accounts has been gradually put into practice since the 1990s in China, in the hope that the above two tasks can be accomplished at the same time, that is, the problem of dual system transformation.

After the exploration through pilot reform and theoretical generation conducted since the mid-1980s, the "Decision" of the Third Plenary Session of the Fourteenth Central Committee of the CPC adopted in 1993 put forward that a hybrid system combining social pooling and personal accounts be implemented for the basic old-age insurance and medical care systems for urban employees in China. According to this approach, China has conducted experimental reforms of the hybrid system by different means in different cities and developed several dozen types of reform. In 1997 and 1998, the State Council, through a comparative summary of the reform types in different places, issued the "Decision on Establishing a Uniform Enterprise Employees' Old-Age Insurance System" and the "Decision on Establishing an Urban Employees' Basic Medical Insurance System", which constituted the basic framework of the two major social insurance systems in Chinese urban areas, old-age insurance and medical insurance.

The combination of social pooling and personal accounts is a type of hybrid mode combining pay-as-you-go and fund accumulation, containing characteristics of both modes. The purpose of combining the pay-as-you-go system and the fund accumulation system in the urban social insurance system is, on the one hand, to meet the demands of completing the transformation of the social insurance system so that the current fund can provide basic insurance to retired people without accumulation, and on the other hand, to enable in-service employees to accumulate a certain amount of social insurance funds, especially old-age pensions, during the 20–30 years when economic growth and the demographic structure were optimal in

- Old-age pension payment
  - Old-age pension for "old people"——Calculated and issued according to the original method——Social pooling fund
  - Old-age pension for "in-service persons"
    - Basic old-age pension——Social pooling fund
    - Transitional old-age pension——Social pooling fund
    - Personal account old-age pension——Personal account fund Π120
  - Old-age pension for "new persons"
    - Basic old-age pension——Social pooling fund
    - Personal account old-age pension——Personal account fund Π120

Fig. 2.1 Diagram of the payment approaches of social old-age pensions in chin

China, so as to alleviate enterprises' fiscal burden and develop the capital market. This institutional design of "completing the whole task in one stroke" has become recognized by most experts, scholars and decision-makers. Compared with the simple pay-as-you-go system or the fund accumulation system, the hybrid system has its own operation mechanism. First, the hybrid system has to guarantee of the payment of retired people ("elderly people"); second, it should provide basic old-age pensions and personal accumulation for in-service personnel ("in-service persons"); third, it should provide basic insurance and complete personal account accumulation for "new persons" (see Fig. 2.1).

The new system increases requirements on value preservation and the appreciation of accumulated funds. To realize the balance of payments is the fundamental principle for the operation of social insurance funds. The partial fund accumulation system requires that social insurance funds realize two "balances of payment"; one balance is to ensure payment to retired people from pooling funds, and the other balance is to realize the long-term dynamic balance of the accumulated fund. This system has to integrate horizontal balance and vertical balance to realize the periodical balance of payment. In the early period, the financing rate is higher than the payment rate so as to realize partial fund accumulation, that is, a reserve fund, in the case that in the advent of the peak period of aging, the peak fund payment demand can be met at a relatively low financing rate, so as to prevent any financial crisis in social insurance funds (see Fig. 2.2).

(ii) Institutional deviation of the hybrid mode of social insurance funds in China

China's social insurance fund hybrid system, to some extent, meets the fund system ideal and the multi-pillar system advocated by the World Bank; however, in practice, these systems are not the same, resulting in a large disparity between the operation mechanism and the operation effect.

First, too much importance is accorded to the role of the fund system. China fails to define the primary and secondary relationship between social pooling and personal accounts in the institutional framework, which means that China is not clear

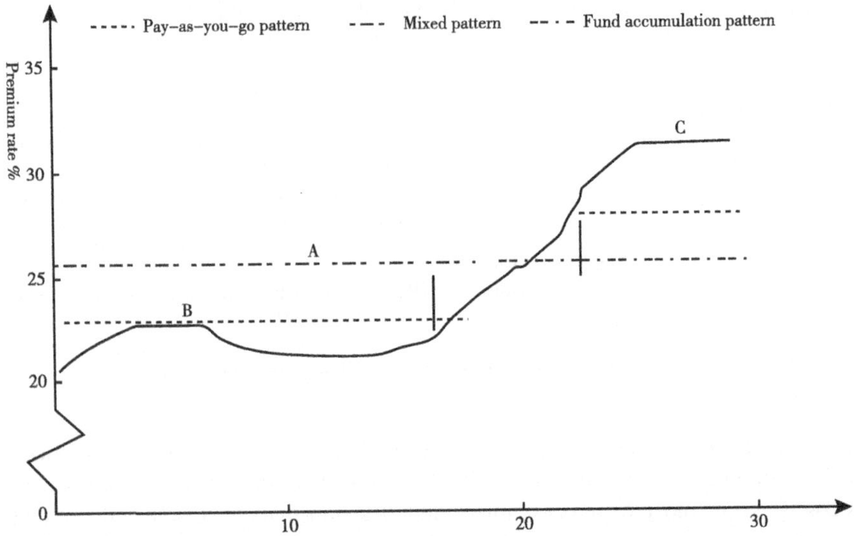

Fig. 2.2 Diagram of variation of premium rates of three financing modes. *Source* Man (1997, p. 169)

with regards to whether the new social insurance system to be established is to be dominated by social pooling (pay-as-you-go) or will be inclined towards developing personal accounts (fund accumulation). In the fund ratio cut of social pooling and personal accounts, no primary and secondary relationship between the two aspects of China's new social insurance system can be discerned. However, as the ratio of personal accounts in China's hybrid mode is larger (see Table 2.4), it can be concluded that the design of China's social insurance fund modes much prefer the fund system commended by the World Bank. However, to complete the "dual system transformation" in the social insurance system, China does not have the practical conditions for realizing the fund system in the short term. Such institutional vagueness is not conducive to the normal operation and sustainable development of the new system.

Second, the design of China's social insurance system has not attached adequate importance to the issue of transitional cost, which affects the effect of personal accounts (the accumulated part of the fund) and is an objective cause for the presence of empty individual accounts. For example, in the design of the old-age insurance system plan, historical debts are under-estimated, and the approach of empty personal accounts going before gradual replenishment is adopted, which leads to empty personal accounts. As future funds are now prepaid, if no solution is worked out, either the institutional design of the mode integrating social pooling and personal accounts will be affected, or a financial crisis will arise. At present, adjustments should be made regarding the old-age insurance system, or the system will be become difficult to sustain.

Table 2.4 Ratio cut of social pooling funds and personal accounts in China's basic old-age insurance and medical insurance

Type of insurance	Social pooling fund		Personal account fund	
	Source of funds	Percentage of the total amount of funds (%)	Source of fund	Percentage of the total amount of funds (%)
Basic old-age insurance	Payment by units (20–16% of the total salary)	13 percentage points of the payment by enterprise, that is, 54.2% of the total amount of insurance funds	The part transferred to personal accounts from enterprise payment (a drop from 7 percentage points to 3 percentage points), personal payment (4–8% of the personal salary base)	11 percentage points, that is, 45.8% of the total amount of insurance funds
Basic medical insurance	Unit payment (16% of total salary)	70% of the enterprise payment (4.2 percentage points), that is, 52.5% of the total amount of insurance funds	The part transferred to personal accounts from enterprise payment (30%), personal payment (2% of the personal salary base)	3.8 percentage points, that is, 47.5% of the total amount of insurance funds

Source Calculated and arranged according to the "Decision on Establishing a Uniform Enterprise Employees' Old-Age Insurance System" (1997) and the "Decision on Establishing an Urban Employees' Basic Medical Insurance System" (1998) of the State Council

Third, China's comprehension of the multi-pillar mode contains deviations. Of the three-pillar system advocated by the World Bank, the first pillar is the pay-as-you-go and public-operated system that ratifies expenditure according to revenue, mainly for providing a social security net for elderly people with a low-income, the second pillar is the compulsory fully-accumulated system that ratifies expenditure according to revenue, with private and competitive fund management, and the third pillar is voluntary savings and annuity providing supplementary retirement income. Though the sources of the second pillar (compulsory personal accounts) are compulsory, its nature is similar to personal savings, its property rights are personal, while its operation and management are conducted by private and competitive fund companies. However, China has not defined the relationship between the two funds or the property right ownership of personal accounts, but practices centralized and interconnected management, thus leaving an institutional loophole for the appropriation of personal accounts by the social pooling fund. Given the difficulty of the social pooling fund to meet the demands of increasing payments, the "gratuitous" appropriation of personal accounts by social pooling accounts has resulted. Not only is it difficult for personal accounts to be fully funded, which become certificated "empty accounts", but fund investment is also unable to be conducted, value cannot be preserved or appreciated, and the accumulation effect of the partial fund accumulation system is lost, all a far cry from the initial objectives of institutional design.

Fourth, the management system for personal accounts (fund accumulation) aspect of China's social insurance fund mode is hindered and not conducive to appreciation on investments. Constrained by many factors such as fund payment pressure and capital market imperfections, the investment channels for the social insurance funds that have been accumulated in China are not smooth, with chaotic management, being barely able to realize value preservation and appreciation. In sum, the hybrid mode of combining social pooling and personal accounts in China, though similar to the fund accumulation system and the multi-pillar system advocated by the World Bank, differs widely from them in terms of operation mechanism and practical conditions. China has confused its system with that advocated by the World Bank, creating many problems in practice.

2.3 Difficulties in the Practice of the Hybrid Mode of Social Pooling and Personal Accounts

The hybrid mode of China's social insurance system attempts to integrate the "fund system" and the "multi-pillar" system. However, the framework of China's new old-age insurance and medical insurance system, which is equipped with the shell of the "fund system" to some extent, does not have the conditions and management mechanism for implementing the fund system; despite its formation as a "multi-pillar" system, it deviates from the "multi-pillar" operational mechanism, thus giving rise to difficulties in fund operation.

(i) The social pooling fund is becoming over-burdened, while old-age insurance personal accounts operate as empty accounts

The expenditure of old-age pensions amounts to the largest amount of expenditure within social security, as all members of society will become old one day, thus requiring an increase in expenditure on old age pensions to meet the pressures of an aging population. At present, though old-age social insurance in China only covers persons employed in urban units, the coverage is considerably widespread (the total number of retired persons in 1999 was 37.3 million, and the total insurance benefits amounted to RMB 336.1 billion). The payment of the old-age insurance fund has turned from "pay-as-you-go" to the hybrid system and historical debts have led to great obstacles when attempting to transform the old-age pension system. Due to the transformation of the old-age security system, a considerable amount of historical debts have had to be paid from the old-age insurance social pooling fund. The expanding expenditure has exerted great pressure on the social insurance pooling fund. Since the implementation of the new old-age insurance system, the social pooling fund has become overburdened, and there is no option but to appropriate funds into individual accounts. As a result, the personal accounts of

Table 2.5 Income and expenditure of China's old-age insurance fund in 1989–1999

Year	Fund income (billion yuan)	Fund expenditure (billion yuan)	Total surplus (billion yuan)
1989	14.67469	11.88292	6.79899
1990	17.88178	14.93363	9.78760
1991	21.57084	17.30714	14.40688
1992	36.5766	32.19145	22.00683
1993	50.35402	47.06303	25.85889
1994	70.74245	66.10902	30.47662
1995	95.00507	84.76087	42.98338
1996	117.17639	103.18689	57.85604
1997	133.791	125.133	68.285
1998	145.9	151.16	61.16
1999	196.5	192.5	73.4

Source The Ministry of Labor (1997, p. 17); the Ministry of Labor and Social Security, and the National Bureau of Statistics (1997, 1998 and 1999)

accumulation accounts cannot be ensured to have adequate funds and can only operate as empty accounts. It was estimated that "empty accounts" in personal accounts have amounted to about 200 billion since 1997. In 1998, the total expenditure of national old-age insurance funds was greater than the total income (see Table 2.5). In this way, not only will personal accounts encounter a tremendous financial crisis, but the social insurance hybrid mode will also face huge institutional risks.

(ii) The nominal social insurance premium is too high, affecting the revenue of social insurance funds

To ensure that the huge fund payment is met, the urban social insurance premium in China has been set very high. With the acceleration of an ageing population, room for further increase of insurance premiums is becoming increasingly narrow. In 1999, urban old-age insurance in China only covered 46.9% of the total number of working people in cities and towns and 55.9% of the number of people who should have been covered by such insurance. Affected by factors such as economic downturns, difficulties encountered by enterprises and insufficient payments, the payment rate of units and individuals that have participated in social insurance has not been satisfactory. For example, the payment rate calculated by Guangdong Province according to the number of insurance participants dropped from 96.9% in 1993 to 91% in 1999. The arrears of social insurance premiums have become more common and the problem is even more serious in economically undeveloped areas. The payment rate in many places is only 70%; arrearages in national basic old-age insurance exceed RMB 36 billion. By regulation, social insurance charges should be deducted from employees' actual salary. But the salary base for premium payments differs widely from the employees' actual salary. In 1999, the average monthly salary base for enterprise old-age insurance in Guangdong Province was

RMB 847, but it was discovered through a survey that the base for old-age insurance premium payments by enterprises only accounted for about 70% of an employees' actual total salary. The World Bank discovered through a survey in 1995 that the actual old-age insurance payment rate of urban employees in China was only about 13% of the total amount of their salary. In that year, the nominal payment rate was above 23.5% (higher than the average rate of about 20% in the world), but the actual payment rate was only 55.3% of the nominal payment rate (World Bank 1998).

The presence of the above problems affected the source of social insurance funding and the stability of income. The average salary of urban in-service employees in 1999 was RMB 8346. Calculated with a coverage of 1.17 billion people and the social insurance premium rate as stipulated by the state (on average about 38–41% of the total salary, with 25–28% for old-age insurance, 8% for medical insurance, 3% for unemployment, and 1% for work-related injury and maternity insurance each), the revenue of urban social insurance in China is enormous, amounting to RMB 539-581.3 billion. If the rate of people participating in the insurance scheme, the fund payment rate and the actual payment rate all surpass 90%, the annual income of the social insurance fund should amount to RMB 377.3–406.9 billion. However, the national income of the social insurance fund only amounted to RMB 220.8 billion in 1999, accounting for only 54%-59% of the due payment, or only 38–41% of the total nominal payment. Due to the excessive discrepancy between the actual amount of collection and actual expenditure in the social insurance fund, China has to stipulate a very high social insurance collection rate, which suppresses an enterprises' initiative for premium payment.

(iii) The social insurance fund is very difficult to manage, with the huge pressure of value preservation and appreciation

The hybrid mode places a set of very high requirements upon fund managers, because it requires the actuarial valuation of the balance of payments of "two funds", the calculation of fund balance at different stages and the management of a large amount of accumulated funds with great risks and high requirements regarding safety. Affected by factors such as institutional design, management systems, management experience and a lack of professionals, the management and value maintenance and appreciation of accumulated funds in the social insurance of China are confronted with increasingly serious problems: On the one hand, the problem of disorderly management and capital loss is so severe that over RMB 10 billion yuan of social insurance funds was illegally appropriated, occupied or embezzled in the mid-1990s (Lianyou 2000). But on the other hand, in righting the wrong, proper limits have been exceeded, without preserving adequate fund investment channels; the fund appreciation rate falls short of inflation or interest rates (see Table 2.6), hardly able to realize the purpose of value maintenance and appreciation.

Table 2.6 Price index, bank interest rate and treasury bill interest rate of 1985–1999

Year	Rise of commodity retailing price (%)	Bank interest rate (%)		Treasury bill interest rate (%)	
		Current	One-year	Annual interest rate	Term (year)
1985	8.8		4.32	9	5
1986	6.0		5.04	10	6
1987	7.3		5.04	10	6
1988	18.5		8.64	10	3
1989	17.8	2.88	11.34	14	3
1990	2.1	2.88	10.08	14	3
1991	2.9	1.8	7.56	10	3
1992	5.4	1.8	7.56	10.5	5
1993	13.0	3.16	10.98	13.96	3
1994	21.7	3.15	10.98	15.86	5
1995	14.8	3.15	10.98	–	–
1996	6.1	1.98	7.47	–	–
1997	0.8	1.71	5.67	9.18	3
1998	−2.6	1.44	4.77	–	–
1999	−3.0	0.99	2.25	2.89	3

Source Arranged according to "China Statistical Yearbook (2000)" of the State Statistics Bureau

2.4 The Approaches and Measures for Deepening the Reform of the Social Insurance Fund System in China

(i) Stick to the principal status of social pooling and reduce the ratio of personal accounts

The problems arising from the operation of China's social insurance fund are related to the fact that we overburden the institutional design of the "fund system" and the "multi-pillar system". Therefore, to improve the social insurance system with Chinese characteristics, we should accord with the national conditions of China, having a backward capital market, a low level of economic development, and old-age pensions which can only meet the most basic necessities for the survival of retired persons, sticking to the principal status of the public insurance fund system, and weakening the over-dependence on personal accounts and lowering the excessively high expectation of value. The scale of the personal account fund should be determined according to the objective reality, which may start from "small accounts", and based on the principle that personal accounts should be funded by personal payments. If an enterprise also pays, it should be at its own discretion (such as enterprise supplementary insurance) instead of being compulsory. In this way, the independence of personal accounts and the supporting reform of the management system can be guaranteed.

(ii) Stick to the multi-pillar design and improve the fund management system

Though the "multi-pillar" system of the World Bank is more suitable for developed countries with a developed capital market and a healthy management system, the design concept of the "multi-pillar" old-age pension system deserves recognition, because it mobilizes the initiative of various parties to participate in endowment insurance and serves as an active measure addressing the ageing crisis. The traditional urban pension system in China relies too heavily on the guarantee from enterprises, institutions and governments. With the development of the market economy, increasing diversification of property rights, increasing improvement of the capital market, and increasing betterment of the legal system, it is necessary and feasible to establish a pension system with a multi-pillar mode.

Besides the basic old-age insurance and basic medical insurance run by the government, China may also carry forward its cultural tradition of frugality and saving, develop various forms of supplementary insurance, and bring into play the initiative in family security, community help and social charity. It is necessary to point out that to develop a compulsory personal account accumulation system (the second pillar), China must follow the requirements of the market economy and international customary practices to establish a management system in which the social pooling fund is independent from personal accounts. Differing from the social pooling fund, personal accounts cannot be mixed up, as their ownership and right to yields belong to individuals. To implement the fund accumulation mode for personal accounts, scattered and competitive social insurance fund investment companies or foundations should be established. The personal account fund should be handed over to independent and competitive market entities (which may be private), that is, fund management companies, for operation. The government may monitor fund operation through laws, regulations and government control so as to ensure the security of accumulated funds.

(iii) Open up sources of non-conventional insurance funds to address the cost of an institutional transition

An important root cause for the institutional crisis in China's new social insurance system is that the government has failed to establish adequate and sound channels for addressing historical debts through the reform of the social insurance system. Two problems were resolved in the transformation of the old-age pension system in Chile: first, the old-age pension debts under the old system were resolved through the fiscal ("endorsed bond") channel, which created an ideal environment for reform; second, planned investment was conducted for the accumulated fund in personal accounts to realize the value preservation and appreciation of the social insurance fund. The method of West Germany providing East Germany with social insurance financial support after the re-unification of Germany can also be taken for reference. In light of inadequate normal (institutional) sources for the social insurance fund now, non-institutional sources should be opened up through multiple channels so as to resolve historical and implicit debts. We think that fund sources may be expanded in the following ways: first, adjust the fiscal expenditure structure and continue to pay the retirement pension for retirees from state-owned units before 2000; second, sell off some state-owned assets, including some state-owned shares or some state-owned land and public housing etc.; third, issue social security national debts, lottery and introduce special taxes (such as inheritance tax).

(iv) Improve revenue and expenditure control, strengthen investment operation, and realize value preservation and appreciation

Currently, there are many problems with the sources, expenditure management and investment operation of the social insurance fund in China, which should be addressed by resolute and feasible measures. In terms of fund sources, we should strengthen institutional construction to establish a stable and sustainable source foundation for the social insurance fund. (1) Continue to expand its coverage. To reform the original coverage of social insurance, employed persons with permanent urban residential registration should all be included. This is a requirement for the socialization of social insurance and also a necessity to lower the dependency ratio and expand the source foundation for the social insurance fund. (2) Lower the nominal social insurance premium rate, and increase the base salary for the payment of the social insurance fund and the successful collection rate so that the rates are maintained at least above 95%. Meanwhile, measures should be adopted to resolve the problem of a false payment base. The payment base of the social insurance fund should be changed from "total salary" to "total income"; just like the collection of individual income tax, various kinds of "normal income" that employees receive from their respective units should be included into the base for the payment of their social insurance premiums. (3) Implement the tax collection system, strengthen the collection of social insurance fund collection, and gradually convert over to social insurance tax. While fund sources are expanding, we must improve and adjust the expenditure system and structure, thus increasing revenue and reducing expenditure. (1) Effectively lower the retirement pension replacement rate so that basic old-age insurance is based on guaranteeing basic needs. The retirement pension rate should be gradually lowered from above 90% to below 60% or about 50% of the salary for payment (instead of the final salary before retirement), so that basic old-age insurance is based on basic old-age support and room for development is reserved for supplementary old-age insurance. (2) Gradually raise the retirement age, and curb early retirement to alleviate the payment pressure of the old-age insurance fund. (3) Regulate the social insurance fund expenditure adjustment mechanism, and weaken the impact of non-institutional measures on the social insurance fund. The expenditure adjustment of the social insurance fund must be conducted through scientific estimation and through institutionalized and law-based channels, so as to prevent the impact of any temporary decision on the expenditure expectation of the whole social insurance fund. (4) Adjust the expenditure structure and conduct scientific fund management. The basic principle of balance of payments should be adopted for the social insurance pooling fund. "Strike a balance between expenditure and revenues, with a slight surplus". It is not good to have no surplus, but excessive fund accumulation is not good either.

Currently, China exercises strict control over the investment of the social insurance fund, which is a passive preventive measure related to capital market imperfections, few investment channels, big risks in industrial investment, backward operation monitoring measures and the insufficient ability to prevent financial risks. However, considering the long-term sustainable development of the social insurance system and international practices, we must relax control over investment operations of the social insurance fund, and expand investment channels on the basis of rationalizing the institutional design of social insurance and the fund management mechanism, so that the accumulated fund of social insurance can enter the capital market, acquire higher return on investment and realize the value preservation and appreciation of the accumulated fund. (1) Establish a professional investment institution for the social insurance fund, and develop a fund investment monitoring framework. The social insurance investment fund mainly consisting of personal accounts and supplementary insurance must have the transition made solely by professional institutions. Such professional institutions should establish a board of directors, expert wealth management teams and develop fund custodians and an adequate monitoring and control mechanism. A proper entry and exit mechanism should be established for fund institutions to develop a competitive pattern under government oversight. (2) Stick to the principle of gradual improvement and create a good environment. (3) Expand investment areas and innovate investment tools. Currently, the government only allows insurance funds to be deposited in banks and for the purchase of treasury bonds, which cannot be adapted to the requirement of value preservation and the appreciation of social insurance. With the increasing expansion of the scale of personal accounts and supplementary insurance funds, it will be an objective need to relax investment restrictions so that such funds can enter the capital market and create room for the expansion of investment and potential areas for investment.[1]

[1]The contents of this chapter are published in the *Economic Research Journal*, 2001 (2).

Chapter 3
Health Problems and Health Equality in the Transitional Period

Despite achieving significant developments in terms of health services in China, the reform of public services has yet to show relevant results, such as how to establish health services in line with the socialist market economic system. With an overemphasis on market-oriented and industrialized medical care, the efficiency and equity of the health reform have even been subject to decline to some extent. The high cost and lack of accessibility of medical treatment caused by rapidly rising medical expenses has become an economic and social hot topic of general concern. This article mainly addresses the causes and roots of the challenges and problems faced by health services in the course of economic transformation. It provides some opinions and suggestions on how to enhance the efficiency and fairness in the development of the health sector in a socialist market economic system, and how to bring into full play the role of medical care and health security in the construction of a harmonious society.

3.1 Health Security Challenges and Outstanding Problems Caused by Economic Transformation

The main task of Chinese health services under the planned economic system is to find a solution to the "scarcity of doctors and medicine" issue. Thanks to the state's efforts, its sound public health system and the clear guiding principles, China has managed to provide basic health security at a very low level to most urban and rural residents and has created a Chinese health care model despite the relatively low level of economic development and the relative shortage of medical and health resources. With the transformation of the economic operation system and social organization system since reform and opening-up, the traditional health care model based on work units or communities face very big challenges.

Y. Wang, *Social Security in China: On the Possibility of Equitable Distribution*, Research Series on the Chinese Dream and China's Development Path, DOI 10.1007/978-981-10-5643-7_3

In terms of the public health system, China used to mobilize government and mass forces to conduct large-scale patriotic health campaigns and health education campaigns, vigorously clean up the environment of health services. Doing so, it would also step up efforts to control infectious diseases and endemic diseases, and properly implement a "prevention-based" health development strategy. Since reform and opening-up, however, patriotic health campaigns have lost their organizational foundation, and government investment in public health services is hardly enough to maintain the normal operation of health institutions; as a result, grassroots medical and health institutions and even many public health institutions have become commercial or market-based. This affects the functioning of public health and changes the status of the government's "prevention-based" strategy to that of a mere "slogan". The frequent occurrence of public health issues in China exposed the challenges and predicaments facing public health services after the economic transformation.

In terms of the medical and health system, rapid development has been achieved in medical and health institutions under a lenient market-based system. Moreover, the ability to provide medical services has been comprehensively improved since reform and opening-up. Except for a very small number of sparsely populated and poverty-stricken areas with inconvenient transportation, the scarcity of doctors and medicine issue has basically been solved. However, the lack of effective guidance and supervision in the introduction of a market mechanism leaded to distorted services and low efficiency in the medical and health sector and seriously increased the cost of medical and health care. This aggravates the medical burdens of urban and rural residents and gives rise of the serious problem of increasingly non-accessible and expensive medical treatment. In terms of results, since reform and opening-up, the extent of the improvement of the health of Chinese residents does not match the rapid increase of medical expenses. Since the 1990s, in particular, the continuous rapid increase of medical expenses has far exceeded the extent of GDP as well as urban and rural income growth for the same period. The average annual increase of total health expenditures from 1978 to 2003 was 12.09%, nearly three percentage points higher than the average growth rate of GDP in the same period (Dezhi 2005). From 1998 to 2003, the average annual income of urban residents increased by 8.9%, and that of rural residents increased by 2.4%, but medical and health expenditures in urban and rural areas increased by 13.5% and 11.8% respectively. The increase rate of medical service expenditures exceeds the increase of per capita income, and medical and health expenditures now rates third in terms of major expenditures for families after food and education. In 2003, total health expenditures amounted to RMB 658.41 billion, accounting for 5.62% of the GDP, while total health expenditures only accounted for 3.17% of the GDP in 1980. It is noteworthy that the proportion of medical expenditures in urban and rural familial income has rapidly risen to over 10%. A considerable number of urban and rural residents (especially rural residents) have to assume these medical expenses on their own because they lack medical insurance. Rapidly rising medical expenses have become a huge economic burden for urban and rural residents (see Table 3.1).

Table 3.1 Growth of medical expenses in China

Year	1980	1990	1995	2000	2001	2002	2003
Total health expenditures (billion yuan)	14.32	74.74	215.51	458.66	502.59	579	658.41
Proportion in GDP (%)	3.17	4.03①	3.69	5.13	5.16	5.51	5.62
National per capita health expenditures (yuan)	14.51	65.40	177.90	361.90	393.80	450.70	509.50
Urban per capita health expenditures (yuan)		158.50	401.30	813.00	841.20	987.10	1108.90
Rural per capita health expenditures (yuan)		38.80	112.90	314.90	244.80	259.30	274.70
Proportion of urban per capita health expenditures (yuan) in residents' income (%)		10.40	9.40	12.90	12.30	12.10	12.20
Proportion of urban per capita health expenditures (yuan) in residents' consumption expenditure (%)		12.40	11.30	16.30	15.80	16.40	17.00②
Proportion of rural per capita health expenditures (yuan) in residents' income (%)		5.70	7.20	14.00	10.30	10.50	10.50
Proportion of rural per capita health expenditures (yuan) in residents' living consumption expenditure (%)		6.60	8.60	18.90	14.10	14.10	14.10②

Note ① According to the estimate of the World Bank, total health expenditures in China accounted for 3.5% of the GDP in 1990. See *The World Bank Development Report 1993: Investing in Health*, China Financial & Economic Publishing House, 1993. ② According to the household surveys conducted by the State Bureau of Statistics, the proportion of medical and health expenditures in urban and rural residents general living expenditures is obviously smaller than shown in the table. For example, in 2002 and 2003, the proportion of urban residents' medical and health expenditures was 7.13 and 7.31% respectively, and that of rural residents was 7.08 and 7.34% respectively. In 1990 and 1995, the proportion of such expenditures for urban residents was 2.01 and 3.11% respectively; that for rural residents was 5.06 and 4.94% respectively. See *The Statistical Yearbook of China* (2004)

Source of data Ministry of Health: *China's Health Statistic Abstract 2005*, p. 31. For the data on urban and rural residents' income, see *The Statistical Yearbook of China* of relevant years

In contrast with the substantial increase in medical expenses, no significant improvement has been found in the health conditions of urban and rural residents, and some health indexes have even dropped. Urban and rural morbidity has been rising. According to the 2003 national health survey, the two-week morbidity rate for the residents in the regions under survey was 143.0‰ (153.2‰ for urban residents, and 139.5‰ for rural residents), and the prevalence of chronic diseases for residents under survey was 151.1‰ (239.6‰ for urban residents and 120.5‰ for rural residents). Besides, the prevalence of major infectious diseases in recent years (such as SARS) has been rising. From 1995 to 2004, the prevalence of infectious diseases in mandatory reporting rose from 176.24/100,000 people to 235.85/100,000 people, and the death rate rose from 0.34/100,000 people to 0.53/100,000 people. The damages and potential risks of infectious diseases are increasing.

In relation to the above problems, efficiency and equity in dispatching health resources has been declining since the 1990s. The relationship between equity and efficiency has always been one of the core issues of economic research. In the course of modern economic growth, the relationship between equity and efficiency can be generally classified into the following four situations: with the rise of economic efficiency, social equity improves; with the rise of economic efficiency, social equity remains unchanged or even weakens; with the decline of economic efficiency, social equity improves; with the decline of economic efficiency, social equity declines. The first situation is the most desired, but it tends to require quite a long development period. The second and third situations, to some extent, reflect the orientation or focus of economic and social policies in different periods of development, and are also acceptable. The fourth situation is most unacceptable. To overcome "egalitarianism" in the era of planned economy, China has established guidelines for reform and development which both "gives priority to efficiency, and gives consideration to equity".

This policy has played an active role in economic development. However, if applied to an economy where market does not play its role, (especially in the field of social development), and without relevant government function (especially strict market supervision), the result of such a policy would be the decline of equity without any guarantee of enhanced efficiency. The health industry has unfortunately become a typical field in which both efficiency and equity decline. Since 1993, National Health Service surveys have clearly reflected the "market failure" and "government failure" that coexist in the health sector. With rapid increase over twenty-odd years, medical facilities and equipment have improved, while clinic visit rate for urban and rural residents has dropped. The two-week clinic visit rate of urban and rural residents was 19.9 and 16.0% respectively in 1993, which dropped to 11.8 and 13.9% respectively in 2003; their annual hospitalization rate was 5.0 and 3.1% respectively in 1993, which changed to 4.2 and 3.4% respectively in 2003. The average number of patients diagnosed and treated by each doctor and the use rate of sick beds in medical institutions are declining on the whole. A main cause for the decline in the efficiency of medical resources use is the rise of medical costs, which cause a considerable number of people in financial difficulty to give up medical services provided by medical institutions. A 2003 survey showed that the hospital visit rate dropped by 18.4% from that of 1998 (a drop of 27.1% in cities and a drop of 15.4% in rural areas). Of the patients surveyed, 51.1% saw a doctor in medical institutions, 35.7% opted for self-medication, and 13.1% did not take any medical measure. 48.9 of the patients did not visit any clinic (57.0% for cities and 45.8% for rural areas). "Expensive medical treatments" exert more serious impacts on low-income people in urban and rural areas. 38.2% of outpatients not adopting any treatment measure chose to do so because of financial difficulties; of the patients who should have been hospitalized but chose not to, 70.0% blamed financial difficulties. This is a direct reflection of the gradually widening income disparity among urban and rural residents in recent years in the health sector. The increase of economic inequalities is also reflected in the decline of equity in health services. In the global health equity rankings by the World Health Organization, China ranks fourth from the bottom, which, to some extent, reflects the decline of health equity in China.

3.2 The Progress and Perplexity of the "Three Reforms" in China's Health Care System

To address health problems in the course of economic transformation, the Chinese government has adopted a series of policies and measures. In the 1980s, mainly market-based measures were adopted to curb the rise of state-funded medical cost and raise funds for the development of medical and health services. Since the 1990s, especially the mid-1990s, as medical expenses soared more rapidly after the adoption of the market-based system, more and more people found it difficult to receive medical treatment. As a result, the government adopted three institutional reforms centered on accelerating the reform of the medical security system, the medical and health system, and the drug production and circulation system. Other representative policies and regulations launched during this period included: the "Decision of the CPC Central Committee and the State Council on Health Reform and Development" (1997), the "Decision of the State Council on Constructing the Basic Medical Insurance System for Urban Employees" (1998), and the "Guiding Opinions on the Reform of Urban Medicine and Health System by the Economic Restructuring Office of the State Council" (2000), among others.

Since 1998, rapid development has been achieved in the construction of the urban medical security system in China. This is mainly reflected in the expansion of basic medical insurance coverage for urban employees. By the end of 2004, the number of people covered by basic medical insurance was 124.04 million, including 90.45 million in-service employees, and 33.59 million retirees. To relieve the medical burden of poor urban residents in cities, in April 2005, the General Office of the State Council forwarded the Opinions on Pilot Work for the Establishment of the Urban Medical Relief System by the Ministry of Civil Affairs, the Ministry of Health, the Ministry of Labor Security and the Ministry of Finance, to promote pilot work for the medical relief system. In light of rural residents without medical insurance and facing non-accessible and expensive medical treatments, China started pilot work on the new rural cooperative medical system. The central government and local governments employ funds from their fiscal funds, and farmers voluntarily participate in medical insurance based on households as units, thus mainly allowing the treatment of serious illnesses contracted by farmers covered by insurance. By the end of June 2005, 641 counties (cities and districts) conducted pilot work on new rural cooperative medical insurance, including 225 million farmers, of whom 163 million participated in cooperative medical insurance, at a participation rate of 72.6%. Farmers covered by cooperative medical insurance were compensated 119 million person-times of, and expenditures in terms of compensation money amounted to RMB 5.038 billion.[1] Though this went beyond the regulations on employees' basic medical insurance in the "three reforms", it implied the gradual expansion of medical security coverage.

The reform of the medical and health system and of the drug production and circulation system is ongoing. However, it may have engendered more problems and doubts than progress. One issue concerning the reform of China's health system is the direction is should take. Although both theoretical circles and practical work departments all recognize "establishing an urban medical and health system meeting the requirements of the socialist market economy" as the general objective of reform, yet they have a different understanding of the implications of this system. One opinion has it that besides medical and health service institutions assuming public health functions, other institutions should be turned into market-based entities from as in the former planned management system so as to gradually industrialize and marketize the health service sector. In the course of economic reform, this line of thinking has become mainstream in theoretical circles, reflected in the implementation of classified reform in hospitals by relevant government departments as stated in the relevant documents on the health system reform, the implementation of "property right" reform in health centers in some places, and the permission and encouragement of private capital and foreign capital to enter the medical and health service system. At the end of 2003, of the 283 thousand medical institutions registered nationwide (excluding village clinics), state-owned (85 thousand) and collective (49 thousand) institutions accounted for 47.3%; private (136 thousand) and joint venture (60) institutions accounted for 52.7%. Quantitatively, medical institutions not owned by the states and of a collective nature have become the majority. According to the classification by departments such as the Ministry of Health, of the above institutions, non-profit medical institutions (135 thousand) accounted for 47.5%, and profit-making medical institutions (146 thousand) accounted for 52.5%. Most of non-state-owned and collective health institutions, especially profit-making health institutions, tend to behave like ordinary enterprises, that is: oriented by market and profits. Of medical institutions which still retain a state-owned and collective nature or are even classified as non-profit organizations, due to insufficient public investment and competition pressurizing the whole medical market, they have been partly marketized or even mainly target at profit making. The industrialization and market-based tendencies of

[1]The first group of pilot counties (cities and districts) initiated in China in 2003 amounted to 304, which increased to 333 by 2004; by 2005, every prefecture (city) had at least one pilot county. Seethe news report "Pilot work on new rural cooperative medical insurance has scored obvious results" on the Ministry of Health website http://www.moh.gov.cn/index.aspx.

medical and health services since reform and opening-up in China have been very obvious. Another viewpoint is that although state and society cannot and do not have to arrange for all medical services, and although the self-regulatory role of market in medical and health services is not negligible, yet industrialization should not be blindly advocated and marketization should not be over-stressed in health development as well as in medical and health service institutions. The main reasons for such an idea include: ① serious information dis-symmetry exists between the supplier and the purchaser in the medical service market, which is not a perfectly competitive market, and where the market mechanism cannot play an adequate role, let alone effectively allocating health resources; Therefore, playing up the market theory in medical services may lead to serious health inequalities. ② Over-emphasis on market orientation in the medical and health sector will cause both inequality and inefficiency in terms of the administration of medical services, susceptible to double distortion in price and supervision. ③ Commercialization and market orientation in the reform of the health system go against the nature of public enterprise, partial public products property and the requirements of social equality. No government in modern society should leave problems in medical and health services to be solved wholly by market forces.

In over twenty years of reform exploration and theoretical summary, despite the existence of some conflict on the reform of the medical and health sector in China, authorities in charge of health have at least realized that the "excessive dependence on market orientation" in practice is not advisable. It has been proved in practice that the reform of the medical and health system may refer to but cannot simply copy the experiences in the market-oriented reform of ordinary commodity (even drugs). The government must take up responsibilities in the public health system and should reserve and even improve community-based public medical and health institutions with reasonable layout, high accessibility and low cost, so as to meet medical demands of poverty-stricken people (who may be given special medical aid) and the masses. Moreover, appropriate fiscal subsidies and policy support may also be given to fields such as medical technologies research. Of course, there is no society able to bear the tremendous amounts of medical expenses caused by the progress of medical technologies. Medical services other than basic medical needs may be developed gradually by market-oriented and industrialized methods under the guidance of regional medical and health plans. In terms of medical and health institutions, the government and the market can divide the work, and both should play an active role. The government should mainly focus on the public health sector and the basic medical field, and therefore should "focus on basic matters and liberalize medical care"; it should focus on public health, community medical care and preventive health care. However, further exploration is required as to how to implement the above opinions in the specific practices of health development and reform.

Another noteworthy problem is how to realize the complementary support of the "three reforms". Despite certain progress made in simultaneous promotional pilot work of "three reforms", the effect is limited on the whole. The specific reform approach in the health system may require major adjustments. The government's medical cost compensation increase for medical institutions may, to some extent, reduce the medical expenditures of urban and rural residents, yet it is still difficult to control the rise of medical expenditures if the operation mechanism of medical institutions is not fundamentally reformed. In the long run, public funds can hardly be sustained. Meanwhile, there are too many problems in drug production, especially in terms of circulation. Abnormally high drugs prices and excessive waste of medical funds increase drug prices, reduce efficiency and increase the people's burdens. As to how to effectively supervise this field despite a highly-involved market, China has not identified truly effective measures or approaches. Despite the rapid development of medical security, especially in terms of basic medical insurance for urban employees, medical security coverage is less than 50% of the total amount of labor in urban areas. The existence of a large number of people who get medical treatment at their own expenses has become an important symbol of the difficulty of achieving basic effect in the "three reforms".

We should say that despite the progress made in terms of health security for urban and rural residents in China, in comparison with the past, China remains a far cry from the objective of establishing a health security system suitable for the socialist market economy and the current economic development stage while also meeting people's basic health demands. Many theoretical and practical problems should be studied and explored.

3.3 Suggestions on Promoting Health Development, Health Equality and the Construction of a Harmonious Society

(i) To develop health services and promote health equality are a fundamental project for the construction of a harmonious society

The right to health is a basic right granted by the constitution to citizens and also an important part of human rights. The improvement of health conditions directly reflects national and social development and progress. The problem of medical and health care is one of the most fundamental problems which must be addressed for human subsistence and development, as it relates to the people's standards and quality of living as well as to the development objectives and the future of a country and a nation. Since the Central CPC Committee clearly stated the objective of constructing a harmonious socialist society in the resolution of the Fourth Plenary Session of the Sixteenth National Congress, to build a harmonious society has become an important objective for the future development of China. Health services and health equality not only shoulder important missions in the construction of a harmonious society, but also provide an important base for constructing a harmonious society.

Developing health services can promote economic growth. In statistical indexes, health expenditures count as consumption expenditures, while expenditures for public health are deemed to be fiscal burdens, social burdens and family burdens not creating wealth. As the health flexibility coefficient is generally larger than 1,[2] health burdens keep rising. Indeed, for the large number of medium and low-income people whose income grows slowly, the rapid growth of medical cost increasingly exceeds their bearing capacity, and medical cost itself has become a huge barrier constraining their access to medical services. However, in terms of the society as a whole, medical expenditures should be deemed as health investments. For individuals, health investments should become an important part of HR capital investment. Families are reduced or reverted to poverty by diseases because the main labor forces of such families are robbed of their health and thus their main source of income is lost. Therefore, health investment is an inevitable basic expenditure for families and society, as well as an important drive for economic development. An important factor for China's economic development since the founding of the PRC is increased investment in health by the state and society, as well as the constant improvement of the people's health conditions, including the increase of life expectancy, large-scale control of infectious diseases and endemics, the reduction of the number of people who are sick, and the improvement of general health conditions. The World Health Organization also thinks that the expansion of key health services coverage may salvage the lives of millions of people each year, alleviate poverty, stimulate economic development and promote global security.[3]

Health equality plays the role of adjusting income distribution and promoting social equality, harmony and stability. There are various definitions or explanations when it comes to health and equality. Health equality should be taken as an important part and objective for economic and social development, and stress should be laid mainly on people's accessibility to basic medical and health services provided by the state and society, whatever the way, approach or process adopted. From the perspective of result equality, though not every social member has the same ability to pay, yet the right to health as a basic human right should be taken as a public objective, instead of allowing this basic right to be eroded by other forces. If some social members cannot enjoy this basic right for personal or family reasons, the state or society should be obliged to help them obtain basic health security. Maintaining health equality means that the state and society should grant certain help to poor people unable to acquire basic medical security, which is an important responsibility of social security, whereby the role of social security in regulating income distribution, narrowing the wealth gap, and promoting social harmony is

[2]According to the estimate of Dezhi (2005), from 1978 to 2003, the average elastic coefficient of per capita health cost versus per capita GDP in China was 1.29.

[3]A WHO Macroeconomics and Health (2002) report held that only USD 14 billion was invested in the intervention of infectious diseases in the most under-developed countries of the world, with which the death of 8 million people could be prevented each year, and 330 million disability adjusted life years (DALYs) could be extended. According to conservative estimate, each DALY got USD 563 and the direct economic benefits of 330 million DALYs amounted to USD 186 billion each year, which amount could be several times higher.

played. Of course, the key to exercising the above functions resides in the realization of health equality.

Health development and health equality are two main pillars safeguarding urban and rural residents' health, and neither are negligible. China has made notable progress in using multiple channels to raise health development funding and in promoting health development since the initiation of reform, but considerable investments in terms of funds, human resources and material resources are still required for the future development of health services, so as to ensure that total health resources keep growing with economic development in order to provide a material basis for securing people's health. Under the socialist market economy, the government should not and cannot be a single entity as it used to be under the planned economic system. Instead, it should draw upon the beneficial experiences in raising health development funding through multiple channels and continue to absorb social, individual and even foreign capital into the health sector. Health investment should be better planned to meet the actual demands and bearing capacity of the level of economic development, instead of being completely market-oriented. In fact, though the insufficiency of social investment channels is a problem facing China's medical and health sector, it is not the main problem, as the worst problem is serious health inequality and efficiency decrease in terms of medical resources use. In particular, improving the efficiency of the use health resources and the equality of health security should become a fundamental project for the construction of a harmonious society.

(ii) The government must fulfill its responsibility for improving health equality

Currently, people have no doubt on the objective of improving health equality. The crux is how to realize the objective of health equality with markets as the main mechanisms for resource allocation. In light of guiding thoughts, the key is that the government should play a guiding role in medical and health services and health security. A review of the history of medical and health services and medical security in all countries of the world, especially developed countries, will find that almost invariably there was a course of development from free market adjustment to centralized social pooling. Because medical and health service security and medical security are fields where "market failure" is relatively prevalent, it is not feasible to rely entirely on free market, and thus the government's role is irreplaceable.

Public health, which means health services provided for all the people and the whole society in a region, is the most fundamental medical and health service to which everyone should be entitled; it implies the social services and public goods with the widest coverage, strongest public interest and best effect, and is also the basis of the entire medical and health security system of a society. As market failure is more serious in the field of public health, without the intervention of the government and society, investment in this field can hardly meet actual demands and serious inequality and overall low efficiency in the use of health resources will ensue. Public health, as public medical care services, has a tremendous external effect, which demands intervention, coordination and integration by a force beyond the market. Preventive public health care and the construction of the medical security system, to some extent, are among the basic unshakable responsibilities of the government.

The government plays a leading role in the three reforms of medical and health care, which are major attempts at establishing a health security system suitable for the socialist market economic system. Constrained by various factors, some progress has been made only in certain aspects, and to carry on the reforms is still a very formidable task. The expansion of medical security coverage requires the powerful promotion of the government; while the deepening of the reforms of the urban employees' basic medical insurance system, the urban residents' medical assistance system, and the new rural cooperative medical system should further resolve the problems affecting the healthy development of the above systems. There is still a longer way to go in the reform of the medical care system, with the crux lying in how micro-operating entities in medical and health services strike a balance between their own interests and social interests, as well as between short-term development and long-term development. This fundamentally requires the government's investment mechanism, as well as reasonable policy guidance, and strict supervision and regulation. In terms of the three reforms, the reform of the field of drug production and circulation allows for the highest degree of marketization, and is also one of the fields with the closest combination of market mechanisms and government regulations. As the reform of the medical and health system has not been fully implemented, and the reform of the drug production and circulation field is entangled in the problem of medical and health care system, many enterprises have not truly become independent entities in the medical industry, lacking the foundation and stamina for healthy development and unable to compete with large-scale enterprises in the world medical circles. As a result, the material and technological support provided for the health of urban and rural residents in China does not meet actual demands.

The government is the formulator and implementer of national and regional health service development plans. The three reforms, which are only periodical reform goals, do not encompass the entire contents of health development and health security. The government's leadership role is indispensable for settling health problems and securing the people's health, as the government has to guide many fields. In some health sectors in which market, society, families and individuals can function more easily and better, the government surely should not over-reach like it did in the period of planned economy, but should shoulder the responsibility for creating an environment, regulating behaviors, conducting supervision and promoting development for them. So to speak, as health issues concern the long-term objective of state and national survival and development, the government of a modern society must play a leading role and shoulder responsibilities in this respect, no matter whether this modern society functions in a planned economy or market economy.

(iii) Several suggestions for promoting health development and health equality

(1) Continue to improve the investment in health services, especially public health services and raise their proportion in terms of total medical expenditures. The absolute amount of fiscal investment in health has been rising year after year in China, and the proportion of government health investment in terms of total health funds has also been growing since 2003; from the perspective of the structure of health funding since the reform, however, the proportion of health expenditures in the government's budget has obviously been declining, while the proportion of individual health expenditures has obviously been rising. Internationally, whether in developed countries or middle-income countries, or even in many low-income countries, government and social health expenditures account for the absolute majority of the total health funds. As it is not enough for health development, especially health equality, to rely on markets alone, as markets have many defects, one of the critical solutions is to step up government investments in health services. The increase of government health investments is not just the proper increase of its absolute value, but should also include a rise of its proportion in terms of total health funding. Only in this way can the relevant financial burdens of the people be alleviated. This is a strong support for the basic medical needs of those patients without sufficient economic bearing capacity, and also the most powerful measure for maintaining health equality. "The issue of whether personal medical and health costs should be borne by individuals or the government makes a big difference. If medical and health costs are mainly borne by the government, poor people can enjoy basic medical and health services, which can help improve the health level of the whole nation and the welfare of the whole society fundamentally." (Shaoguang 2003). Given the fast increase of payment for medical care, in accordance with international experience as well as China's national conditions, we should strive to approximately double the proportion of government health expenditures in total health expenditures during the 11th Five-Year Plan period. In the meantime, the proportion of governmental, social and individual health expenditure in the national total is expected to be around one third respectively. With the adjustment of the structure of health expenditures, the public nature of health services and the equality of health security will be obviously improved.

(2) Deepen the reform of the medical and health system so that the main bodies in medical and health service providers recover their nature as public institutions instead of being industrial or business entities. In the course of reforming the health system, though the property rights of health resources are mainly publicly owned or state-owned, yet the absolute majority of medical and health institutions, including a substantive number of state-owned and collective institutions, are subject to major transformations due to insufficient fiscal investments and the "industrialization" slogan, the latter which so excessively pursues commercialization and market profits that their nature of public institutions is lost—obviously a major behavioral distortion. Medical and health service institutions as public institutions, and especially medical professionals

as employees of public institutions, should reverse their tendency to excessively pursue commercial interests so that the main bodies of medical and health service providers restore their nature as public institution and discard the industrial or business nature. To realize this point under the market economy, we should gradually separate revenue and expenditure in the business projects of medical and health service institutions and fundamentally cut off their income channels by adopting a market-based approach towards their service items.

(3) Strengthen supervision over the drug production and circulation industry and the behaviors of medical and health service providers, as well as increase the entry threshold and fines for non-compliance. In fact, the best constraint for some medical services exceeding basic medical demands is the personal payment system. Under such a condition, some market-based medical and health service institutions should be allowed or even encouraged to develop. China has a large population with complicated medical demands, so the development of the drug and health industry is indispensable. Meanwhile, a large number of health service institutions should also conduct cost accounting with reference to market prices. All these cannot be separated from the development of the medical market. However, as a typical market of incomplete competition with information asymmetry, and in addition to the fact that medical and health services are life-and-death matters, all countries should conduct very strict regulation over this market. The behaviors of both service agencies and relevant personnel should be strictly regulated.

(4) Strive to improve efficiency in terms of the usage of medical and health resources. The fiscal budget and society cannot bear the sole expansion of the total amount of health investments without the improvement of efficiency in the use of health. We should establish full-time institutions and expert consultation committees for "deepening the reform of the health sector", strengthen the leadership of the health reform, and study the overall approach and development plans for the health reform under the new situation. We should make regional health plans meet the reality in China and truly guide and supervise health facilities and staff. We should integrate health resources, strengthen the uniform management of the public health system, and break the isolation and blockade between traditional healthcare institutions and in the whole system. We should deepen and effectively promote the reform of the drug production and circulation system and the medical and health service system, strengthen the supervision of the entities in drug production and circulation and medical and health services, rigorously conduct health supervision and law enforcement, and strictly prosecute any violator. We should shoulder the responsibility of planning for the allocation of health resources and expand the main or leading role of government investment in rural health and urban community work by means of moderately cutting government investment in urban healthcare. We should improve the social and public interest and the welfare nature of rural health services, especially national public health services, by increasing government investment in rural health services, particularly rural

health services in West China, and guide medical resources in changing their focus from "treatments neglecting prevention" to preventive health care. We should actively explore the reform of the public health investment system and gradually turn from investment in medical and health service institutions towards the provision or purchase of public health services for urban and rural residents, providing compensation funds according to the effect of medical services and encouraging medical and health service institutions to be oriented not towards profit but towards the safeguarding of residents' health. To truly change the system of combining medical treatment and medicine, we should ensure that the fiscal compensations for public health institutions meet basic demands so that public health institutions and medical service entities prioritize the provision and the development of basic medical services. The central government should increase transfer payment for public health in West China and rural health services to effectively solve the "scarcity of doctors and medicine" in these places. We should mobilize the transfer of medical professionals towards West China, step up the training of health technical personnel and improve health services.

(5) We should improve the mandatory implementation of the medical security system, and especially the medical assistance system, in order to provide the most basic medical and health services to poor people in our society. Under the conditions of the market economy, the establishment of a sound medical security system is one of the primary measures for the government to interfere with the medical and health sector, besides direct fiscal investment. Meanwhile, this is also a key measure for improving health equality. While securing and promoting public health services and new cooperative medical care, the government should focus on social pooling for serious diseases and continue to explore different types of rural medical security systems. For all farmers, serious diseases are the main health threat. Therefore, it is appropriate for new cooperative medical care to focus on serious disease insurance, as such a practice can effectively prevent a most serious phenomenon, that is: impoverishment, or backsliding to poverty due to illness. However, on the other hand, "serious illness insurance" under the prerequisite of voluntary insurance coverage will inevitably lower coverage rate, and the higher the minimum payment line, the narrower the scope of income. New rural cooperative medical care should explore the security mode of balancing both serious and minor diseases on the basis of insuring serious illness. In the management of serious illness insurance funds, the mode of operation management in commercial insurance companies may be introduced to ensure the effective use of the funds. This is in fact a sort of semi-commercial and semi-social security medical insurance. Similar practices can be found at home and abroad. In the light of the narrow coverage of urban basic medical insurance and new rural cooperative medical insurance, we should step up the establishment of an urban-rural medical assistance system. Medical assistance is one part of the medical security system and an important content of the entire social security system, as well as an effective measure for providing welfare medical security to poor people, and

plays an important role in freeing them from being impoverished or backsliding to poverty ergo illness. Medical assistance plans should be implemented for rural poor people within a region or a district. Medical assistance plans may be integrated with the whole social security system. For example, the scope of targets for implementing medical assistance could be determined by using the standard of the rural subsistence security system. In this way, not only could poor people be truly relieved but also the plan would be conveniently implemented as well as organizational costs reduced. On the whole, in the construction of the medical security system, not only should the government play a leading role, but also a multi-level and multi-type medical security system should be established according to farmers' actual demands and bearing capacity, and on the basis of respecting farmers' wishes.

(6) We should mobilize the public, especially public service organizations, to participate in patriotic health campaigns and effectively address urgent health problems in the course of economic and social transformations, such as health services for the migrant population, treatment of large-scale public health events, control of new modern infectious diseases, and increasingly serious mental health problems. In the establishment of a medical security system, we should closely combine medical security and public health, focusing on preventive health care so as to maximize the benefits of limited medical and health resources. With the state's strengthening of public health investment and improvement of the medical security system, medical and health services should be based on grassroots community services, efforts should be made to improve the training quality and professional skills of grassroots medical personnel, effectively solve the problem of people blindly crowding big hospitals and not going to community health centers, and truly implement the strategy of prevention first. Meanwhile, we should increase funding, investment and efforts to prevent new main infectious diseases and properly cope with emergency public health incidents. In light of the health problems of the migrant population, we should adopt a new mechanism with the objective of gradually including them into the management and services of their communities. We should mobilize social forces and citizens to participate in the construction of public health. As the absolute majority of public health problems are closely related to residents' awareness and behavior, through public participation, not only can public health resources be expanded but also more effective health education can be conducted in the course of their participation to promote the construction of the health environment and the changes of citizens' health-related behaviors.[4]

[4]This article is published in *China Industrial Economics*, Vol. 12, 2005.

Chapter 4
Establishing a Basic Rural Medical Security System

Since 1998, the establishment of an urban employees' basic medical insurance system has been considered one of the key reform projects in China, for which significant progress has been achieved. However, still no clear approaches or policies address the medical security problems of farmers, who make up of the absolute majority of the population. Due to profound changes in the social and economic structure, the cooperative medical system has been subject to overall decline since the 1980s, causing about 90% of the rural population to be without any medical security and to pay medical expenses out of their own pockets. Although the state put forward the task of restoring and reconstructing cooperative medical services in the 1990s, yet for various reasons this decision has yet to bear any fruits. The slow growth of farmers' income cannot keep up with the rapid increase of medical costs. Numerous poor farmers are plunged into such a predicament as they find themselves without resources to obtain medical treatments and purchase drugs. In recent years, the health of a significant number of farmers has even been deteriorating. A large number of farmers have been reduced or reversed to poverty due to illness, which not only directly imperils the life of these poor families but also affects the results of China's poverty alleviation strategy. Farmers' health problems have become major problems that cannot be ignored.

4.1 The Feasibility of Establishing a New Rural Medical Security System

Despite the awareness of the importance and necessity of establishing a medical security system in China's rural areas, people have yet to reach consensus on whether a rural medical security system meeting national conditions can be established at the present stage. The issue is whether China has sufficient financial resources and reliable institutions for the establishment of rural medical security.

Y. Wang, *Social Security in China: On the Possibility of Equitable Distribution*,
Research Series on the Chinese Dream and China's Development Path,
DOI 10.1007/978-981-10-5643-7_4

Those opposing rural medical security hold that as limited financial resources have rendered it very difficult for China to establish an urban medical security system, it would be impossible to establish a rural medical security system based on the state's financial resources; meanwhile, due to the reform of government institutions, government organs and personnel have been streamlined, and grassroots governments do not have institutions on which rural medical security needs to rely upon. Besides, China's traditional rural cooperative medical system existed under the conditions of planned economy; profound changes have taken place in China's urban and rural economic and social structure, rendering it impossible to establish a cooperative medical system according to traditional ways. There is no experience to draw upon for the establishment of a new rural medical security system suitable for the socialist market economic system.

The above opinion, so to speak, reflects that to comprehensively establish a rural medical security system in China at the current time is no easy matter, but rather one beset with difficulties. However, such difficulties can be overcome if real importance is given to farmers' health issues and effective measures adopted. Therefore, we need not ask ourselves whether we can establish rural medical security, but rather whether we want to or not. In our opinion, we are not only able to develop rural medical security; in China's new situation, doing so is necessary.

First, by developing the rural economy and increasing farmers' income, the financial resources for establishing rural medical security have been accumulated. Medical security requires funds, and a higher level of security requires more funds. In over twenty years since the initiation of reform and opening-up, farmers' per capita net income has increased tenfold from less than RMB 200 to over RMB 2200. If farmers could bear the expenditure of cooperative medical security in the time of planned economy with very low income, they could also bear the establishment of rural medical security to some extent, according to their current income. In terms of the government's financial resources, recent years have seen rapid increase of tax revenues in China; national tax revenues amounted to RMB 1.266 trillion in 2000. Therefore, the government should be able to inject some funds in rural medical security. Of course, due to the decline of the grassroots collective economy and the implementation of the system of tax distribution, in most regions of China, public finances below the county level, especially township finances, are in difficulty, which is the objective reality. However, this is only an issue of fiscal structure; in terms of economic power, China should now have more financial resources to establish rural medical security than twenty years ago.

Second, the issue concerning the establishment of institutions for the development of rural medical security can also be overcome. Cooperative medical care during the period of planned economy mainly relied on people's communities and production brigade organizations which grasped political and economic resources etc. Since reform and opening-up, although township governments and villagers' autonomous organizations' control of economic resources and their intervention in economic activities have been substantially weakened, these organizations still exist. Meanwhile, the number of rural doctors has increased and their professional qualifications have largely improved in comparison with the time before reform.

Table 4.1 Composition of China's medical security system in 1998, *Unit* percentage

Survey index	Urban and rural total	Urban	Rural				
		Total	Total	Class I	Class II	Class III	Class IV
Free medical care	4.95	16.01	1.16	1.07	0.76	1.98	0.26
Labor protection medical care	6.22	22.91	0.51	1.40	0.54	0.15	0.03
Semi-labor protection medical care	1.62	5.78	0.20	0.64	0.10	0.07	0.05
Medical insurance	1.88	3.27	1.41	2.39	1.63	1.16	0.12
Social pooling medical care	0.39	1.42	0.05	0.15	0.03	0.01	0.00
Cooperative medical care	5.54	2.74	6.50	22.21	3.24	1.62	1.83
Out-of-pocket medical care	76.40	44.13	87.44	71.79	93.17	94.77	81.49
Other forms	2.98	3.73	2.73	0.34	0.52	0.23	16.22

Source Initial Report on the Main Results of the Second National Health Service Survey in 1998

More than that, great development has also been achieved in other types of social organizations, such as rural financial institutions. If we expand our vision, we would find that there do exist institutions establishing the rural medical security; If we raise them from the village level to the county level (which is the direction of development), we will have richer organizational resources, as a county (municipal) unit enjoys relatively independent organizations resources of various types, such as a medical security system and a financial insurance system.

Finally, as for the lack of experience in establishing rural medical security under the new situation, the practice experiences of relevant regions have fully proven that a multi-level and multi-type rural medical security system can be established. Although there no longer exists a nationwide cooperative medical system, cooperative medical care is still maintained in South Jiangsu and Shanghai, while a variety of rural medical security initiatives have been taken and newly developed, such as rural labor insurance medical care, cooperative medical insurance and social pooling for serious illness. The results of the "Second National Health Service Survey" held by the Ministry of Health in 1998 showed that nationwide 61.50% of rural residents participated in cooperative medical care, and about 6.11% participated in some other type of medical security (see the following Table 4.1). This demonstrates that although it is difficult to restore the traditional cooperative medical care system in the rural areas,[1] yet it is necessary and feasible to develop a multi-type and multi-level medical security system in rural areas, where there is a huge space for development.

[1]For relevant analysis, see the author's article "A Report on the Rural Medical Security System", in Chen Jiagui ed. (2001), *The Development of Social Security in China: a Report*, Social Sciences Academic Press.

4.2 Suggestions and Measures for Establishing a New Rural Medical Security System

(i) Principles for establishing a new rural medical security system

To establish a basic medical security system for farmers in the new situation of socialist market economy, we should stick to the following basic principles: First, we should stick to the principle of state support. A mechanism in which the state and farmers make joint investments and share risks should be established, so that the limited fund investments by the state can guide farmers in their participation in the medical security system. Meanwhile, we should lay emphasis on a mechanism of diversified investments, and substantiate farmers' medical security fund by using the donations from community economies, enterprises, charity institutions, foreign-funded institutions and individuals. In terms of state investments, the majority may be diverted from state health service funds and some from tax revenues. Second, measures can be adjusted to local conditions. China has a vast territory with great disparity in economic and social development; as this cannot be changed on the short term, we cannot and should not adopt a "sweeping approach" or "unified pattern" for the nationwide establishment of farmers' medical security. We should allow all regions to start from their own reality and actively explore a multi-form and multi-level medical insurance system, especially a cooperative medical insurance system addressing the local characteristics of rural areas. Third, we should stick to the principle of socialization. We should promote the participation of farmers through national legislation (instead of just relying on "voluntary participation") based on county-level regions (instead of villages or townships), which would help expand the scale of medical security funds and enhance the ability to resist risks. Meanwhile, we may draw upon the form of personal accounts in urban employees' medical care to establish farmers' family medical security accounts, promote farmers' fund saving and lessen the risks of illness. Fourth, we should stick to the principle of insuring against serious illness. Farmers' illness threats mainly come from serious illness, a risk which they cannot bear. However, due to limited state investments, it is impossible to establish comprehensive and advanced medical security; therefore, such limited funds may only be applied to most urgent needs, that is: the most serious illnesses which pose the biggest threats to farmers. As the state has established the "basic medical insurance" system for urban employees, it should also establish the "essential serious illness security" system for farmers.

(ii) State attention and support are the basis and prerequisite for establishing farmers' medical security

With the disintegration of collective economy, the absolute majority of rural grassroots community organizations has lost or lacks the ability to collectively invest in farmers' medical security, which is a fundamental cause for the decline of community-based cooperative medical care. Since the initiation of reform in the tax-sharing system, financial resources have been concentrated in upper level governments, while grassroots governments have weaker funding to the point that a significant number of township governments operate in debt, while many counties and cities maintain payroll finance or "subsidized" finance. Reforming grassroots government agencies and combining townships could indeed reduce administrative expenditures, but leaves the issue of increasing financial resources for grassroots community authorities unaddressed. A root cause is that the state employs its main financial resources to solve large and medium state-owned enterprises issues, and it practices the "one country two systems" policy for urban and rural areas, which includes seriously urban-biased policymaking in terms of education, health, electricity, roads, credits, water conservancy, post and telecommunications and other infrastructure.[2] Rural resources are being abused while investment in these areas is inadequate, leading to financial difficulties for township enterprises, small and medium enterprises, and farmers' household economies, as well as to shrinking county economies. A substantial number of grassroots governments are weighed down with education expenditures, employees' salaries and retirement pensions, etc. The state may lack determination to solve the issue of farmers' medical security, but grassroots governments not only unable to address farmers' medical security but also have no such a wish or motive.

Currently, the state has included the establishment of a socialized urban employees' basic medical insurance system as one of the five key reform projects, which shows that the state has assumed the burdensome responsibility of urban employees' basic medical insurance. This is a basic reflection of state functions and also an inevitable requirement for establishing a fair society. Based on the objective reality of the great urban-rural disparity in China, it is impossible to completely unify the urban-rural medical security system within a short period, and the urban-rural gap in the scope and level of medical security will persist for a long time. However, such factual disparity cannot excuse the state from shirking its responsibility for securing farmers' health. In a way, farmers whose income is lower need more support and protection from the state in medical security than urban employees. Our health policy should not merely focus on enhancing the health of a few healthy people, but should enable those without health security to have access to the most essential health security. Meanwhile, medical security, particularly public health care, is typically considered as a social "public goods", and should be made available to the whole society instead of its access being limited to urban residents. This is an objective requirement for establishing a complete market economy system and also a public investment producing maximum benefits for the whole society. Additionally, to establish a medical security system for all people, especially farmers, is a necessary development in order to maintain the healthy

---

[2]The Research Team of the Academy of Macroeconomic Research, SDPC (2001), Problems of Rural Tax Reform: A Study, Review of Economic Research, 2001 (24).

operation of the basic medical insurance system for urban employees. With rapid industrialization and urbanization in China, the rural population has been migrating to cities and towns (the ratio of urban population has exceeded 36% according to the 2000 census data). If farmers' medical security issue is not soon settled, the impact on the urban medical security system will be tremendous, and the stable operation of the urban medical security system will be affected.

(iii) The establishment of farmers' basic medical security should focus on security for serious illness

New approaches are required for the settlement of farmers' medical security problems under the conditions of the market economy. In light of the extreme complexity of the medical security system and difficulty in managing medical consumption, we cannot do for farmers' medical care as was done for solving the issue of urban employees' medical insurance. Our foothold is to establish and resolve farmers' most essential medical security, especially security for risks of major illness which farmers can hardly bear. On the whole, farmers' medical security relies mainly on self-protection based on families, because of low productivity and also because of the large proportion for which farmers account nationally. In this regard, the situation cannot be compare with that of developed countries in the West. However, we cannot leave all the burdens of medical security to self-protection based on farmers' families, because farmers' families have limited bearing capacities. For ordinary and minor ailments, families can manage to bear medical costs. As for major and serious illnesses, low-income farmers absolutely cannot afford treatment. It should be noted that currently rural families are becoming smaller, thus farmers' income increases slowly, while various taxes are constantly rising, posing excessive burdens. From 1994 to 1999, farmers' per capita income increase rate (12.16%) was lower than the increase rate of their burdens, which actually reduced their families' self-protection abilities, especially the ability to resist serious illnesses.

Therefore, to alleviate farmers' burdens, as well as reduce management difficulties and the cost of the medical security system, we advocate that we should first establish farmers' serious illness insurance based on counties (or townships) in rural areas. The sources of funds for farmers' serious illness security would mainly be comprised of funds contributed by farmer households and fiscal subsidies. To establish a farmers' serious illness security fund, the ratio of contributions may be adapted to actual local conditions. Compared with traditional cooperative medical care, farmers' serious illness security—which has such advantages as a high level of social pooling, strong resistance against risks, low level of fund raising, as well as facility in fund raising, management and settlement—is a basic rural medical security system adapted to new situations. Of course, in regions with better conditions (such as suburban villages in South Jiangsu, Shanghai, and medium and large cities), more comprehensive medical security (including outpatient services) may be developed on the basis of farmers' serious illness insurance.

(iv) Several measures for establishing the rural medical security system

(1) We should enhance the awareness of the government as well as that of the whole society on the issue of rural medical security. We have noted that whether the farmers' medical security system can be established mainly depends on awareness levels. Only when awareness is enhanced will great importance be attached to this issue, and thus will feasible measures be actively explored and adopted to be implement in the system. We stress the major responsibilities of the state in resolving farmers' medical security problems, not just because the state should more proactively adopt measures in terms of the institutional design of and fiscal investment for farmers' medical security, but more importantly because we wish to arouse the close attention of the government and that of the whole society. The state is obliged to settle farmers' medical security problems, which is also an inevitable path to modernization.

(2) We should adjust the government's medical and health investment structure to focus on supporting disadvantaged groups and patients. With the reform of the health system and especially the emergence of a large number of private hospitals, the state's focus on health investment should gradually shift from health service providers to medical service consumers; that is because the current problem is not the "scarcity of doctors and medicine", but rather that people in most regions lack even the most essential medical security. State support may promote the growth of medical consumption, drive the development of the medical industry, and increase employment opportunities so that people can enjoy better medical services and living standard. Except for remote areas and some medical institutions and public health institutions which the state must control, medical institutions' access restriction may be lifted so that medical institutions can raise funds in market and become independent market players who assume sole responsibility for their own profits or losses. This can not only promote medical service institutions such as hospitals to improve their service quality and better their service attitude but also reduce state investments, which can be diverted to the establishment of medical security for the people. As a whole, the state's total investments in medical and health services would not increase significantly, but the effect would become more significant and fairer.

(3) Reasonably distribute health resources and effectively reduce medical costs. "Shortage" (poor facility capacity) and "redundancy" (disorderly scattering of service professionals and service centers, and loss of control over scale) coexist due to seriously unreasonable allocation of medical and health resources in China, which lead to the rise of medical costs. To control the rise of medical costs, we should focus on controlling the expansion of the scope of medical services and the rise of internal costs. Based on the scope of regional health care, we should strictly enforce the examination and approval of new medical institutions, control the expansion of the current scope, remerge unreasonably overlapping institutions, and adjust and rationalize service functions. In light of the disorderly situation in the medicine and medical market, to strengthen the supervision of pharmaceutical production, sales link and medical institutions is

an important step in order to control the rise of medical costs and alleviating farmers' burdens. The reform and supervision of urban and rural medical markets should be conducted simultaneously to plug up loopholes and improve efficiency.

(4) Strengthen public health work and improve the public health system. Preventive healthcare is for everybody and it has the nature of low cost, good efficiency and significant effect. "In line with the principle of cost-effectiveness and fairness, preventive healthcare can obviously reduce risks of illness, disability and death, improve life quality, effectively protect social productivity, and promote social and economic development," and thus should remain a priority in terms of rural healthcare work, with strengthened input in funding, personnel and facilities. Significant achievements have been made in public health (mainly marked by epidemic prevention, health supervision and patriotic health campaigns), maternal and children's health care, and medical preventive health systems. However, the three systems overlap and are separated so that their limited resources cannot be effectively utilized. We should, while keeping in view the implementation of regional health planning and the adjustment of medical service institutions, and basing ourselves on the current situation of township health centers and village health stations with integrated management, establish a health care system of "one network with multiple uses". Based on the nature of provided services (public health care and preventive care or general operating business, health care for poverty relief or ordinary treatment, etc.), we should reasonably solve the issue of the compensatory mechanism for public health and preventive care, and enable public preventive care to have stable funding, as well as ensure the normal development of preventive health care.

(5) Establish a medical assistance system and strengthen health care for poverty relief. The rural medical security system with Chinese characteristics should also include a medical assistance system. The role of the government is not just "to add flowers to the brocade", but more importantly to "provide fuel in snowy weather" by including poverty relief through health care for poverty-stricken areas and people as one of the key contents for promoting rural health care. This is necessary in order to realize the objective of "making health available to everyone" and to develop production and prevent people from "being reduced or reversed to poverty" because of illness. The poverty relief plans implemented in China focus on economic poverty relief. Economic poverty relief and health poverty relief should be integrated. With the support of the central government and developed regions, we should first solve the health care facility construction and "scarcity of doctors and medicine" issues in poverty-stricken areas, and allocate a part of the state's special fund for poverty relief and relevant support funds to specially address the medical poverty relief in poor regions. As for rural poor people in different regions and areas, medical assistance plans should be implemented. Medical assistance plans are part of the medical security system, which is an important part of the whole social security system. We should incorporate health poverty relief into social

security, especially the social assistance system, and integrate medical assistance plans into the whole social security system. For example, the scope of targets for medical assistance may be determined by using the standard of the rural subsistence security system. In this way, we can truly assist poor people, while reducing organizational cost so that such a practice becomes convenient and feasible.[3]

[3]This article is published in Research on Economics and Management, Vol. 3, 2001.

Chapter 5
Analysis of Factors Affecting Rural Residents' Satisfaction with Medical Services

5.1 Introduction

With the development of the rural economic society, rural residents have growing demands in terms of medical services, and the quality of medical services provided to rural residents has been drawing more and more attention. Medical service satisfaction is an important index for evaluating the quality of medical services, and it can, to some extent, reflect the people's potential medical demands. Satisfaction generally comprises a series of indexes. Yiren and Pengde (2005), through questionnaire surveys of patients in a certain hospital in Nanjing, classify patients' satisfaction indexes into five dimensions by using the factor analysis method, that is: medical effect, medical professionals' technique and capability, medical professionals' attitude, medical environment, and medical support and expenditure. In recent years, especially since the implementation of the new rural cooperative medical care system (Hereinafter referred to as New Rural Co-op), many scholars have, on the basis of field surveys, studied the medical service satisfaction of rural residents as well as the factors affecting satisfaction. A survey conducted by Liming et al. (2009) on 245 farmer households in three provinces shows that the satisfaction of farmers who subscribe to the New Rural Co-op on medical services is relatively high, but their satisfaction concerns more the "volume" of supply than the "quality" thereof. Wang et al. (2006) has found out through research that farmers' overall satisfaction with the implementation of the New Rural Co-op program is related to their age, policy awareness, medical service expenditures, satisfaction on reimbursement, and their expected coinsurance rate. Liu et al. (2008) have found out through research on the New Rural Co-op that farmers' age, marital status, education background, occupation, self-rated health conditions and self-rated happiness in life have a significant impact on their satisfaction with the New Rural Co-op, while gender has no significant impact. Zhou and Shi (2009) have found out through research that the satisfaction with the New Rural Co-op reimbursement system shows a significant positive correlation with the New Rural Co-op

Y. Wang, *Social Security in China: On the Possibility of Equitable Distribution*,
Research Series on the Chinese Dream and China's Development Path,
DOI 10.1007/978-981-10-5643-7_5

reimbursement ratio and procedures, and a significant negative correlation with whether farmers subscribe to other health insurances, their family's yearly medical expenditures, and personal expectation on the amount raised.

In light of past studies, besides the quality of medical services per se, the personal traits of medical service users and their economic, social and cultural background are also important factors affecting their satisfaction with medical services. However, different factors affect satisfaction with medical services differently, with some directly affecting satisfaction with medical services while others coming into play via an intermediate variable. However, in extant literature, many studies analyze all factors as factors directly affecting satisfaction with medical services, instead of differentiating the direct factors and the indirect factors affecting satisfaction with medical services; therefore, it is very difficult for them to analyze how different factors affect satisfaction with medical services.

Studies on satisfaction with medical services cannot be separated from the rating of medical services by rural residents, who are the direct consumers of medical services. How do rural residents comment on the current medical services? How many are satisfied, and how many are not? What factors affect their satisfaction with medical services? This article will use the data of a questionnaire survey by a task force of the Chinese Academy of Social Sciences (CASS) on "the study of the demand for medical services by medium and low-income people in China and innovation of service modes" conducted in 2009, and adopt the path analysis method to analyze factors affecting rural residents' satisfaction with medical services and how each factor affects such satisfaction.

5.2 Course of Survey and Framework of Research

(i) Course of survey

The data used in this article are the initial data concerning rural areas concluded by the task force of the Chinese Academy of Social Sciences (CASS) on "the study of the demand for medical services by medium and low-income people in China and innovation of service modes" conducted in 2009. This survey mainly addressed medium and low-income rural and urban residents in China. Limited by funding, human resources and time, representative regions were sampled, including six urban areas and four rural areas (ten areas in total) in seven provinces (municipalities) in Northeast China, North China, Northwest China, Southeast China, Southwest China and Central China. The four rural regions were respectively Miyun County, Beijing, Xinzheng City, Henan, Yuzhong City, Gansu, and Kaiyuan City, Yunnan. These regions cover different levels of income in rural areas while including three geographical units in the eastern, central and western parts of China.

This survey adopted the method of visiting homes with questionnaires. The survey was conducted from July to October, 2009. During the course of the survey, strictly trained interviewers asked questions and filled out questionnaires by themselves, and gave explanations to questions raised by interviewees. Over one hour was spent on filling out each questionnaire on average, and the project principal checked each questionnaire, and even re-visited interviewees one by one to ensure the accuracy and validity of the data. Finally, this survey acquired the information of 903 rural residents and their families (including some local residents whose household register was not rural), among whom there were 441 rural households which met medium and low-income standards, and 462 (relatively) high-income rural households. As this survey did not adopt the method of random sampling nationwide, the results of the research were deficient to deduce the overall situation, but it was hoped that they could illustrate rural residents' satisfaction with medical services nationwide to some extent.

(ii) Framework of research

This research held that rural residents' rating on medical institutions, medical professionals, drugs and the medical insurance system directly affected their satisfaction with medical services, whereas their social and demographic characteristics such as age, gender, region and educational background, as well as family income, family members' health status, diagnosis and treatment methods after taking ill, use of medical services, accessibility of medical resources, ratio of medical and health care expenditure, and time interval of medical expense reimbursement, etc., mainly affected their satisfaction with medical services through the above four factors. Therefore, this study takes these four factors (such as rating of medical institutions) as intermediate variables, and factors such as social and demographic characteristics as initial variables, and adopts a path analysis to disclose the courses of initial variables and intermediate variables affecting satisfaction with medical services (see Fig. 5.1 for the framework of analysis).

The dependent variables are interval variables, which are measured by the method of direct value assignment to answers, with 1 ~ 5 points assigned to answers ranging from "very dissatisfied" to "very satisfied" (the highest point being 5). The intermediate variables are all interval variables, which are measured through a series of indexes. The rating for medical institutions consists of variables

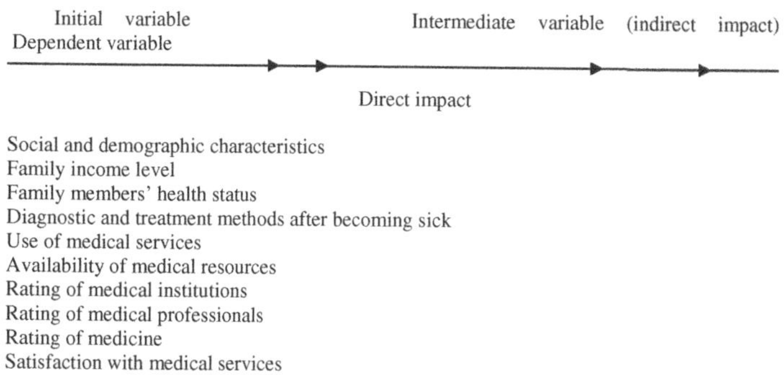

Fig. 5.1 Framework of Research

such as quantity of institutions, medical environment, convenience and medical equipment; the rating for medical professionals consists of variables such as technical accomplishments, explanation of state of an illness and service attitudes of medical professionals; the rating for drugs consists variables such as types, quality and prices of drugs; the rating for the medical insurance system consists of variables such as the level of contribution, convenience in reimbursement, amount of reimbursement and catalog of reimbursed drugs.

Besides the interviewees' personal, social and demographic characteristics, initial variables mainly appeal to the family characteristics of interviewees, mainly out of the consideration that in one family, whenever a member is taken ill, the other members will generally be involved in the care of the sick one; therefore, to some extent, families are basic units using medical services. Initial variables mainly include: ① Social and demographic characteristics, including interviewees' age, gender (male or female), national geographical location (east, central or west), education background and occupation; ② Family income level (low, medium or high)[1]; ③ Family members' illness status, including the main types of diseases caught by family members in the previous years (chronic diseases, acute diseases or other diseases) and the incidence of disease; ④ Treatment and diagnosis methods adopted after family members are taken ill, including not adopting any measure, self-diagnosis and treatment as well as seeing a doctor in a medical institution; ⑤ Use of medical services, including the medical institutions mainly used (grassroots medical institutions, pharmacies, town health centers and county hospitals) and drug use frequency in the previous year; ⑥ The proportion of medical and health expenditures, referring to the ratio of year-round medical and health care expenditures against total expenditures; ⑦ Accessibility of medical resources, including the distance to the nearest big hospital and the distance to the nearest village clinic; ⑧ Time interval of reimbursement of medical expenses, including spot reimbursement and off-the-spot reimbursement.

The following hypothesis is proposed in this article based on experiences and available literature: ① Satisfaction with medical institutions, medical professionals and drugs exerts more impact on satisfaction with medical services than satisfaction with the medical insurance system. ② Gender has no impact on satisfaction with medical services. ③ Age, location, occupation and education background have a significant impact on satisfaction with medical services. ④ Family income levels indirectly affect satisfaction with medical services in that the higher income rural residents have, the lower their satisfaction with medical services is. ⑤ Types of diseases are not related with satisfaction with medical services; the incidence of

[1]The task force, in the beginning, defined "medium and low income" as income higher than the local minimum subsistence level, and lower than 50% of the local rural net per capita income, and classified "medium and low income" into medium income and low income according to research needs. Medium income refers to the income level above 50% of the medium and low-income standard (that is, 25% of the per capita income of the previous year), while low income refers to the income level below 50% of the medium and low-income standard. The families under survey whose income is above "medium and low income" standard are called high-income families.

diseases is related with satisfaction with medical services in that the higher incidence of diseases rural residents have, the lower their satisfaction with medical services is. ⑥ The conditions of medical institutions used exert a direct impact on satisfaction with medical services in that the higher level of medical institutions rural residents use, the higher their satisfaction with medical services is; the frequency of drug use has no impact on satisfaction with medical services. ⑦ The accessibility of medical resources indirectly affects satisfaction with medical services mainly by affecting satisfaction with medical institutions. ⑧ The ratio of medical and health care expenditures against total expenditures directly affects satisfaction with medical services. ⑨ The time interval of medical expense reimbursement indirectly affects satisfaction with medical services by affecting satisfaction with the medical insurance system.

5.3 Results of Research and Analysis

(i) Statistical description of variables

(1) Basic description of rural residents' satisfaction with medical services

In light of the survey results, rural residents currently are not highly satisfied with medical services. The average score is 3.46 points, between "so so" and "fairly satisfactory"; 35.3% of the interviewees choose "so so"; 43.3% of them choose "fairly satisfied"; 12.7% of them choose "dissatisfied", that is, giving a score less than 3 points; while only 8.3% of them choose "very satisfied".

(2) Statistic description of intermediate variables

Table 5.1 indicates that the average rating for medical institutions is 13.54 points, of which rural residents have higher rating on the convenience of getting medical care than on the quantity, environment and equipment of medical institutions; the average rating for medical professionals is 9.94 points, of which rural residents have higher rating over the service attitudes of medical professionals than on their medical skills and explanation of diseases; the average rating for drugs is 9.13

Table 5.1 Statistical description of intermediate variables

	Total score	Average value	Minimum value	Maximum value	Standard deviation
Rating for medical institutions	20	13.54	5	20	2.32
Rating for medical professionals	15	9.94	3	15	1.92
Rating for drugs	15	9.13	4	13	1.44
Rating for the medical insurance system	20	11.50	4	20	2.43

points, of which rural residents have the highest rating on types of drugs and the lowest rating on prices of drugs; the average rating for the medical insurance system is 11.50 points, of which rural residents have the lowest rating on the scope of reimbursement. On the whole, rural residents' ratings on the medical insurance system differ the most, whereas their ratings on drugs differ the less.

(3) Statistic description of initial variables

Tables 5.2 and 5.3 indicate that of the 903 interviewees, mid-aged people are dominant, and their average age is 45; in terms of gender, females outnumber males; in terms of geographical location, people from the western region are most numerous; in terms of education background, most have only received primary school education or below; in terms of occupation, most work in the field of agriculture (mostly farmers). The family income level of most interviewees is above the middle level in local rural areas; the diseases afflicting their family members are mostly acute diseases, and most adopt the measure of "seeing a doctor in a medical institution" after a disease is contracted, opting mostly for rural grassroots medical institutions; the distance to the grassroots medical institution closest to the interviewees is 2.69 km on average; the medical expenses can be reimbursed directly (directly deducted from the New Rural Co-op fund) after the interviewees and their family members see a doctor.

(ii) Multivariate regression analysis of intermediate variables on rural residents' satisfaction with medical services

According to the framework of analysis, intermediate variables are used first to conduct a multivariate regression analysis of satisfaction with medical services. The explanatory power of the model is 26%, with relatively satisfying goodness-of-fit. According to the results of the analysis, with the exception of the rating of the medical insurance system, the rating of medical institutions, the rating of medical professionals and the rating of drugs have all passed the significance test. The rating with the biggest impact is that of medical professionals, with a standardized regression coefficient of 0.355, followed by the rating of medical institutions, with a standardized regression coefficient of 0.14 (see Table 5.4). Therefore, in the subsequent path analysis, the rating of the medical insurance system will not be incorporated into the regression model.

(iii) Multivariate regression analysis of the impact of initial variables on intermediate variables and dependent variables

The multivariate regression analysis method adopted in this article is the optimal scaling regression analysis method, which allows independent variables to be classified variables and gives each class an appropriate quantitative rating. Based on the framework of models expected to be fit, this method analyzes the changing degrees of impact of different classified variables on dependent variables and adopts certain nonlinear transformations to reiterate original classified variables, so as to find the best quantitative rating for them and then fit an optimal equation.

Table 5.2 Statistical description of initial variables (1)

Variable		Assignment	Number of samples	Effective percentage
Gender	Male	1	425	52.93
	Female	2	477	47.07
Location	East	1	250	27.68
	Central	2	199	22.04
	West	3	454	50.28
Education background	Primary school and below	1	392	43.61
	Junior middle school	2	301	33.48
	Senior middle school and above	3	206	22.91
Occupation	Agricultural management personnel	1	48	5.34
	The self-employed	2	40	4.45
	Rural migrant workers	3	17	1.89
	Agricultural practitioners (farmers)	4	794	88.32
Family income level	Low income	1	137	15.17
	Middle income	2	304	33.67
	High income	3	462	51.16
Main types of diseases that family members had in the previous year	Chronic diseases	1	108	12.27
	Other diseases	2	164	18.64
	Acute diseases	3	608	69.09
Main method of diagnosis and treatmentadopted after a family member is taken ill	Not adopting any measure	1	21	2.47
	Self-diagnosis and treatment	2	206	24.21
	See a doctor in a medical institution	3	624	73.32
Medical institutions mainly used in the previous year	Township health centers	1	161	21.70
	Rural grassroots medical institutions	2	401	54.04
	County hospitals	3	71	9.57
	Pharmacies	4	109	14.69

(continued)

Table 5.2 (continued)

Variable		Assignment	Number of samples	Effective percentage
Time interval for reimbursement of medical expenses	Spot reimbursement	1	386	70.57
	Off-the-spot reimbursement	2	161	29.43

Note In this table, the sums of samples of each group of classified data are not inter-equivalent and are not necessarily equivalent to the number of effective samples (903), which is caused by the large amount of sample missing value. However, in order not to lose the information of missing cases, this article preserves case records with missing value and incorporates samples with missing value into the regression model in optimal scaling regression

Table 5.3 Statistical description of initial variables (2)

Variable	Average value	Minimum value	Maximum value	Standard deviation
Age	45.35	16	84	13.89
The distance to the large hospital closest to the interviewee's home (km)	45.85	1	260	40.73
The distance to the community health center (village clinic) closest to the interviewee's home (km)	2.69	0	24	3.04
Frequency at which family members were taken ill in the previous year	2.36	0	11	1.37
Frequency at which drugs were use in the whole family in the previous year	135.55	0	3285	336.05
Ratio of medical and health care expenditure against total expenditures (%)	26.97	0	705.88	48.84

Table 5.4 Multivariate regression analysis of the direct impact of intermediate variables on satisfaction with medical services

	Unstandardized regression coefficient	Standardized regression coefficient
Rating of medical institutions	0.052	0.140***
Rating of medical professionals	0.161	0.355***
Rating of drugs	0.049	0.081*
Rating of the medical insurance system	0.021	0.059
Constant term	0.465	
F	68.278***	
R^2	0.256	

Note *** and * show the significance level of 0.1% and 5% respectively

In light of the multivariate regression analysis of initial variables to intermediate variables and dependent variables, the four regression models all have a relatively good fit. Table 5.5 indicates that the explanatory power of the initial variables to several intermediate variables are all above 15%, of which the one with the strongest

Table 5.5 Multivariate regression analysis of the impact of initial variables on intermediate variables and dependent variables (standardized regression coefficient)

Initial variables	Intermediate variables			Dependent variables
	Rating of medical institutions	Rating of medical professionals	Rating of drugs	Satisfaction with medical services
Age	0.166*	0.198**	−0.001	0.271***
Gender	−0.028	0.027	−0.039	−0.100
Location	0.345***	0.303***	0.260***	0.273***
Education background	−0.143*	−0.094	0.036	−0.045
Occupation	0.213***	−0.243***	0.217***	0.172***
Family income level	−0.058	−0.119*	−0.024	−0.159***
The distance to the large hospital closest to the interviewee's home (km)	−0.129	−0.080	−0.138	−0.109
The distance to the village clinic closest to the interviewee's home (km)	−0.015	0.012	0.129*	−0.018
Main types of diseases contacted by family members in the previous year	−0.150**	0.112*	0.165***	−0.077
Number of times family members were taken ill in the previous year	0.038	−0.135*	−0.042	0.019
Main method of diagnosis and treatment adopted after a family member is taken ill	0.102*	0.143**	0.064	0.069
Main medical institutions used in the previous year	−0.056	0.070	−0.172***	−0.082
Frequency of drug use by the whole family in the previous year	0.011	−0.015	−0.086	0.003
Proportion of medical and health care expenditure in the previous year	−0.085	−0.076	0.067	−0.076
Time interval for medical expense reimbursement	0.075	0.054	0.044	−0.003
F	1.931**	1.486*	1.584*	1.671*
R^2	0.182	0.150	0.154	0.164

Note ***, ** and * respectively indicate the significance level of 0.1%, 1% and 5%

explanatory power is that initial variables against the rating of medical institutions; the direct explanatory degree of the initial variables to dependent variables is 16%, obviously lower than the explanatory power of intermediate variables to dependent variables. This shows that directly applying initial variables to explain dependent variables is subject to very big defects, as initial variables affect dependent variables mainly through intermediate variables, which also illustrates that the above preset framework of research is reasonable. In light of the regression results, the initial variables significantly affecting the rating of medical institutions are age, location, education background, occupation, main types of diseases contracted by family members in the previous year, and main method of diagnosis and treatment adopted after a family member is taken ill; initial variables significantly affecting the rating of medical professionals are age, location, education background, occupation, main types of diseases contracted by family members in the previous year, and main method of diagnosis and treatment adopted after a family member is taken ill; initial variables with significant impact on drug ratings are location, occupation, distance to the closest village clinic, main types of diseases contracted by family members in the previous year, and main medical institutions visited in the previous year. Initial variables with significant and direct impact on satisfaction with medical services are age, location, occupation and family income level.

(iv) Path analysis of the impact on satisfaction with medical services

Table 5.6 indicates the course in which initial variables impact dependent variables, of which indirect impact = the standardized regression coefficient of an initial variable to an intermediate variable × the standardized regression coefficient of the intermediate variable to dependent variables; total impact = indirect impact + direct impact; in accordance with Table 5.5, the standardized regression coefficients with $p > 0.05$ are not included in the table.

The results of path analysis show that location exerts the greatest impact on satisfaction with medical services (according to the absolute value of the path coefficient), with its coefficient reaching 0.450; age comes next, with a coefficient of 0.365; family income level ranks the third, with a coefficient of −0.211. Gender, distance to the closest large hospital, frequency of drug use by the whole family in the previous year, proportion of medical or health care expenditure in the previous year and time interval for medical expense reimbursement have no impact on rural residents' satisfaction with medical services.

Next, let's further analyze the impact of various factors on satisfaction with medical services.

(1) Age exerts a positive impact on satisfaction with medical services, that is, rural residents' satisfaction with medical services increases with their age. For one thing, current medical services can meet the demands of elderly people but fail to meet young people's demands; for another, elderly people probably have lower requirements for medical services than young people.

Table 5.6 Path analysis of initial variables on satisfaction with medical services

	Total impact	Indirect impact			Direct impact
		Rating of medical institutions	Rating of medical professionals	Rating of drugs	
Age	0.365	0.023	0.071	–	0.271
Gender	–	–	–	–	–
Location	0.450	0.048	0.108	0.021	0.273
Education background	−0.020	−0.020	–	–	–
Occupation	0.134	0.030	−0.086	0.018	0.172
Family income level	−0.201	–	−0.042	–	−0.159
Distance to the closest large hospital	–	–	–	–	–
Distance to the closest village clinic	0.010	–	–	0.010	–
Main types of disease family members contracted in the previous year	0.032	−0.021	0.040	0.013	–
Frequency at which family members were taken ill in the previous year	−0.048	–	−0.048	–	–
Main method of diagnosis and treatment adopted after a family member is taken ill	0.065	0.014	0.051		–
Main medical institutions used in the previous year	−0.014	–	–	−0.014	
Frequency of drug use by the whole family in the previous year	–	–	–	–	–
Ration of medical and health care expenditure in the previous year	–	–	–	–	–
Time interval for medical expense reimbursement	–	–	–	–	–

(2) In terms of location, the satisfaction with medical services of rural residents in western regions is higher than that in central regions, while the satisfaction with medical services in eastern regions is the lowest.

(3) Educational background exerts a negative impact on satisfaction with medical services; that is, the better rural residents' educational background is, the lower their satisfaction with medical services is. Educational background affects rural residents' satisfaction with medical services mainly by affecting their rating of medical institutions. This is probably because residents with better educational background have very high expectations on medical services, which in turn reduces their satisfaction.

(4) In terms of occupation, agricultural management personnel are the least satisfied with medical services, while farmers are the most satisfied. This is probably because people engaged in different occupations have different expectations when it comes to medical services. Farmers, who did not have such medical security before the implementation of the New Rural Co-op feel quite satisfied with the availability of medical security, which is an important reason for their enhanced satisfaction with medical services.

(5) Family income level exerts a negative impact on satisfaction with medical services; that is, the higher rural residents' family income level is, the lower their satisfaction with medical services is. This is mainly because high-income families have higher demands in terms of medical services, while a certain gap exists between such demands and the current service level, thus affecting their satisfaction with medical services.

(6) Distance to the closest village clinic has a positive impact on their satisfaction with medical services; that is, the farther rural residents live from their village clinic, the higher their satisfaction with medical services is. This is mainly because the farther rural residents live from their village clinic; the less likely they are to visit it, thus the fewer problems they discover, which in turn increases their satisfaction.

(7) Frequency at which family members contracted diseases in the previous year has a negative impact on their satisfaction with medical services; that is, the more often family members are taken ill, the lower their satisfaction with medical service is.

(8) In terms of main types of diseases contracted by family members in the previous year, rural residents' families whose members mainly contact acute diseases have a higher satisfaction with medical services than those whose members mainly suffer from chronic diseases and other diseases. This is probably because acute diseases under survey are mainly influenza, for which there are very mature drugs and medical techniques, thus improving patients' satisfaction.

(9) In terms of the main treatment and diagnosis methods adopted after family members are taken ill, rural residents who see a doctor in a medical institution after having been taken ill have a higher satisfaction with medical services than those resorting to self-diagnosis and treatment (buying drugs themselves or self-recuperation). This is probably related to the medical institutions attended. Rural residents choosing self-diagnosis and treatment generally visit pharmacies. In this research, rural residents who often attend pharmacies have a lower satisfaction with medical services that those visiting other types of medical institutions.

(10) In terms of main medical institutions used in the previous year, rural residents using township health centers have the highest satisfaction with medical services, while those using pharmacies have the lowest satisfaction with medical services. This is mainly because township health centers are designated medical institutions for the New Rural Co-op, where medical facilities and doctors' skills are better than grassroots medical institutions and pharmacies; also, such health centers are closer to county hospitals and are less costly, thereby rural residents are more satisfied with them.

5.4 Conclusion and Policy Implications

This article attempts to analyze the factors currently affecting rural residents' satisfaction with medical services by mean of the path analysis method and referring to the survey data of 903 rural households in China. The results of this analysis indicate that currently rural residents have a low satisfaction with medical services. Such intermediate variables as the rating of medical institutions, rating of medical professionals and rating of drugs directly affect rural residents' satisfaction with medical services; in terms of initial variables, the age, location, occupation and family income level of rural residents directly affect their satisfaction with medical services while educational background, main types of diseases family members suffer from, and diagnosis and treatment methods after being taken ill indirectly affect their satisfaction with medical services.

Therefore, to improve rural residents' satisfaction with medical services, efforts should be made in the following aspects: first, in terms of provision of medical services, rural residents' medical service demands should be met mainly by medical institutions, medical professionals and drugs; second, ways for diversified medical services to meet the medical service demands of rural residents of different ages, income level and education background should be explored. With the development of the rural economy and society, rural residents' disparity in income and educational background become more and more significant. This leads to the diversification of their demands in terms of medical services. The past "sweeping approach" to rural medical services can no longer meet the requirements of the development of rural medical services. As a result, we need to be more insightful in terms of rural residents' medical demands and diversify rural medical service products on the basis of providing basic medical services, thus satisfying the diverse medical demands of the rural residents and improving their satisfaction with medical services.[2]

[2]This article, written in collaboration with Jiang Cuiping, is published in *Chinese Rural Economy*, 2010 (8).

Chapter 6
Analysis of Social Security Expenditures by the Chinese Government

Since reform and opening-up, the Chinese government has been constantly increasing fiscal investments in social security. Significant results were achieved, which in turn play an important role in providing for people's basic life needs, maintaining social stability and promoting economic development. However, there is still a sizable gap between fiscal investments in social security and people's demands for social security. Not only is the total amount of fiscal expenditures insufficient, but also the structure of expenditures is unreasonable, and fiscal expenditures in social security does not play a satisfactory role in adjusting income distribution.

6.1 Introduction

Social security—an important system for alleviating poverty, ensuring people's livelihood, promoting economic and social development, and maintaining social stability, social fairness and justice—is also a key area of modern government expenditures and a main part of public expenditures. Due to differences in developmental stages and developmental modes, the total volume, structure, scope, key points and operation mechanism of different countries' social security expenditure vary. Great disparity can also found in one country's different periods in terms of social security expenditures. By studying the changes in the development of the status of social security expenditures, we can discern the importance attached by the government to the construction of social security. This reflects the stages and levels of economic and social development of a country or a region and deepens our understanding of a country's path and mode of development.

Different countries' concept of a social security system differs widely. Welfare states in Europe generalize social security as social protection expenditures or social expenditures, while in the United States social security mainly refers to various poverty-relief expenditures and security expenditures under the direct charge of

Y. Wang, *Social Security in China: On the Possibility of Equitable Distribution*, Research Series on the Chinese Dream and China's Development Path,
DOI 10.1007/978-981-10-5643-7_6

government finances. In China, social security is a huge concept covering social assistance, social insurance and social welfare, but often excludes affordable housing, basic health services and education services. This article classifies the fiscal expenditures of the Chinese government for social security into three types. The first type refers to retirement pensions in traditional public institutions, social welfare and relief expenditures, and social security subsidy expenditures (hereinafter referred to as Caliber I); this is the caliber currently used for statistics of fiscal social security expenditure. The second type includes social insurance, social welfare, social care and social assistance expenditures, for which funding is mainly comprised of state fiscal expenditures and various social insurance funds not included in fiscal management (hereinafter referred to as Caliber II). The third type is social security expenditures in the broad sense, including government expenditures in education, medical care and health (hereinafter referred to as Caliber III); this is similar to some countries' social expenditures.

Since reform and opening-up, China has been deepening its understanding of the social security system and its functions in the course of building a socialist market economic system. In the 1980s, some pilot reform projects were conducted mainly for the purpose of serving the reform of state-owned enterprises (SOEs). However, on the whole, security provided by state-owned enterprises and government departments and public institutions to their employees constituted the main part of social security. State finances only provided subsistence security for the strictly defined population in absolute poverty, and provided limited social welfare to targets entitled to preferential policies. In 1992, China's expenditures in social special care, welfare and relief amounted to RMB 6.645 billion, accounting for 1.78% of fiscal expenditure and 0.25% of GDP.[1] From the 1990s to the early 21st century, centering on building the socialist market economy system and on the basis of reform experimentations, China gradually established the basic institutional framework for modern social security. Though the individual contribution and multi-agent responsibility sharing mechanism was introduced in the social insurance system, yet with the constant expansion of social security and improvement of security levels, the government expenditures directed at social security kept increasing. In 2002, the Chinese government spent RMB 37.297 billion on social special care, welfare and relief; in addition to the retirement pensions of public institutions, the national fiscal expenditures in social security, in the narrow sense, amounted to RMB 263.622 billion, accounting for 11.95% of the total fiscal expenditures of the year; meanwhile, the expenditures from social insurance funds in the same year was RMB 347.15 billion. Increasing expenditures from social insurance funds have become an important part of social security expenditures.

After the Sixteenth CPC National Congress, the Party and the government attached more importance to the development of social security and increased government expenditures in social security. In the second half of 2003, China started pilot projects as part of the new rural cooperative medical system. By 2008,

[1]Calculated on the basis of relevant data of *China's Fiscal Statistic Yearbook 1993*.

this system had covered 90% of the rural residents in China. In 2007, the State Council suggested that an urban residents' basic medical insurance system be established. By the end of 2009, this system had covered over 1/2 of urban residents. Rural residents' minimum subsistence system had covered all rural areas nationwide by the end of 2007. In 2008, the State Council studied and deployed pilot work for new rural social old-age insurance. In 2009, pilot projects were conducted in over 300 counties nationwide. The scope of related fiscal expenditures also kept expanding. By the end of 2008, fiscal expenditures in social special care welfare and relief amounted to RMB 680.429 billion, accounting for 10.96% of fiscal expenditures of the same year; though the proportion was basically the same as that of 2002, the absolute scope was not at the same level. Revenues and expenditures in terms of social insurance funds increased more rapidly. In 2008, expenditures in five social insurance funds was RMB 992.51 billion (the revenues being RMB 1.36961 trillion), with an accumulated surplus of RMB 1.5176 trillion.[2] While developing social insurance and increasing government social security expenditures, the Chinese government attached more importance to the development of social services such as education and health. The funding for nine-year compulsory education in rural areas was entirely included in fiscal security. In 2009, it was decided to conduct a new round of drug and health system reform in preparation for a RMB 850 billion increase in fiscal investments within three years. To cope with the world financial crisis, constructing low-rent housing and reconstructing urban and rural buildings in a state of disrepair became important fields in terms of large-scale treasury bond investments. In 2008, China planned to invest RMB 900 billion to construct affordable housing in three years, part of which was from fiscal funds. In 2009, the central finances arranged for a fund of RMB 55.1 billion specially establishing to subsidize affordable housing; in 2010, RMB 63.2 billion was arranged. Housing security, like education and health, has become a content of social security in the broad sense that cannot be ignored in China. In 2008, state finances invested RMB 1.176725 trillion in education and health services.[3]

6.2 Constant Increase in Social Security Expenditures by the Chinese Government

On the whole, since reform and opening-up began, fiscal expenditures of the Chinese government in social security have been constantly increasing. In absolute terms, special care and social welfare, relief expenditures, retirement pensions of public institutions, and expenditures in social security assistance (fiscal

---

[2]Related data are based on *Statistical Bulletin on the Development of Human Resources and Social Security Services* in past years.

[3]Related data are based on *Financial Statistics Yearbook* in 2008.

expenditures in social security in the narrow sense) increased by 401.26 times from RMB 1.891 billion in 1978 to RMB 760.668 billion in 2009 (Caliber I). On the basis of fiscal expenditures in social security in the narrow sense, the scope of expenditures in provenance from social insurance funds (minus fiscal subsidies) (Caliber II) also rapidly increased by 7.2 times, from RMB 221.098 billion in 1998 to RMB 1.813295 trillion in 2009. If consideration is given to the fact that the Party and the state have taken public service equalization as an important objective for constructing a socialist harmonious society, social security expenditures should include fund security and basic public services. Including state financial expenditures in education and health, we can see that the state's total expenditures in social security will be further increased. Fiscal social security in the narrow sense, social insurance expenditures, and fiscal education and health investments, added together (Caliber III), increased from RMB 452.734 billion in 1998 to RMB 3.256368 trillion in 2009, with quite a significant overall scale.[4]

In terms of the proportion of fiscal expenditures in social security against total fiscal expenditure, Caliber I expenditures in 1978 accounted for 1.65% of total fiscal expenditures, which rose to 9.97% in 2009; Caliber II expenditures accounted for 17.81% of total fiscal expenditures in 1998, which rose to 20.88% in 2009; Caliber III expenditures accounted for 11.53% of total fiscal expenditures in 1978, which rose to 37.51% in 2009. The proportion of expenditures of various calibers against total governmental fiscal expenditures increased the fastest in 1998, mainly resulting from the increase in subsidy expenditures for social insurance funds centering on the reform of state-owned enterprises; the proportion was the highest in 2002 (mainly resulting from the substantial increase of subsidy expenditures for social insurance funds by state finances), while the proportion after 2003 was relatively stable. In light of the proportion of social security expenditures in the GDP, Caliber I expenditures in 1978 accounted for 0.52% of GDP, which rose to 2.23% in 2009; Caliber II expenditures in 1998 accounted for 2.62% of GDP, which rose to 5.33% in 2009; Caliber III expenditures in 1978 accounted for 3.55% of GDP, which rose to 9.56% in 2009. In terms of the proportion in fiscal revenues, Caliber I expenditures accounted for 1.67% in 1978, which rose to 11.1% in 2009; Caliber II expenditures accounted for 22.39% in 1978, which rose to 26.46% in 2009; Caliber III expenditures accounted for 45.84% in 1998, which rose to 47.53% in 2009. In light of the proportion in the sum of fiscal revenues and social insurance fund revenues, there was no significant change, with Caliber II having been maintained at around 20%, and Caliber III between 35 and 40% (see Table 6.1). It should be noted that the proportion of fiscal expenditures in social security dropped somehow in 2008 and 2009, mainly as a result of other investments aimed at coping with the financial crisis.

Obvious periodical characteristics have been found in China's social security fiscal expenditures since reform and opening-up. In the early period of reform and

[4]Calculated by the author according to relevant statistics, not including housing security due to the difficulty of acquiring data.

Table 6.1 Social security expenditure of the Chinese government

Unit billion yuan; %

Year	Caliber I	Caliber II	Caliber III	Proportion in total fiscal expenditures			Proportion in GDP		
				Caliber I	Caliber II	Caliber III	Caliber I	Caliber II	Caliber III
1978	1.891		12.94	1.65		11.53	0.52		3.55
1986	3.558		43.253	1.61		19.62	0.35		4.21
1992	6.645		91.677	1.78		24.50	0.25		3.41
1994	9.514		145.62	1.64		25.14	0.20		3.02
1996	12.803		200.535	1.61		25.26	0.18		2.82
1998	59.563	221.098	452.734	5.52	17.81	36.47	0.71	2.62	5.36
2000	151.757	360.452	649.356	9.55	20.05	36.13	1.53	3.63	6.54
2002	263.622	559.043	960.493	11.95	22.36	38.41	2.19	4.65	7.98
2004	311.608	722.371	1236.839	10.94	22.16	37.95	1.95	4.52	7.74
2006	436.178	995.023	1689.814	10.79	21.63	36.73	2.06	5.18	7.97
2008	680.429	1509.851	2686.576	10.87	21.30	37.90	2.26	5.02	8.94
2009	760.668	1813.295	3256.468	9.97	20.88	37.51	2.23	5.33	9.56

Unit %

Year	Proportion in total fiscal revenues			Proportion in the sum of fiscal revenues and social insurance fund revenues	
	Caliber I	Caliber II	Caliber III	Caliber II	Caliber III
1978	1.67				
1986	1.68				
1992	1.91				
1994	1.82				
1996	1.73				

(continued)

Table 6.1 (continued)

Unit %

Year	Proportion in total fiscal revenues			Proportion in the sum of fiscal revenues and social insurance fund revenues	
	Caliber I	Caliber II	Caliber III	Caliber II	Caliber III
1998	6.03	22.39	45.84	19.23	39.37
2000	11.33	26.91	48.48	22.47	40.48
2002	13.95	29.57	50.81	24.36	41.85
2004	11.80	27.37	46.86	22.45	38.44
2006	11.25	25.67	43.60	20.99	35.65
2008	11.09	24.62	43.81	20.12	35.81
2009	11.10	26.46	47.53	21.43	38.48

Note Caliber I includes special care and social welfare, relief expenditures, retirement pensions of administrative institutions, and expenditures in social security assistance; Caliber II is expenditures of social insurance funds (minus fiscal subsidies) plus Caliber I, and the denominator for calculating the proportion of Caliber II (total fiscal expenditures) includes social insurance fund expenditures minus fiscal subsidies. Caliber III is education and health expenditures plus Caliber I; it should be noted that the proportion of social security fiscal expenditures in 2002 was relatively big as a result of the substantial increase in state fiscal subsidies for social insurance funds

Source of data based on relevant data in *Chinese Financial Statistics Yearbook*, *China Statistics Yearbook*, and *China Health Statistics Yearbook* of past years; the data in social insurance fund expenditures from 1998 to 2008 are from *China Financial Statistics Yearbook 2008*; the data of 2009 are from the Report on the Final Accounting of Expenditure that year; due to different statistical calibers in different years, there are some differences in the data of some years opening-up, the absolute value of social security fiscal expenditures and its proportion in total fiscal expenditures were both low. With the acceleration of reform and opening-up as well as economic and social development, social security fiscal expenditures increased year after year. Since the start of the 21st century, China has been attaching more importance to the development of services for people's livelihood; the framework of the social security system has been gradually developed and improved; and the increase in the scale of social security fiscal expenditures has been further accelerated. Meanwhile, due to the rapid increase of economic and fiscal revenues of the state during this period, the proportion of social security expenditure by the government has been relatively stable. However, with the increase of future social security demands, expenditures in education, medical and health care, and housing, in particular, should be further increased.

6.3 Gradual Expansion of Social Insurance Fund Revenues and Expenditures

China has not taken social insurance funds as a budgetary management item. With the deepening of the SOE reform and the development of the socialist market economic system, the traditional unit security system has been gradually turned into the new social insurance system, and social insurance funds have become an important part in total social security funding. China's current social insurance system mainly includes two types. Type I is old-age insurance, medical insurance, unemployment insurance, work-related injury insurance and maternity insurance for regularly employed urban employees; type II consists of the new rural cooperative medical care system (New Rural Co-op), urban residents' basic medical insurance and the new rural old-age insurance (NROAI) under pilot test, as well as the to-be-launched urban residents' basic old-age insurance system. Different from social services such as social relief and medical and education services which mainly rely on state fiscal investments, the social insurance system has established a mechanism with tripartite investments—the employer, the participating individual and government finances—in which the three forces play different roles in different types of social insurance. With the development of employees' social insurance starting from the 1990s, urban and rural residents' basic old-age insurance and the basic medical insurance system have been gradually established, the coverage of social insurance has been expanding in China (see Table 6.2), and the scale of revenues and expenditures of social insurance funds has been expanding (see Table 6.3). Table 6.4 shows the proportion of government social security expenditures, including expenditures of five social insurance funds, in the revenues of social insurance funds and fiscal revenues of the year; in 2000, the proportion of government social security expenditures, including the expenditures of five social insurance funds, in the revenues of social insurance funds and fiscal revenues was 40.48%, which dropped to 38.48% in 2009 (the drop was related to the accumulation of social insurance funds).

Table 6.2 Number of people participating in social insurance in China. *Unit* million people

Year	Employees' basic old-age insurance	Employees' basic medical insurance	Unemployment insurance	Work-related injury insurance	Maternity insurance	New rural cooperation medical care	Urban residents' medical insurance	New rural old-age insurance
1995	109.79	7.459	82.38	26.148	15.002			
1998	112.031	18.787	79.279	37.813	27.767			
2000	136.174	37.869	103.263	43.503	30.016			
2002	147.366	94.012	101.816	44.056	34.882			
2004	163.529	124.036	105.839	68.452	43.838	80.00		
2006	187.663	157.318	111.866	102.685	64.589	410.00		
2008	201.369	199.956	123.998	137.872	92.541	815.00	118.26	55.95
2009	235.50	219.37	127.15	148.96	108.76	833.00	182.10	86.91

Source of data The data for 1989-2008 are from *China Labor Statistics Yearbook 2009*; the data of new rural cooperation medical care are from *China Health Statistics Yearbook 2009*; the data of new rural social old-age insurance are from *Statistical Bulletin on Labor Security* of past years. The data of 2009 are from relevant statistical bulletins of 2009

Table 6.3 Revenues, expenditures and balance of China's employees' social insurance funds. *Unit* billion yuan

Year		1989	1995	1998	2000	2002	2004	2006	2008	2009
Old-age insurance	Revenues	14.67	95.01	145.9	227.85	317.15	425.84	630.98	974.02	1149.1
	Expenditures	11.88	84.76	151.16	211.55	284.29	350.21	489.67	738.96	889.4
	Accumulated balance	6.8	42.98	58.78	94.71	160.8	297.5	548.89	993.1	1252.6
Medical insurance	Revenues		0.97	6.06	17.0	60.78	114.05	174.71	288.55	367.2
	Expenditures		0.73	5.33	12.45	40.94	86.22	127.67	201.97	279.7
	Accumulated balance		0.31	2.0	10.98	45.07	95.79	175.24	330.36	427.6
Unemployment insurance	Revenues	0.68	3.53	7.26	16.04	21.56	29.1	40.24	58.51	58.0
	Expenditures	0.2	1.89	5.61	12.34	18.66	21.1	19.8	25.35	36.7
	Accumulated balance	1.36	6.84	13.34	19.59	25.38	38.6	72.48	131.01	152.4
Work-related injury insurance	Revenues		0.81	2.12	2.48	3.2	5.83	12.18	21.67	24.0
	Expenditures		0.18	0.9	1.38	1.99	3.33	6.85	12.69	15.6
	Accumulated balance		1.27	3.95	5.79	8.11	11.86	192.9	33.5	40.4
Maternity insurance	Revenues		0.29	0.98	1.12	2.18	3.21	6.21	11.37	13.2
	Expenditures		0.16	0.68	0.83	1.28	1.88	3.75	7.15	8.8
	Accumulated balance		0.27	1.03	1.68	2.97	5.59	9.69	16.82	21.20
Sum of five items	Revenues	15.36	100.6	162.31	264.49	404.87	578.03	864.32	1369.61	1611.6
	Expenditures	12.09	87.71	163.69	238.56	347.15	462.74	647.74	992.51	1230.3
	Accumulated balance	8.16	51.68	79.11	132.75	242.34	449.34	825.59	1517.6	1894.2

Note The balance of revenues and expenditures of urban employees' basic medical insurance funds in 2007 and 2009 included urban residents' basic medical insurance. Source of data: the data of 1989–2007 are from *China Fiscal Statistics Yearbook 2008*; the data of 2008 are from *China Labor Statistics Yearbook 2009*; the data of 2009 are from *Statistical Bulletin of Human Resources and Social Security 2009*

Table 6.4 Government social security expenditure including social insurance expenditure. *Unit* trillion yuan; %

Year	2000	2001	2002	2003	2004	2005	2006	2007	2008	2009
The sum of expenditures on five types of insurance and government fiscal expenditures on social security (A)	0.6494	0.783	0.9605	1.0647	1.2368	1.4606	1.6898	2.1172	2.6866	3.2564
The sum of revenues of five types of insurance and fiscal revenues (B)	1.604	1.9488	2.2952	2.6598	3.2177	3.8625	4.7403	6.2134	7.5026	8.4634
A/B	40.5	40.2	41.9	40.0	38.4	37.8	35.7	34.1	35.8	38.5

6.4 Structure and Characteristics of the Chinese Government Social Security Expenditures

The structure of the social security fiscal expenditures in China is mainly characterized by the following points:

First, the increase of social security expenditures in the narrow sense obviously outpaces that of the investments in education and health services. In terms of the structure of fiscal expenditures, the proportion of fiscal expenditures in social security in the narrow sense is relatively small, while investments in education and health are the focus of government public expenditures. In 1994, education and health investments accounted for 23.5% of fiscal expenditures. Since then, the absolute amount of education and health expenditures in government fiscal expenditures increased still, but its proportion dropped substantially, which has maintained basically around 18% ~ 19% since the start of the 21st century. During this period, the Chinese government vigorously developed social insurance and social security, and the amount of fiscal investments in social security in the narrow sense and its proportion in fiscal expenditures increased gradually (see Table 6.5). In 2006, the proportion of social welfare benefits, retirement pensions of public institutions, and fiscal subsidies for social security accounted for 10.8% of fiscal expenditures of the same year. Fiscal subsidies for social security accounted for 5.25%, which became the biggest expenditure in social security fiscal expenditures in the broad sense after education expenditures. As the social insurance system was just established then and was also faced with fund risks, subsidy expenditures on social insurance funds became a focus of subsidy expenditures on social security. Fiscal subsidy expenditures on social insurance funds increased by 81.4 times from RMB 2.155 billion in 1998 to RMB 177.67 billion in 2009, and the fiscal subsidies for social insurance funds amounted to RMB 1.09158 trillion from 1998 to 2009.[5]

Second, the increase of social security fiscal expenditures in China has promoted the transformation of the social insurance system from a pay-as-you-go system to the partial fund accumulation system. In terms of social security, in the earlier stage of reform and opening-up, the pay-as-you-go mode was mainly practiced, characterized by ratifying revenues according to expenditures on a balanced budget with a small surplus. In the course of establishing a modern social security system, China has established an institutional mode combining "social pooling and personal accounts" for employees' basic old-age insurance and basic medical insurance. Besides, personal accounts (such as enterprise annuity and housing provident fund) or family accounts (New Rural Co-op and NROAI) systems have also been introduced to other social insurance systems in China. As a result, China's social insurance system has become a partial fund accumulation system. To cope with the demands of a future aging population, the National Council for Social Security Fund was established in 2000 to manage social security funds allocated from state

[5]Related data are based on *China Fiscal Statistics Yearbook* of past years.

Table 6.5 Structure of Social Security Fiscal Expenditures in China. *Unit* billion yuan; %

Year	Education expenditures		Medical and health care expenditures		Expenditures on special care, social welfare and relief		Retirement pensions of public institutions		Expenditures on social security subsidies	
	Absolute value	Proportion	Absolute value	Proportion	Absolute value	Proportion	Absolute value	Proportion	Absolute value	Proportion
1978	7.505	6.69	3.544	3.16	1.891	1.69	–	–	–	–
1982	13.761	11.19	6.899	5.61	2.143	1.74	–	–	–	–
1986	27.472	12.46	12.223	5.54	3.558	1.61	–	–	–	–
1990	46.245	15.00	18.728	6.07	5.504	1.78	–	–	–	–
1994	101.878	17.59	34.228	5.91	9.514	1.64	–	–	–	–
1998	172.63	15.99	59.006	5.46	17.126	1.59	27.436	2.54	15.001	1.39
2000	217.952	13.72	70.952	4.47	21.303	1.34	47.857	3.01	82.597	5.20
2002	310.599	14.08	90.851	4.12	37.297	1.69	78.884	3.58	147.441	6.69
2004	385.11	13.52	129.358	4.54	56.346	1.98	102.812	3.61	152.45	5.35
2006	516.905	12.79	177.886	4.40	90.768	2.25	133.02	3.29	212.39	5.25
2008	901.021	14.39	275.704	4.40	104.192	1.66	181.249	2.90	248.465	3.97
2009	1043.754	13.68	399.419	5.23	97.683	1.28	209.295	2.74	275.748	3.61

Note The proportions in the table refer to the proportions in fiscal expenditures; due to changes in government fiscal revenues and expenditures items in 2007, expenditures on special care, social welfare and relief, retirement pensions of public institutions, and social security expenditures were combined as "social security and employment expenditures". *Source of data China Fiscal Statistics Yearbook* and Report on the Final Accounting of State Revenues and Expenditure of past years finances and raised by other channels, also responsible for partly managing social insurance accumulated funds. From the year 2000 to the end of 2009, the net fiscal allocation to national social security funds amounted to RMB 380.256 billion.[6] By the end of the year 2009, the cumulative balance of national social insurance funds was RMB 1.5721 trillion; the accumulated amount of national social insurance funds reached RMB 776.62 billion; the cumulative balance of enterprise annuities was RMB 253.3 billion; the cumulative balance of new rural cooperative medical care funds was RMB 18.51 billion; and the cumulative balance of rural social old-age insurance funds was RMB 68.1 billion. The sum of cumulative balance of the above items amounted to RMB 2.68863 trillion in 2009, accounting for 7.9% of GDP (see Table 6.6). If we consider the accumulation of housing provident funds, this sum and proportion is even bigger. The management and investment of funds have become an important task and a difficult problem in the course of developing the social security system.

Third, the increase of social security fiscal expenditures expanded the coverage of minimum subsistence security. Since reform and opening-up, urban and rural residents' incomes have been rising and their living standards have been improving. In 2008, the Engel coefficient for rural families in China was 43.7%, having dropped by 24.0 percentage points from 67.7% in 1978. The Engel coefficient for urban families in China dropped to below 40% by 2000.[7] The Engel coefficient for rural families in China dropped to below 50% by 2000. The absolute poverty incidence in rural areas kept dropping. In 1978, the absolute poverty incidence in rural areas was 30.7%, which dropped to 4.2% by 2008. Nevertheless, there are still a large number of poor people in China. In quite a long period of time, China only offered minimum subsistence security to extremely poor people unable to subsist (such as households of the five guarantees system). In the course of the SOE reform, a large number of laid-off workers became part of new poverty-stricken groups whose problems could not be resolved by the traditional social relief system. From the mid-1990s, regions such as Shanghai started to establish a minimum subsistence security system for poverty-stricken people. By the end of the 1990s, the government had started to implement the policy of "realizing universal coverage for all eligible residents", constantly increasing fiscal investments in the minimum subsistence security system. The rural subsistence security system had basically covered all the rural areas nationwide by 2007. In 2009, 23.477 million urban residents and 47.593 million rural residents received minimum subsistence allowances from the government.[8]

Fourth, the increase in social security fiscal expenditures in China, to some extent, affects both basic subsistence security and developed security. The

[6]Source of data: Website of the National Council for Social Security Fund (http://ww1ssf1gov1cn/zjcj/dzqk/201005/t20100510-26851html).

[7]National Bureau of Statistics of the People's Republic of China: Urban and Rural Residents' Lives Are Improved from Poverty to Prosperity". See the website of the National Bureau of Statistics (http://www1stats1gov1cn/tjfx/ztfx/qzxzgcl60zn/t20090910-4025858491html).

[8]Source of data: *Statistical Bulletin on the Development Civil Undertakings* in China of past years.

Table 6.6 Cumulative balance of national social insurance funds from 1989 to 2008. *Unit* billion yuan; %

Year	Five social insurance funds	National social security funds	Enterprise annuity	NRCMCS funds	Rural social old-age insurance funds	Accumulated total	The proportion of accumulate total in GDP
1990	11.73					11.73	0.6
1995	51.68					51.68	0.9
1998	79.11					79.11	0.9
2000	132.75					132.75	1.3
2002	242.34	124.19				366.53	3.0
2004	449.34	171.14		1.12	28.5	650.1	4.1
2006	825.59	282.77	91.0	5.78	35.4	1240.54	5.9
2008	1517.6	562.37	191.1	12.23	49.9	2333.2	7.8
2009	1572.1	776.62	253.3	18.51	68.1	2688.63	7.9

Source of data The data of the five social insurance funds are taken from the Data Center of the DRCNET, including urban basic old-age insurance, basic medical insurance, unemployment insurance, work-related injury insurance and maternity insurance; the data of national social insurance funds are taken from the annual reports of the National Council for Social Security Fund; the data of enterprise annuities and rural social old-age insurance are taken from *Labor Statistical Bulletin* of past years; the New Rural Co-op data are based on *Green Book on Social Security* in China 2010, and the data for 2009 ended by September traditional social security system has a narrow coverage with a low level of security, mainly addressing the issue of the subsistence of extremely poor people. With the gradual improvement of the social security system and the increase of state fiscal investments, while stepping up investments in education and health, there is, to some extent, a will to allocate more fiscal investments of social security in China to both basic subsistence security and developmental security projects. Though fiscal expenditures in terms of employment subsidies amounted to RMB 114.168 billion for the period from 1998 to 2007, the fiscal investments in terms of social security for developmental projects were insufficient; during the ten-plus years of economic transformation in which the focus was particularly set on ensuring basic subsistence, the government's fiscal investments in education and health services increased slightly. The proportions of education expenditures and medical and health care expenditures saw no improvements and even dropped somehow, directly leading to problems such as "expensive medical services" and "schooling difficulties". That is an important reason why China has no other choice but to further increase investments in education and health services now.

6.5 Fiscal Expenditures of Social Security in China: Problems and Countermeasures

(i) Main problems in China's social security fiscal expenditures

First, the total amount of social security fiscal investments is insufficient. Since reform and opening-up, the total amount of social security fiscal expenditures in China has been increasing. However, the current investments are insufficient to meet the growing social security demands of urban and rural residents. Compared with the social security expenditures of some other countries, China still lags behind in terms of social security fiscal expenditures (see Table 6.7).

Second, social security fails to play a satisfactory role in adjusting the distribution of residents' income. From 1981 to 2009, farmers' per capita net income increased by 22.1 times, while the disposable income of urban families increased by 36.1 times, so that the income disparity of urban and rural residents became more and more serious. Old-age insurance, an important item in the overall social insurance and social security system, instead of playing the role of narrowing the gap between different groups and ensuring different groups to fairly share old-age insurance benefits security, widens, to some extent, the gap between different groups. In 1990, the ratio of per capita monthly pension for urban enterprise employees, employees in public institutions and civil servants was 1:1.06:1.10, which showed that the benefits they received were basically the same; by 2005, the monthly per capita pension of public institutions increased to 1.89 times that of urban enterprise employees; meanwhile civil servants' monthly per capita pension expanded to 2.06 times that of enterprise employees'[1].

Table 6.7 Proportion of social security expenditure in GDP in some OECD countries. *Unit %*

Year	1960	1980	1985	1990	1995	1998	2001	2005
Canada	–	14.3	17.4	18.6	19.6	18.4	17.8	16.5
France	13.4	21.1	26.6	26.6	29.2	29	28.5	29.2
Germany	20.5	23	23.6	22.8	27.5	27.4	27.4	26.7
Japan	5.8	10.2	11	11.2	13.5	14.5	16.9	18.6
Mexico	–	–	1.8	3.8	8.1	8.8	11.8	7.4
Sweden	12.8	28.8	30	30.8	33	30.4	28.9	29.4
Turkey	–	4.3	4.2	7.6	7.5	11.1	–	13.7
The United Kingdom	13.9	17.9	21.1	19.5	23	21.5	21.8	21.3
The United States	10.3	13.3	13.0	13.4	15.5	14.5	14.8	15.9

Note The data in the table are based on related data of OECD. The data for Japan in 1960 is replaced by the data in 1970; the per capita GDP of the United Kingdom, Sweden, the United States, France and Germany in 1960 was USD 1,363, USD 1,641, USD 2,783, USD 1,297, and USD 1,345 respectively. China's per capita GDP in 2004 was USD 1,532. *Source of data* Task force of the Division of Social Security of the Ministry of Finance: International Comparison of Social Security Expenditure, *Public Finance Research*, 2007, Vol., 10, pp. 36–42; *International Statistics Yearbook*; OECD database

Third, the focus of social security fiscal investments is not clear, which does not well address the adjustment of income distribution. Currently, a large part of fiscal investments in social security is used to subsidize social insurance funds and complement national social security funds. On one hand, due to imperfections in the design of the social insurance system, the benefits brought by social insurance subsidies to high-income people are more than those to low-income people, creating a "rob the poor to support the rich" situation, thus exacerbating income disparity; on the other hand, although a large amount of funds is accumulated, it is, however, not well used, leading to difficult problems in the management and investment of accumulated funds, promoting fund security, as well as maintaining and increasing fund value. Other projects in urgent need of fiscal investments, such as medical and health care services, do not have sufficient investments. In recent years, the proportion of government budgetary expenditures in total health expenditures has been dropping. In 2008, government expenditures on medical and health care only accounted for 4.4% of yearly total fiscal expenditures. The proportion of education expenditures in government fiscal expenditures has been stumbling and even dropping to some extent. By 2006, fiscal expenditures in education in the Chinese government just surpassed 3% of GDP. The proportion of government education expenditures in total education expenditures is declining. Besides, investments in security housing should also be strengthened. By the end of 2006, only RMB 4 billion of public finance was used in the construction of low-rent housing, which increased to RMB 72.6 billion in 2009. However, as far as the demands of the many low and medium-income people are concerned, it is just like a drop in the bucket, while huge amounts of housing provident funds have not even been brought into full play.

Fourth, the proportion of central and local fiscal expenditures is not reasonable. Compared with the fiscal revenues of central and local governments, the proportion of fiscal expenditures in social security is out of balance, with the proportion of local government expenditures far exceeding that of central government. In light of central and local governments' social security expenditures in 2008, the central government's expenditures on social security and employment (social security expenditures in the narrow sense) only accounted for 40.3% of the fiscal expenditures of the whole country, 30% of medical and health care expenditures, and 17.8% of education expenditures. In light of fiscal revenues, in 2008, the fiscal revenues of the central government accounted for 53.3% of the total fiscal revenues, while local fiscal revenues accounted for only 46.7%.[9]

(ii) Suggestions on strengthening and improving social security fiscal expenditures in China

First, we should further increase fiscal investments in social security and improve the level of social security. In the future, we should further increase fiscal investments in social security and gradually explore the establishment of a long-acting mechanism for social security fiscal investments. While improving the public finance mechanism, we should establish and improve social security budgets. Currently, social security in China is mainly subsistence security, with a low level and narrow scope of security. To further improve the equity and sustainability of economic and social development in China, we should establish a developed social welfare system for the benefits of all people. It is estimated that by 2012 we will realize the objective of basically establishing a new social welfare system for the benefit of all people and the full coverage of the social security system, which will require a fiscal investment of about RMB 2.6 trillion. By 2020, we should basically realize the full coverage of all people, which will require a fiscal investment of about RMB 5.74 trillion (He et al. 2009). Increases fiscal investments in social security should be managed in accord with the actual conditions of economic and social development, and social investments and personal contributions should be mobilized to develop social security.

Second, we should optimize the structure of fiscal expenditures in social security and improve the performance of such expenditures. Investments in subsistence security are the most fundamental investments, but they accounts for a relatively small proportion in fiscal expenditures, and other security projects may be developed and improved to reduce the amount of poor people and minimum subsistence security demands. Government medical and health care expenditures should be raised to 6% of fiscal expenditures as soon as possible, and should continue to be raised step by step. By 2020, we should strive for that figure to reach 8% ~ 10% of

[9]Source of data: National fiscal revenues and expenditure final account report of China 2008; the total fiscal revenues and expenditure data are from *China Statistics Yearbook 2009*.

fiscal expenditures. In terms of education investments, the proportion of state fiscal education expenditures should account for 4% of GDP by 2012 (Zhu 2008), and by 2020 the proportion should reach over 5%, and the proportion in fiscal expenditure should reach 20%. In terms of housing security, considering the tremendous demands for low-rent housing by low-income families, fiscal investments in this regard should be increased urgently; by 2012, the investments in housing security should reach about RMB 260 billion, and by 2020 about RMB 700 billion. In terms of old-age security, according to the demands of old-age security and considering the accelerated growth of the aging population, by 2012, the fiscal expenditures in terms of old-age security should reach about RMB 800 billion, and by 2020 about RMB 1.4 trillion (He et al. 2009); the focus of recent investments is old people without security in urban and rural areas as well as rural residents. In the course of adjusting the structure of fiscal expenditures in social security, we should not only ensure the equitable fiscal expenditures, but also improve the efficiency of fiscal expenditures. We should establish a performance assessment system of social security fiscal expenditures in order to improve the political, economic and social performance of social security fiscal expenditures (Lin 2007).

Third, we should improve the governmental responsibility sharing mechanism of social security fiscal investments at different levels. To strengthen fiscal investments in social security, the central government should not take the whole responsibility, while the burdens of local governments should not be aggravated. Instead, responsibilities should be reasonably allocated between the central government and local governments. We should, on the basis of clarifying the responsibilities for social security between the central government and local governments, define the responsibilities of governments at various levels in terms of fiscal investments in different social security items. In China, due to the constraint of the economic development level and the government's control over financial powers, the central government delegates more expenditure responsibilities to local governments so that local governments have to take up the main responsibility for expenditures in the absolute majority of expenditure items, which is a direct cause for the fact that fiscal expenditures of the central government only accounts for 30% of national fiscal expenditure (Kou and Zhou 2007). We should further increase social security fiscal expenditures by the central government and try to balance local governments' fiscal expenditures through transfer payment.

Fourth, we should improve the function of social security fiscal expenditures in income distribution adjustment and narrow the gap among different residents. To improve the function of social security in adjusting income distribution, we should make efforts in various aspects. On one hand, we should try to maintain social equity and justice through the social security system by improving the institutional design of social security; on the other hand, we should allow social security fiscal expenditures to play their role in adjusting income distribution and narrowing wealth disparity. The function of social security in adjusting income distribution can be realized by adjusting the investment structure and directions and clarifying the key projects, regions and groups of people for fiscal investments. Fiscal investments should be channeled towards urban and rural low and medium-income people, meet their social security demands, and improve their income level; and meanwhile they should also be channeled towards rural areas and the central and western parts of China.[10]

[10]This article is published in *Finance and Trade Economics*, 2011, Vol. 1, written in collaboratin with Long Yuqi.

Chapter 7 Several Major Issues in the Reform and Development of China's Social Security System: Comments and Suggestions on China's Social Security Report

Of the many research results on social security, China's Social Security Report (hereinafter referred to as The Report) stands out as one of the achievements in the first phase of "China Economic Research and Consultation Projects" for its selection of key issues and strong lineup of researchers. Besides internationally famous experts on social security such as Nicholas Barr, the participants included Chinese experts such as Li Jian'ge, Gao Xiqing, Zheng Silin, Xiang Huaicheng, Zhou Xiaochuan, Liu Zhongli, Wu Jinglian, Lou Jiwei, Guo Shuqing, Yu Yongding, HouYongzhi, Li Shaoguang and Zheng Beingwen. Resulting from several years' study, The Report is quite original in that it draws on the latest international experiences as reference, examines China's national conditions, compares and analyzes the advantages and disadvantages of different modes of old-age insurance, and suggests that the "Non-financial (Notional) Defined Contribution" (NDC) system which is practiced in some European countries be implemented in China, in attempts to straighten out the thinking for the reform of China's social security system and resolve problems such as the pension fund financial crisis. This report also gives a series of policy suggestions for establishing a uniform social security management system, raising retirement age, allocating state-owned assets, expanding coverage, improving the capital market, and promoting social equity. It is a report analyzing China's reform on its social security system from a very broad perspective, and also a very deep report about China's reform on its social security system. In light of my own understanding, I would like to put forward some of my opinions focusing on the key points of this report.

7.1 The NDC Issue

The NDC system put forward in China's Social Security Report is the central concept of the whole report, and also has the strongest impact of all other suggestions because it addresses the issue of selecting a system and mode for China's

Y. Wang, *Social Security in China: On the Possibility of Equitable Distribution*, Research Series on the Chinese Dream and China's Development Path,
DOI 10.1007/978-981-10-5643-7_7

urban employees' basic old-age insurance. Since the establishment of the basic old-age insurance system combining social pooling and personal accounts in China, the issue on the scale of personal accounts, the issue of the management system, the issue of notional accounts and the issue of investment, among other issues, have become focuses of controversy and difficult obstacles in the process of establishing of a new system. Although ten years of exploration have passed, a system integrating social pooling and personal accounts with healthy operation and meeting China's basic national conditions has yet to be found. This has been a major factor impeding the government from making breakthrough in China's urban employees' basic old-age insurance system. The Report suggests the adoption of the NDC system to resolve the institutional dilemma, as it is indeed a great breakthrough and a new development from the World Bank's suggestions on China's implementation of the "three-pillar" mode.

The Report suggests that the main arguments for China's adoption of the NDC system include: ① the NDC system maintains the role of personal accounts but actually does not allow for real fund accumulation, nor does it require this generation to contribute to the richer next generation, thus avoiding unreasonable inter-generational income re-distribution. ② The NDC system is operated by the public old-age pension administrative department, and is not subject to the constraint of the inadequate financial capability or management capability of any private sector while it is able to avoid the fluctuation of assets value in the capital market within a short term; as a result, insurants are subject to less risk, which is especially important when the banking and financial market system is still at the developmental stage. ③ The NDC pension system currently does not require any rise in contribution or any increase of central fiscal subsidies. ④ As China has a very high savings rate, and its capital market is not sound, it is not necessary to fully fund "notional personal accounts" into a form of complete fund accumulation, while maintaining that notional personal accounts can provide a basis for a future transition to accumulation personal accounts. We should say that the above reasons are sufficient and highly persuasive.

The conclusion from the above reasons is that China does not have to fully fund personal accounts and may maintain the current basic mode of "mixed account management" of social pooling and personal accounts. From the perspective of feasibility, this is perhaps a realistic choice for reforming the current basic old-age insurance system. However, if the absolute majority of provinces in China still carry on the practice of not fully funding personal accounts, they are actually adopting the NDC mode. The presentation of the NDC system will provide a theoretical explanation or "extrication" for the viewpoint that it is not necessary to fully fund personal accounts in the current period. From the perspective of report drafters, the proposal of the concept of NDC may free the system from the empty account entanglement problem arising in the recent decade, while maintaining the personal account system design put forward as a reform measure. As the "personal accounts" of basic old-age pension are maintained, its scale would not shrink so much as to finally lose the significance of the "personal account" system. This is a compromise with which personal accounts are actively maintained but do not have to be "fully funded". Although this concept will help to transform fixed income into fixed contribution, clarify that the social insurance premium that each person submits is related to their future welfare income (Feldstein 2009), clear up the misunderstanding that accounts have are constituted of a single type of full accumulation system, and maintain the position of large scale personal accounts in the basic old-age insurance system given the fact that it is basically impossible to fully fund big accounts in China. However, as far as I am concerned, from the perspective of improving China's old-age insurance system and operation mechanism, the NDC system, instead of a deep reform of the institutional mode combining social pooling and personal accounts (it is by nature still a pay-as-you-go system), delays the solution of the problem concerning the "full funding" of personal accounts. In the issue of the personal account system, some basic notions should be clarified.

(i) In terms of institutional design, should it consider this system as part of the basic old-age insurance system or as a new supplementary system? Should we stick to mandatory participation or opt for voluntary participation by those eligible? Should it be turned into a system universally enjoyed by all workers participating in the basic old-age insurance system or a system mainly covering people whose employment or income is more stable? Since designing the personal account system, China has actually taken it as an organic part of the basic old-age insurance system and insisted that it be universal and mandatory. As a result, it is inevitable that personal account funds be managed along with social pooling funds instead of being independently managed. Consequently personal accounts cannot become a full fund accumulation system in the true sense, but only in the notional sense, thus not significantly different from the NDC other than in name. Currently, though some provinces are conducting pilot projects on fully funding personal accounts, yet it is still difficult to completely separate personal accounts from social pooling funds due to institutional design, and little progress has been made in this regard; the proportion of fully-funded personal accounts is increasingly dropping, and in practice, it is increasingly difficult to manage personal accounts in parallel with social pooling funds. The practice of fully funding personal accounts illustrates that if personal accounts are fully funded, the scale of funding cannot be big (as it is unnecessary and impossible) and only small-scale funding can be conducted at an appropriate ratio (the ratio of personal accounts that are fully funded is only 2.5% in Sweden, accounting for 13.5% of total old-age pension contribution). Meanwhile, once personal accounts are fully funded, they should be managed as per the full fund accumulation system, instead of being tied up with social pooling funds. In light of the fact that personal accounts can only cover a small proportion and noting that it is difficult to cover all workers participating in the basic old-age insurance system, we can see that the personal account system is a subordinate and supplementary system in the whole old-age insurance system, and thus should not be designed as a basic system on par with the pay-as-you-go social pooling system. Pay-as-you-go has been and remains still the main mode in terms of basic old-age insurance system worldwide, especially with great international powers. The large population and the huge scale of old-age security funds in big powers determine that the market mechanism cannot be fully relied upon to establish old-age security funds for the personal account system, as that would cause risks of enormous inflation for accumulated old-age pension funds and weaken the re-distribution function of old-age insurance funds. Besides, maintaining huge personal accounts and high premium collection rates for the issuance of current old-age pensions is not conducive to the expansion of the coverage of the basic old-age insurance system. To maintain the universality of personal accounts, this system can be made mandatory to some extent, but this should be mainly be reflected by tax preferential policies. Moreover, it is impossible to cover all workers.

(ii) In terms of the fund management system, the management of personal account funds still lacks a clear institutional guarantee. Given that personal accounts are not fully funded, such funds are jointly managed along with social pooling funds. The problem as to whether they should be managed independently or on a market basis is not very prominent. However, once personal accounts are fully funded according to the fund accumulation system, the management and investment problems about personal account funds will surface, and a commensurate management system will have to be established. We maintain that given that personal accounts are gradually fully funded, a management system relatively independent from social pooling funds should be established. Personal account funds should be pooled and managed on a provincial basis, to be entrusted to qualified investment institutions for investment. National centralized management over such funds is not appropriate. To some extent, the management of personal account funds could be inspired of that of enterprise annuity and occupational annuity funds, or be appropriately combined with them.

(iii) If personal accounts are fully funded, it is worth asking what the appropriate size should be. On the whole, in light of the impact of such factors as the huge historical debt gap in China's old-age pensions, a capital market that is not sound enough and a relatively high overall savings rate, the size of personal accounts after being fully funded should not be too large. Currently, except for Liaoning, which funds personal accounts at 8%, all the remaining pilot provinces generally fund personal accounts at 5 or 3% (equivalent to 11–18% of the current total contribution rate of old-age insurance). We may deem practice as more persuasive than theories and policies, as a too high ratio will make it too difficult and risky to fully fund personal accounts, while a too low ratio will lose practical significance. It is appropriate for each province to establish personal accounts at a ratio of 3–5%.

In sum, in light of the NDC system suggestion put forward in The Report, we think that the direction of further reform in China's basic old-age insurance personal account system is a transformation into a supplementary system with a moderate scale. This system may be mandatory to some extent or comprise tax reductions or exemptions, but most importantly should address regularly employed personnel. To avoid the impact of the financial market, personal account funds may be appropriately concentrated in provincial personal account management centers, but should be managed uniformly nationwide. Old-age pension funds in the full fund accumulation system should stick to market-based investments and operations, and insurants should have certain decision-making authority in terms of investments in their respective account funds.

II. The Problem with the Expansion of Old-age Insurance Coverage and the Framework of the Old-age Insurance System

It is exactly correct for The Report to put forward the suggestion of expanding old-age security "coverage". This suggestion is unequivocally summarized in the report of the 17th CPC National Congress as "all people should are entitled to old-age care", which illustrates that this has become a consensus both in theoretical circles and at the policymaking level. This is of great significance for the promotion of the construction of China's old-age pension system.

No schedule has been set up to expand the coverage of the old-age pension system. Currently, besides government departments and public institutions, almost all people regularly employed in the city have been included into the employees' basic old-age insurance system. In principle, government departments and public institutions should also accelerate the socialized reform of old-age pensions, so as to accelerate the construction of a uniform labor market system. The reform of public institutions' old-age insurance system has been ongoing since 2009, with specific schemes being identical with enterprise employees' basic old-age insurance. Besides, the construction of various types of rural social old-age insurance systems has been ongoing in various places. More typically, Beijing has established a rural basic old-age insurance system based on 10% of annual income, and meanwhile established an old-age allowance system with which urban and rural old people above 60 years old without any pension benefits can receive a fiscal subsidy of RMB 200 each month, thus realizing full coverage. Theoretical circles have proposed the development strategy of "three types of insurance and one allowance" for China's old-age security system. Specifically, the public employees' basic old-age pension system, the employees' basic old-age insurance system, the farmers' basic old-age insurance system and the urban-rural residents' old-age allowance system should be co-established in order to set up old-age security system covering all the people without any loophole so that everybody enjoy the right to old-age care. (Gongcheng 2008).

Old-age security is classified into two types: contributory social insurance and non-contributory social benefits. For the latter, China only had social assistance of non-contributory social benefits (the subsistence security system) in the past, and was lacking an old-age allowance system that each person could enjoy. For a very long period, China's social insurance system could hardly cover all jobholders, and old people above 60 years old without any pension benefits amounted to 50–60 million, of whom most were rural old people. To alleviate old-age poverty, China should establish a minimum income security system for old people, which should cover both urban and rural areas. Of course, at the starting stage, security benefits may be maintained at a low standard, while the age of entitlement may be higher than the retirement age as is regarded appropriate.

Regarding jobholders, the contributory social insurance system is undoubtedly a main part of the old-age security system. Multiple types co-exist in the current old-age insurance system, including: the retirement pension system of government departments and public institutions, the employees' basic old-age insurance system, the flexible jobholders' old-age insurance system, as well as the migrant workers' old-age insurance system and the rural social old-age insurance system in some places, among others. There is a great diversity of systems at a low level of social pooling. Provincial pooling has not been realized in most places and localized management is conducted for funds, thus making it difficult to transfer social insurance across different regions. This situation is not conducive to the flow and transfer of laborers and retirees.

The Report develops conceives the expansion the urban social insurance system and the improvement pooling levels, but does not define ways to realize these objectives. In fact, we still lack a complete and clear approach for the overall design of China's old-age insurance system. From the perspective of social insurance legislation, various types of jobholders whose income reaches a certain standard in China should be covered by the basic old-age insurance system. The crux is whether to establish one system, one mode, or multiple systems, multiple modes, or a national uniform basic system (basic old-age pension system) supplemented by several other relevant systems. The answer to this question will determine China's approach to establishing a basic old-age insurance system for job holders. The United States started to establish a national uniform basic system (basic old-age pension system) in 1935, providing basic old-age security for all insurants, while establishing a flexible occupational annuity system. This is of reference value for China. In light of such factors as the large population, urban-rural disparity and path-dependent reform modes in China, I suggest that China basically stick to the institutional framework of multiple systems and multiple modes, and establish different systems for public servants, enterprise employees, flexible workers, individual industrialists and businesspeople, and rural employees (especially agricultural workers). However, a basic old-age pension system which is roughly identical nationwide should be established for all insurants, so that when they reach relevant conditions such as the statutory retirement age, basic or fundamental old-age pension with a roughly balanced substitution rate and reaching on the whole above the basic subsistence level is provided to these people. That is to say, a diversified and multi-level basic old-age insurance system with uniform basic old-age pension should be established for urban job-holders. The foundation of this system includes two points: first, establishing an old-age allowance system for urban and rural old people without retirement pensions, and providing a certain amount of old-age pensions (fiscal allowances) to all old people at various levels; second, gradually establishing a national uniform basic old-age pension system for urban and rural laborers, especially non-rural job-holders. As per the requirements of raising the level of pooling, basic old-age pensions should be pooled nationwide, and be directly managed by a department in the charge of the central government.

To establish a diversified and multi-level basic old-age insurance system for basic old-age pensions cannot be separated from the reform of the basic old-age insurance of public servants. Currently, government departments and public institutions still function according to the retirement pension system which does not require the payment of old-age insurance premiums and so must be reformed as it cannot be adapted to the current situation. The reform of old-age pensions for all public servants, people working with public institutions, and employees in public institutions whose salary originates mainly in public finances, that is, civil servants provided for by public finance, should be considered and planned for as a whole for comprehensive reform and coordinated promotion. As state employees, they are entitled to basic old-age insurance, assume the obligations for premium payment, as well as touch the basic old-age pension and the balanced "occupational annuity" security relevant to their occupation and with certain incentive functions.

III. The Problem with the Development and Mode Selection of Rural Social Security

While developing urban social security, China did not neglect the development of rural social security. However, the development of China's rural social security obviously lags behind due to great urban-rural disparity and regional disparity. The rural subsistence security system was not established nationwide until 2007, which is about ten years later than the establishment of the urban subsistence security system; pilot projects started in 2003 for rural new cooperative medical care, which realized basic coverage by 2008, that is 5–10 years later than the urban employees' basic medical insurance system. The "personal account-based" rural social old-age insurance established in line with the principle of "being mainly based on personal contribution, supplemented by collective subsidies and supported by government policies" started early (1991) and developed rapidly, but has become basically stagnant since the 1997 Asian economic crisis. It is not until the latest few years that some coastal developed provinces started pilot work on the construction of a new rural social old-age insurance system. No uniform system has been developed by the state. See Table 7.1 for the development of rural social old-age insurance from 2002 to 2008.

There are two main rural social old-age security policies at the state level. One is the old-age security policy for rural families practicing birth control. Since 2004, rural couples adhering to the birth control policy and who had only one child (or two daughters) have been entitled to a monthly subsidy no lower than RMB 600 as reward until their death. The subsidies are jointly paid by the Central Government and local governments (Information Office of the State Council, The People's Republic of China 2004). The other is the comprehensive social security system for farmers who have lost land. In line with the principle of "exchanging land for security", farmers whose land has been requisitioned can generally join the urban social security system, but at a security standard lower than urban employees. By the end of

Table 7.1 Development of rural social old-age insurance

Year	2002	2003	2004	2005	2006	2007	2008
Number of insurants (million people)	54.62	54.28	53.78	54.42	53.74	51.71	55.95
Funds accumulated (billion yuan)	23.3	25.9	28.5	31.0	35.5	39.2	49.9
Number of people receiving old-age pensions (million people)	/	1.98	2.05	3.02	3.54	4.12	5.12
Amount of old-age pensions paid (billion yuan)	/	1.5	/	2.1	3.0	4.0	5.7

Source Statistical Bulletin on the Development of Labor and Social Security Services (2002–2008)

2008, social security for land-requisitioned farmers was provided in 1201 counties and cities in 27 provinces nationwide, and 13.24 million land-requisitioned farmers had been included into the basic subsistence or old-age security system.

The Chinese government has promised to establish a social security system ensuring that "every old person is taken care of" and covering both urban and rural areas, as well as to guarantee that "everyone is entitled to social security". The construction of the rural social old-age insurance system is one of the key and most difficult points, of which one difficulty is the selection of modality. As to the institutional mode of rural social old-age insurance, theoretical circles have mainly put forward the following ideas:

- Establishing the "universal old-age allowance system" on the basis of the subsistence security system. That is to say, rural people reaching a certain age, regardless of their employment history or income, should be able to receive a guaranteed monthly old-age pension based on national public finances.
- "The personal account full fund accumulation system". The funds contributed by farmers all enter their personal accounts and fund accumulation is practiced.
- "Be included in urban social insurance". Fiscal subsidies are used to emulate employers' contribution to include farmers into urban social insurance.
- "Basic old-age pension + personal accounts". Basic old-age pension consists in the inclusive old-age pension supported by public finances, while personal accounts are old-age pension of full fund accumulation from personal contribution.
- "Material objects in exchange for security". Material objects that farmers have such as agricultural products, land and equities are transformed into insurance premiums, for which practical and feasible social old-age insurance systems have been respectively designed. The insurance mode in rural areas of Beijing (i.e., "basic old-age pension + personal accounts") is receiving more and more attention and recognition.

Based on China's current economic and social developments and future developmental trends, I think the developmental mode of combining insurance and welfare should be maintained for rural social security in China. In this way, some old people, low-income groups and poverty-stricken people can obtain subsistence despite their inability to pay premiums, while middle-income people engage in obligatory contributions, and high-income people in rural areas can enjoy a higher level of security benefits according to the contributions they make. As a result, not only can all the farmers enjoy appropriate social security benefits but also no excessive burden is imposed on national public finances; this developmental mode not only allows for the combination of rights and obligations, but also for the realization of the developmental objective of "all people sharing" and the promotion of the sustainable development of the rural social security system. We should flexibly combine insurance and welfare according to the diverse farmer groups and their income differences. A welfare-focused institutional mode should be implemented for specific regions and people, while an insurance-focused institutional mode should be implemented for other regions and people. The welfare-based social security institutional mode should be implemented for old people in rural regions, low-income people and poverty-stricken people, whereas subsistence security and old-age allowances should be developed and the social assistance system improved in the way that it will be mainly funded by national public finances. Regarding people living in rural regions with relatively high income and a certain capability to pay premiums, such as employees in township enterprises, people with off-farm employment, and migrant workers, their social insurance system should be integrated with urban social security with consideration to the diversity in rural economic development. In terms of fund-raising methods, we suggest that rural social insurance funds be raised by premium payment, as they help better clarify rights and obligations and are also a main source of funds for social insurance in China. Funds for welfare projects are mainly borne by national public finances. Although the central government and local governments share responsibilities, the central public finances taking up the main responsibilities. We should step up transfer payment from the central public finances with priority given to central and western regions and regions inhabited by ethnic minorities, especially remote mountain areas, poverty-stricken areas, old revolutionary areas, areas suffering from resource depletion, areas with harsh natural conditions and counties of ethnic minorities, while appropriately considering some distressed areas in the east. As for distressed areas in the eastern region, provincial public finances should further raise the ratio of special subsidies, principally for financially distressed counties and cities within the province. In light of the rapidly aging population, on one hand, we should accelerate the development of rural social security; on the other hand, we should be far-sighted, make scientific decisions and prudently design the rural social security system, instead of setting up too high security standards.

As for the social security of migrant rural workers in cities, some people in theoretical circles maintain that an independent system be established, which I think not very appropriate. In principle, they should be included in the urban social security system. As their employment is not stable and their income low, migrant workers' social security system should be designed on the basis of reality. First, we should resolve the problems of work-related injuries and major disease security, which should be directly included into the urban social insurance system. The basic requirements for migrant workers' old-age insurance system are low premiums, wide coverage, as well as connectivity and transferability. We should formulate and implement as soon as possible the measures for the transfer and continuation of migrant workers' old-age insurance relations. We should encourage governments in places where conditions permit to involve migrant workers with stable jobs into the urban employees' basic old-age insurance system. It should be defined whether they participate in the employees' basic old-age insurance system or the rural laborers' basic old-age insurance system according to their respective work arrangements. All resident rural workers with stable employment in cities, regardless of their household registers, should participate in the local employees' basic old-age insurance system. Migrant workers with no stable employment should have the right to independently select the type of basic old-age insurance system they wish to participate in.

IV. The Problem with the Management System of Old-age Security Funds

The sources of funds for the two major old-age security systems in China—that is, contributory social insurance and non-contributory social welfare (subsistence security system and old-age allowance system)—differ. The funds for non-contributory social welfare are directly taken from public finances, directly collected by taxation departments, and directly disbursed according to financial resources and the needs of the security system. It is a fiscal security system supported by taxation, and the management of such security funds is generally not involved in the self-sustainability of expenses.

Three systems coexist currently in the contributory social system. First, in the case of regionally managed social insurance pooling funds, except for a few provinces which practice centralized provincial management, social pooling at the provincial level has not been realized. The main practice is to manage social pooling at the county level and prefecture city level. Second, in the case of the personal account system, personal accounts are basically not fully funded; in pilot provinces which have fully funded personal accounts, provincial special financial accounts are mainly used for management. Third, in the case of enterprise annuities, the number of enterprises and employees with annuities nationwide is not large, and the scale of funds collected is limited (about RMB 90 billion in 2008). The trust management mode is generally selected for enterprise annuities, and an expert committee formed by the enterprise annuity management department selects a qualified financial institution for investment. Similar to expanding commercial insurance, the funds of enterprise annuities are managed through the market.

Of the above two major types of old-age security systems, the first type and the third system in the second type are two extreme types, in which no significant difference or controversy is found between the management and operation systems at home and abroad, and for which it is not necessary to reform the fund management mode. What causes serious disputes still is the selection of the management system for social pooling funds and the personal account funds under the urban employees' basic old-age insurance system. As the main part in China's old-age security system, the urban employees' basic old-age insurance fund management system is a key to deepening the reform of China's old-age security system. With the issue of personal accounts being studied in the previous part, here we will mainly discuss the management system for employees' basic old-age insurance social pooling funds.

Currently, two systems coexist for the collection of employees' basic old-age insurance funds, with the human resource and social security departments and local taxation departments collecting respectively about half. This peculiar dual collection system was developed ten years ago when it was difficult to collect social insurance premiums against the backdrops of the economic crisis; it was recognized by the State Council through the promulgation of the "Regulations on the Collection of Social Insurance Funds" in 2000. In 2007, the two departments competed for the power to collect social insurance premiums. As neither party would give in, the final result was to maintain the dual collection system, which has been in operation for nearly ten years now.

The Report suggests that old-age insurance premiums should be collected by the taxation department, and that the definition of income for old-age insurance premium payment should be the same as that of the base for income tax. This proposal intends to transform the "dual collection system" that has been operating in China for ten years into a unitary collection system and thus link old-age insurance premium to income tax rather than to the total salary issued by a unit or the employees' individual salary. This proposal, if successfully implemented, should be able to help straighten out the old-age security fund collection system and base. However, The Report shuns the disputes on the "dual collection system" in China's social insurance funds, without giving sufficient reasons for transforming the "dual collection system" into a collection system by the taxation department, the feasibility of which is dubious, without mentioning that such a transformation could hardly dispels the misgivings of the human resource and social security department, nor does it address the resistance against the reform of the social insurance collection system. In fact, social insurance premium collection systems vary in different countries worldwide; there is no fixed and uniform mode.[1] However, with consideration given to convenience, the collection of one tax or fund fees is generally completed by one department. It is more common for taxes to be collected by the taxation department and fees collected by the social security department.

[1]The study of Researcher Zhou Hong from the Chinese Academy of Social Sciences proves that the tax collection mode, the social security department collection mode and tax and fees hybrid collection mode are found for social insurance in various countries worldwide.

Currently, one of the focuses in the disputes on the "dual collection system" in China is whether social insurance funds are "fees" or tax. Under general conditions, social insurance funds should be special purposes "fees"; collection rates and payment benefits are determined by scientific estimates to ensure the balance of collection and payment. From this perspective, it is right for the social security department to collect social insurance funds. However, as for "social pooling funds" in social old-age insurance, the boundary between "fees" and "tax" is not very clear; in particular, with the constant rise of social pooling in old-age insurance, social pooling funds in social old-age insurance is slowly evolving from "fees" to "tax". In this light, it is reasonable for the taxation department to collect social pooling funds for social old-age insurance. Therefore, whether the nature of social pooling funds in social old-age insurance is defined as "fees" or "tax" is an important basis for whether they should be collected by the taxation department or the social security department.

Before the establishment of social old-age insurance, various enterprises and employers issued retirement pensions for their retirees from their own income. With the establishment of the social old-age insurance system, old-age pensions for retirees are issued from social old-age insurance funds. In 1997, it was decided to classify old-age insurance funds into social pooling funds and personal account funds, to establish localized management for employees' old-age pensions (provincial pooling), and to gradually raise the pooling level of old-age insurance funds. Retirement pensions were transformed into old-age pensions so that unit-based security was transformed into social security. Pooling at the departmental, industrial and district and county government levels were all redirected to the prefecture and even province level, which meant that old-age insurance funds came to have more rigid constraints and gradually turned into social security funds as defined by state policies or laws. Currently, the pooling level of old-age insurance is not high enough, and different regions show different contribution ratios and management methods. If it was determined that national pooling be practiced for social pooling funds of old-age insurance in China (with basic old-age pensions being issued), and the rates and the management system be centralized, they would not be any different from the national "social security tax", and it would be justified for the taxation department to collect fees nationwide. Therefore, determining which department should collect social insurance funds seemingly depends on the nature of the collected funds more than any other factor.

Besides fund collection and the rationalization of the old-age security fund management system, two other problems must be solved: first, the establishment of a national uniform old-age pension management system; second, the establishment of scientific and reasonable issuance adjustment mechanism for old-age pension benefits. These two problems have both been mentioned in The Report, for which principles were proposed. The establishment of a national uniform old-age pension management system under the direct charge of the central government is an important measure for resolving such problems as low pooling levels for old-age insurance funds, great differences in premium payment between different regions, difficulties in adjusting local surplus funds, and regulating the issuance of old-age pension benefits. I think we should push forward the development of this system, and in particular national uniform laws and regulations, such as the "Social Insurance Law", should be promulgated and implemented as soon as possible. However, this system should not be too complex, and we should mainly manage the collection, supervision and issuance of old-age insurance social pooling funds under centralized national management. As to non-large scaleold-age insurance personal account funds, it is suggested that the National Council for Social Security Funds be entrusted with the management of these funds, or that provincial personal account funds management committees manage them respectively so that they can be separated from the funds managed by the government and become market-based funds under strict supervision conditions. As for the old-age pension benefit adjustment mechanism, in-depth discussions cannot be held due to its complicated nature. If national pooling is practiced for basic old-age pensions, such retirement pensions should be of a pay-as-you-go nature, and the issuance standards should be raised as appropriate. The basic old-age pension replacement rate of insured employees reaching retirement conditions will at least reach above 40% of their salary before retirement; as for the insured whose statutory retirement age and contribution years are raised and prolonged as appropriate, their replacement rate may be raised accordingly, but should not exceed 50%. Attention should be paid to the principle that "certain differences may exist in benefit standards between various regions, but such differences should not prevent the transfer of old-age pensions and mobility of laborers nationwide" as proposed in The Report.

In sum, if national pooling is practiced for the future basic old-age pension system, a department under the central government should be assigned to its uniform management. As for the basic old-age pensions of all of the eligible insured people, the state should be responsible for its uniform management, as well as for fund raising and benefit issuance. The transfer and renewal of social insurance among various regions will not be as difficult as it is now. As for personal account funds, due to their shrinking in scale, it is proposed that they be combined with occupational annuities, for which decentralized management and investment should be conducted on a provincial basis; market-based investment institutions are employed for their operation and remunerated from the amount of payment and return on investment. As the return on investment is personal, the transfer and continuation problem of social insurance relations in personal accounts would barely exist.

V. The Problem with Managing the Debt of Old-age Security Funds and State-owned Share Transfer and Holding

A problem that can hardly be bypassed in the course of reforming China's old-age security system is the problem of explicit and implicit old-age security fund debts. The explicit debts are caused by the fact that old-age insurance funds currently collected, especially social pooling funds, are inadequate to pay retired people's pensions; the implicit debts refer to the deficits in the personal accounts of "in-service persons" and "new persons" not fully funded (which have to be paid once these people reach retirement age). Moreover, there are potential deficits in the balance of payments resulting from expanding old-age security expenditures (such as old-age allowances and subsistence security expenditures) and from the expansion of the old-age security system as well as that of the rapidly aging population.

The issue of the actual social pooling funds debts and the implicit debts in personal accounts is mainly resolved by improving the old-age security system so that old-age security funds gradually become self-sustainable. Various measures discussed now, to some extent, also serve this objective. In accordance with China's aging population and the changes in its demographic and labor structure, The Report makes the suggestion of raising the "age for receiving old-age pensions". The main reasons given include the rapid rise of the burden rate of non-laboring population over the laboring population (from 1:1.3 in 1980 to 1:3 in 2002 to 1:2 in 2030); as well as international lessons and experiences (the actual retirement age in developing countries is young, while the retirement age in developed countries has been raised to over 65) showing that the retirement age for workers is low in China, and even so there exists a serious issue of early retirement. With the actual retirement age lower than the statutory retirement age, the retiring population not only exerts pressure on the payment of current old-age security funds but also aggravates old-age security debts, which is not good for the long-term equilibrium of social security funds. Therefore, The Report proposes that "regardless of gender, the minimum age for receiving full pension from social pooling should be gradually raised to 65, the practices of encouraging or forcing early retirement should be stopped, and old-age pension benefits should be reduced pro rata for those with inadequate employment years." This proposal is forward-looking and insightful. The opinions put forward in The Report merit the attention of the social security administrative department, which should carefully study the appropriate time and specific methods for implementing these proposals (the implementation may be delayed several years in light of the pressure of the employment peak). I approve of the opinion on gradually raising the retirement age, but consideration should be given to the characteristics and demands of different occupations; the boundary between retiring from the labor market and receiving "statutory old-age pensions" should be defined; and the problem of early retirement should be resolved. Employing the appropriate measures, the statutory retirement age should be gradually raised to the level of developed countries in order to overcome the pressure of early payment of old-age security funds.

Old-age security expenditures resulting from the expanding coverage of the old-age security system are generally yet limitedly supported by tax and public finances, and such subsidies will gradually be withdrawn in the future and thus will not pose a big problem. Currently, the fiscal department allocates subsidies amounting to several tens of billions RMB for social insurance, especially old-age insurance funds, so as to offset the deficits in old-age pensions. In the short term, the normal operation of the old-age insurance system may be maintained in terms of fiscal subsidies and social insurance funds with expanding coverage. Of course, with the establishment of social security budgets, the deficits in social security funds of the current year may have institutional solutions. The social security debts posing the most serious problem are the expanding deficits in personal accounts and the balance of payment risk from the aging population. As we have already discussed about the personal accounts, how to cope with the risk of the aging population will be focused on as follows.

To cope with the above debts of old-age security funds, the Chinese government established the National Council for Social Security Fund in 2000, which is responsible for raising and operating national social security funds. Through nearly ten years' accumulation, the national social security funds have amounted to RMB 562.37 billion, a small amount in scale with consideration given to the huge social security fund debts. The enormous state-owned assets, state-controlled enterprises and state-holding enterprises in China provide the national social security fund with the material base for raising funds from state-owned enterprises and state-owned assets; the key point is to find the method and approach suitable for the transfer of state-owned assets and shares into the national social security funds. Due to the difficulty to cash state-owned assets, it is now very difficult to directly transfer state-owned assets to the national social security funds for management and operation. A more realistic approach is for national public finance to inject funds and transfer funds from listed state-owned enterprises to national social security funds. National public finances inject some funds each year but on a limited scale; the key funds are from the transfer of state-owned shares. The Chinese government decided in 2003 to transfer some state-owned assets, especially some state-owned shares of listed companies and non-listed shareholding companies to replenish national social security funds. The idea several years earlier was to transfer funds after cashing state-owned shares by selling through the capital market to the national social security funds. As the overall scale of China's capital market is limited, and because it is difficult for China to bear the pressure of selling a large amount of state-owned shares within a short period, it is very difficult to sell and cash state-owned shares. This may bring violent fluctuations in the capital market. It is difficult to have the national social security fund play an effective role by selling state-owned shares.

The proposal in The Report is to change "selling state-owned shares" to "transfer state-owned shares to substantiate social security funds". Social security funds should hold these shares for a long period and pay old-age pensions by bonuses. As strategic shareholders, they can maintain their owners' rights, including bonuses at a reasonable level through company supervision, voting rights and a seat at the Board of Directors, etc. Social security funds must hold shares for a long period, have well-defined responsibilities and independent management authority, and regularly publicize audited account details. To transfer state-owned shares to substantiate social security funds may prevent the loss of state-owned assets similarly to what occurred in Russia. Meanwhile, as long-term strategic shareholders, old-age pension funds may play an important role in supervising corporate operation and improving governance structure. This proposal is very valuable in that it is highly persuasive, pertinent and operable.

In June 2009, upon the approval of the State Council, the Ministry of Finance, the State-owned Assets Supervision and Administration Commission, the China

Security Regulatory Commission and the National Council for Social Security Fund jointly promulgated and implemented the "Implementation Measures for the Transfer of Some State-owned Shares from the Domestic Securities Market to the National Social Security Fund". According to the "Implementing Measures", after the implementation of the policy of separating the new from the old in the share-trading reform, a joint stock limited company with state-owned shares which makes IPOs and gets listed in the domestic securities market shall, unless it is otherwise provided for by the State Council, transfer some of its state-owned shares to the NCSSF, namely 10% of the actual number of the IPO stocks. If the number of shares held by the state-owned shareholder is less than the number of shares which should be transferred, the transfer shall be made on the basis of the number of the shares actually held by it. For state-owned shares of domestically listed companies transferred to social security funds, social security funds will take up the obligations of the original state-owned shareholders in the lock-up period. As for shares transferred by companies which have IPO and are listed after the implementation of the policy of separating the new from the old in the share-trading reform and before the promulgation of these measures, the lock-up period shall be prolonged for three years. After state-owned shares are transferred to social security funds, social security funds have the rights to earnings and disposals with regards to the transferred shares, but shall not interfere with the daily management of the listed companies operations. According to the implementing measures for the transfer of state-owned shares, altogether 131 listed companies were involved, thus 8.394 billion shares should have been transferred, with a market capitalization of about RMB 63.933 billion, which should have amounted to RMB 83.56 billion by the end of transfer, cumulating in a 30% increase. The transfer of state-owned shares this time coincided with the proposal of The Report, which shows the foresight and practicability of the proposal. The transfer of state-owned shares, to some extent, can alleviate the pressure of selling state-owned shares that has been troubling the Chinese stock market for a long time, and help substantiate social security funds. It is also an important measure for improving the social security system and benefiting all people. Of course, the transfer of state-owned shares to substantiate social security funds is only one of the possible measures for resolving the issue of long-term debts of social security funds. There is still a large amount of difficult work and thinking to do, such as how to raise savings social security funds through multiple channels based on demands and reality, and realize value preservation and increase during a long period of time. This is a major preemptive strategy that China must take in order to cope with its aging population.[2]

[2]This chapter is published in *China Industrial Economics*, 2009 (8).

Chapter 8
A Study on the Income Redistribution Effect of Social Security in China: A Case Study on Social Insurance

Social security is an important tool for regulating income distribution. Some scholars have studied the role of income redistribution of social security in China, and have come to different and even conflicting conclusions due to different sources of data, time of investigation, and research perspectives. In 2012, a task force of the Chinese Academy of Social Sciences conducted an urban and rural household questionnaire survey using an experience stratification method and non-strict random sampling in six provinces, namely: Sichuan, Heilongjiang, Hunan, Shanxi, Jiangsu and Hainan. 3417 effective questionnaires were recovered to conduct macro theoretical analysis and empirical analysis on the income redistribution effect of social security.

8.1 Problem Introduction and Literature Review

The expanding income gap has become a major problem drawing extensive concerns from various social circles in China. In the mid-1980s, China's Gini coefficient stood at 0.16, which rose to 0.44 in 2000 and to about 0.49 in 2008.[1] The reasons for the expansion and exacerbation of the income gap are multifold; some are reasonable, while many others are unreasonable; some are about primary distribution, while others are about redistribution. Some experts hold that a very important reason for the expanding income gap among residents is the unhealthy and unfair social security system.[2] Social security is an important tool for the redistribution of residents' income, which important role in income distribution

---

[1]Li Shi and Yang Sui (2009), The Impact of China's Urban Subsistence Security Policy on Income Distribution and Poverty, *Chinese Journal of Population Science*, 2009 (5).
[2]ZhengGongcheng (2010), Social Security: Basic Institutional Guarantee for Regulating Income Distribution, *Chinese Cadres Tribune*, 2010 (6).

Y. Wang, *Social Security in China: On the Possibility of Equitable Distribution*, Research Series on the Chinese Dream and China's Development Path,
DOI 10.1007/978-981-10-5643-7_8

among residents is fully reflected in both international and domestic social security and income distribution practices.

In light of past studies, the redistribution effect of social security has been verified in many countries. David Jesuit and Vincent Mahler, through a comparative study of fiscal redistribution based on the LIS datain 13 developed countries from 1980 to 2000, discovered that national social security outperforms taxation in regulating the income distribution gap. In Sweden, a welfare state, the role played by social security in income distribution accounts for over 80%, while that of taxation only for about 10%.[3] Social security contributed to over 40% in the drop of the Gini coefficient in the United States.[4] Japan's social security system plays a key role in regulating the income distribution gap, and the Gini coefficient after the regulation of social security is about 0.02–0.07 lower than the Gini coefficient before redistribution, with the redistribution rate reaching over 4%.[5] In 2004, after redistribution, the Gini coefficient in the United Kingdom dropped from 0.52 to 0.38, at a rate of 36.8%, to which various direct social security measures made the biggest contributions, alone reducing the Gini coefficient by 15%.[6] When reviewing the OECD data, we discover that in 2010 the Gini coefficient underwent very obvious changes in some countries after the regulation of taxation and transfer payment. The Gini coefficient after the regulation of taxation and transfer payment (mainly social security) dropped by 0.2 on average, while the drop of the Gini coefficient in Austria, Belgium, Finland, France, Germany and Slovenia was over this average.

China's social security is a comprehensive system including social insurance, social welfare and social assistance. In recent years, some experts and scholars have studied the topic of social security and income distribution from different perspectives. Due to their different grasp of national conditions, different sources of data, different research perspectives and different research methods, they have come to different conclusions, causing disagreements, disputes and even conflicts over the specific role of social security in regulating income distribution in China.

Many scholars think that the effect of social security on income distribution regulation is not satisfactory. A "contrary regulation" effect on income distribution can even be observed, showing an important regression effect.[7] Some scholars think

---

[3]David Jesuit and Vincent Mahler (2004), "*State Redistribution in Comparative Perspective: A Cross-National Analysis of the Developed Countries*". Luxembourg Income Study Working Paper.

[4]Ervik, R. (1998), "The Redistributive Aim of Social Policy: A Comparative Analysis of Taxes, Tax Expenditure Transfers and Direct Transfers in Eight Countries". LIS Working Paper, 1998 (184).

[5]Liu Leshan (2008), Overseas Fiscal Measures for Regulating Income Gap and Their Implications, paper delivered at the 18th Annual Conference of the Chinese Society of Laws of Economics.

[6]J.IgnacioConde-Ruiz and Paola Profeta (2007), "*The redistributive design of social security systems, The Economic Journal*", 117(April), 686–712.

[7]Xiang Ling (2007), Several Problems Concerning the Redistribution Regression Effect in the Old-age Insurance System, *Fujian Forum (Humanities and Social Sciences Edition)*, 2007 (1).

that the transfer payment of social security widens income gap between rural residents and urban residents, and that after the transfer payment of social security, the gap between low-income households and medium-income households become wider than before transfer payment, as for that between medium high-income households and high-income households.[8] With a social security system of separate practices in rural and urban areas, social security has further aggravated urban-rural inequality. The per capita social security transferred income of urban residents in 2000 was 10.04 times that of rural residents; the same ratio was 15.45 in 2003 and 13.37 in 2005; if all the welfare "implicitly subsidized" to urban employees is taken into account, the actual income gap of urban-rural residents will expand 5–6 times.[9] The benefits of China's basic old-age and medical insurance for residents of medium and high income far exceed those of residents of low income, thus expanding the income gap.[10] Under the 2005 reform scheme, people above 40 in 2002 had obvious tendency of reverse income transfer.[11] Compared with the original old-age insurance system, the new old-age insurance system obviously weakens the intra-generational redistribution effect and may give rise to serious intergenerational inequalities.[12] In terms of income redistribution, China's current medical security system lacks a regulatory mechanism and fails to bring into play its regulating function for income redistribution. Under the "low insurance premiums and high coinsurance rate" mode, inequalities exist among those receiving benefits from the cooperative medical services.

Many other scholars think that despite the many problems and inadequacies in the institutional design of China's social security, other types of securities such as China's subsistence security, old-age security, medical security, unemployment security and education security all play a positive role in regulating income distribution in China. A research based in Baoji, Shaanxi Province has found that the transfer income from social security has reduced the Gini coefficient between urban and rural residents' by 4.53%; furthermore, the Gini coefficient for urban residents has dropped by 22.76%, while income gap among rural residents has dropped by 1.82%.[13] The current arrangements in China's social old-age insurance system play

---

[8]Wang Maofu and XieYongcai (2012), A Study about Negative Regulation of Income Distribution by Social Security, *Studies on Mao Zedong and Deng Xiaoping's Theories*, 2012 (6).

[9]Gu Cheng and Li Junyi (2004), Expansion of the Gap between Urban and Rural Income Distribution and the Integration of China's Social Security System, *Journal of the Dongbei University of Finance and Economics*, 2004 (4).

[10]Wang Xiaolu and Fan Gang (2005), The Trend of Income Gap in China and Analysis of Influence Factors, *Economic Research Journal*, 2005(10).

[11]He Lixin (2007), The Effect of Income Distribution by the Reform of the Urban Old-age Insurance System in China, *Economic Research Journal*, 2007 (3).

[12]PengHaoran and ShenShuguang (2007), A Comparative Study of the Income Redistribution Effect of China's Old-age Insurance System before and after the Reform, *Statistical Research*, 2007 (2).

[13]GaoWenshu (2012), The Effect of Social Security on Regulating Income Distribution Gap: an Empirical Study Based on the Data of a Survey over Residents in Baoji, Shaanxi, *Social Security Studies*, 2012 (4).

an obvious role of income redistribution.[14] Old-age pension property has exerted a major redistribution effect on property distribution in families of enterprise employees in China's urban areas by reducing the Gini coefficient of family property distribution by 8% points and reducing family property distribution inequalities by 20%.[15] After the institution of compensations for new rural cooperative medical services, inequalities have been alleviated to some extent.[16] Compensations for new rural cooperative medical services are more inclined towards sick people, and those with low income receive higher compensations than those with high income. The subsistence security system can improve the living conditions of some low-income people, and play a certain effective role in alleviating urban poverty; therefore, the subsistence security system constrains, to some extent, the income gap within cities and within rural areas.[17]

Thus, we can conclude that China's research on the role of social security in income redistribution is not very mature, and major disputes and conflicts exist as to how to evaluate the role of the social security system in regulating income gap. Some studies only discuss the role of China's social security in income distribution theoretically or by employing simple statistic data, or even jump to qualitative judgment and conclusion on the role of social security in income distribution by subjective observations. Quantitative studies on the role of social security in income distribution are lacking, and an investigation basis is lacking for subjective evaluation on the role of social security in income redistribution. Thus different research conclusions have been drawn as a result of different sources of data, different survey time and different research perspectives. The income redistribution effect of the entire social security system is different from that of different single social security project, thus leading into some contradictory results. This situation is not ideal for the accurate understanding and grasp of the role of social security in income distribution in China, which is so complicated that hardly any absolute standard can be employed for measurement. Therefore, we should give full consideration to real national economic and social conditions as well as residents' value judgment; as we objectively measure the effect of social security in income redistribution, we should fully examine the subjective evaluation by the public.

Based on current research, this study wishes to examine the important role of social security in residents' income distribution; employ the data of questionnaire surveys to conduct quantitative analysis of the current role of social security in

[14]Wang Xiaojun and Kang Bowei (2009), Analysis of the Effect of China's Social Old-age Insurance System on Income Redistribution, *Statistical Research*, 2009 (11).

[15]Yang Zhenlin and Wang Yake (2007), An Empirical Analysis of the Redistribution Effect of China's Enterprise Old-age Insurance System, *China Soft Science*, 2007 (4).

[16]Ren Ran and Jin Feng (2007), A Study on the Health Service Accessibility and Medical Service Burdens after the Implementation of New Rural Cooperative Medical Care, *China Health Economics*, 2007 (1).

[17]Chen Jiandong, Yang Wen and Feng Ying (2001), An Empirical Study on the Income Distribution Effect of Subsistence Security and Individual Income Tax, *Reform of Economic System*, 2001 (1).

income distribution; and analyze the practical evaluation of different residents on the role of social security in income distribution by taking social insurance as an example, in an attempt to comprehensively analyze and grasp the role of social security in income redistribution in China from both subjective and objective perspectives. The task force of the Chinese Academy of Social Sciences conducted urban and rural household questionnaire surveys using an experience stratification method and non-strict random sampling in six provinces, namely: Sichuan, Heilongjiang, Hunan, Shanxi, Jiangsu and Hainan. 3417 effective questionnaires were recovered. The questionnaire's content concerning the role of social security in income redistribution mainly included items such as the basic conditions of interviewees, their current social security (including social insurance, social welfare and social assistance), and their subjective evaluation, relevant problems and suggestions on social security, as well as its role in income distribution. This article consists mainly of five parts: first, problem introduction and literature review; second, examination of the role of China's social security in income redistribution; third, an objective measurement of the role of social security (social insurance) in income redistribution; fourth, subjective evaluation of the role of social security in income redistribution; fifth, conclusion and suggestions.

8.2 China Attaches Great Importance to the Effective Role of Social Security in Income Re-Distribution

(i) China attaches great importance to the role of social security in income redistribution

Since the start of the 21st century, the CPC Central Committee and the State Council have been attaching great importance to the excessive income gap by actively taking various measures to narrow income gap and promote social equality and justice. Since the 18th CPC National Congress, China has been according more importance to resolving the excessive income gap and deepening the reform of the income distribution system and the social security system in the course of comprehensively deepening reform, and attaching more importance to the role of social security in income redistribution. The 18th CPC National Congress, the Third and the Fifth Plenary Sessions of the 18th CPC Central Committee have all put forward that we should further step up efforts in redistribution regulations and improve the redistribution regulatory mechanism which is mainly based on taxation, social security and transfer payment.

The nature of social security is to maintain social equality and justice, as its function is to distribute and redistribute people's income. With the constant economic and social development in China, people have increasing demands in terms of social security. Various social security systems have been established and improved, the coverage of social security has been constantly expanding, and the fund scale of social security has been expanding. Social security takes up an important position in the distribution pattern of people's income, and its important role in regulating residents' income distribution has become increasingly prominent.

In recent years, China has been gradually establishing and improving various social security systems. In terms of old-age security, the rural residents' and the urban residents' old-age insurance systems have been established successively, and efforts have been channeled to promote the integration of the urban-rural residents' old-age insurance system and construct a multi-level old-age insurance system; while attention is paid to fund security, more and more importance has been accorded to old-age service security. It is especially noteworthy that in 2015, the central government decided to implement the reform on the old-age insurance system in government departments and public institutions, which is conducive to alleviating the "benefit gap" and promoting social equality. In terms of medical security, outpatient social pooling for urban residents' basic medical insurance has been basically established; exploration is being made on the establishment of a major disease insurance system; and the urban-rural medical insurance systems are being gradually integrated. Important steps have been taken in the establishment of unemployment, work-related injury and maternity insurance systems. In terms of subsistence security, the number of people covered tends to be stable, a dynamic regulatory mechanism for urban and rural subsistence security standards has been established, and supervision and service for subsistence security have been improving.

With the establishment and improvement of various social security systems, a social security system covering urban and rural residents has been basically developed, and full institutional coverage has been realized. The medical insurance system, which has taken the lead to cover all the people in China, has developed the largest medical security network in the world. By September 2015, the number of people covered by basic old-age insurance, basic medical insurance, unemployment insurance, work-related injury insurance, and maternity insurance was respectively 852 million, 658 million, 171 million, 211 million, and 178 million. In terms of social assistance, the number of urban residents covered by subsistence security has been maintained at about 20 million, the number of rural residents covered by subsistence security has been maintained at about 53 million, and the number of old people provided for by the Five Guarantee System has been maintained at about 5 million.[18] With the constant improvement of the social insurance system and its expanding coverage, the scale of income and social security expenses has been expanding. By the end of 2014, the income of the five social insurance funds (urban and rural residents' basic old-age insurance, medical insurance, unemployment insurance, industrial injury insurance, and maternity insurance) amounted to RMB 3.9828 trillion, a RMB 457.5 billion increase from 2013 at a rate of 13.0%. Fund

[18]Source of data: *Statistical Bulletin on the Development of Social Services in China 2014*.

expenditures amounted to RMB 3.3003 trillion, a RMB 508.6 billion increase from 2013 at a rate of 18.2%.[19]

With China's increasing fiscal investments in social security, the benefits of social security have obviously improved, and the income redistribution effect of social security is becoming increasingly obvious. China has consecutively raised old-age pensions for enterprise retirees 11 times. As a result, the basic old-age pension for enterprise retirees has risen from a monthly average of RMB 647 in 2004 to over RMB 2000. The consecutive substantial increase of the basic old-age pension has played an active role in improving enterprise retirees' living standards and promoting social equality. The minimum standard for the basic old-age pension of national urban and rural residents' basic old-age insurance has been improved to a monthly pay of RMB 70 for each person. In terms of medical insurance, in 2014, 1.52 billion person-time urban employees received medical services, and 420 million person-time urban residents received medical services. The reimbursement ratio of inpatient medical expenditures within the coverage of employees' basic medical insurance and urban residents' basic medical insurance policies reached above 80% and around 70% respectively. The highest limit of payment from funds was improved to six times that of the local employees' average annual salary and local residents' annual per capital disposable income, which, to some extent, alleviated the problem of overpriced medical treatment. In terms of unemployment, work-related injury, and maternity insurance, the number of people receiving benefits and the amount of benefits have also been substantially improved. Subsistence security levels have been stably improved. In terms of rural poverty relief, in 2011, the state defined the new rural poverty relief standard as RMB 2300 for farmers' per capita net income. Increasingly more poor people have been covered by poverty relief efforts, and come to share the results of reform and development in China.

(ii) The expenditure scale of social security in China and its role in income redistribution

After the 1990s, with the establishment and improvement of various social security systems in China, the coverage of social security gradually expanded, security levels gradually improved, and the social security system became an important tool for China to regulate laborers' and national income distribution, with a more obvious impact on income distribution. In terms of the social security expenditure ratio in fiscal expenditures, since 2000, the social security ratio in the narrow caliber (caliber I) has been maintained at above 10%, the social security ratio in the medium caliber (caliber II) at above 20%, and the social security ratio in the wide caliber (caliber III) including the expenditure of education and health at above 36%, reaching 40% in 2012. In terms of the social security expenditure ratio in GDP, since 2000, the social security expenditure in the narrow caliber has been basically maintained at above

[19]Source of data: *Statistical Bulletin on the Development of Human Resources and Social Security Services in China* of past years.

2%, reaching 2.4% in 2012; with the rapid development of China's social insurance system, social security expenditures in the medium caliber has been increasing quicker, with the ratio from 2.6% of GDP in 1998 to 6% of GDP in 2012; the social security expenditure ratio in the wide caliber increased from 5.4% of GDP in 1998 to 11.4% of GDP in 2012 (see Table 8.1). Of course, various factors should be considered in terms of the impact of social security income on income distribution. Only with a sound institutional design and a scientific operation mechanism can the goal of income distribution through social security be effectively achieved, the "negative regulation" of income distribution by social security avoided, and the "positive regulation" by social security truly realized.

With the improvement of the social security system and the rise of the ratio of social security fund income and expenditure in national economy, social security systems such as subsistence security, old-age security, medical security, unemployment security and education security have come to play an active role in income distribution in China. Different social security items have different mechanisms for and effects on income redistribution. As social insurance funds are collected according to income in primary distribution, and are paid according to the risk level in secondary distribution, the lower the income is, the higher the replacement rate of social insurance is; therefore, social insurance has a very strong income regulation function. According to our survey, with the establishment and improvement of the social insurance system in China, more and more people have become beneficiaries of social insurance, and social insurance benefits have become an important part in individual and family income. In 2011, all individual social insurance benefits accounted for 14.5% of individuals' annual income; the ratio of social insurance benefits in retirees' income was even higher, being 43%. Social assistance is the state's subsistence security provided for people without or with low income due to disasters or poverty; the recipients do not have to pay premiums, payment is mainly made in cash or in kind by national public finances. Such assistance is distributed according to subsistence needs without requiring the beneficiaries' reciprocity in rights and obligations, thereby with a more direct and obvious redistribution effect. Social welfare consists in subsidies and services mainly addressed to specific weak people such as children, old people and the disabled; these are all funded by national public finances and social donations, and distributed according to the needs of these specific people, thus also having a significant function in terms of narrowing income gap.[20]

In practice, social security may not only promote income redistribution and narrow the income gap, but may also give rise to negative regulation and widen income gap. The positive or negative role of social security in income redistribution depends on relevant factors such as institutional mode, coverage, institutional design, institutional transition, and management services. We should bring into full play the positive regulation role of social security in income redistribution, as well

[20]As to the analysis of the specific mechanisms of different social security items for income redistribution, please refer to our other works.

Table 8.1 Social security expenditure in China (*unit* billion yuan; %)

Year	Caliber I	Caliber II	Caliber III	Ratio in total fiscal expenditure			Ratio in GDP		
				Caliber I	Caliber II	Caliber III	Caliber I	Caliber II	Caliber III
1978	1.89	–	12.94	1.7	–	11.5	0.5	–	3.6
1992	6.65	–	91.68	1.8	–	24.5	0.3	–	3.4
1996	12.8	–	200.54	1.6	–	25.3	0.2	–	2.8
1998	59.56	221.10	452.73	5.5	17.8	36.5	0.7	2.6	5.4
2000	151.76	360.45	649.36	9.6	20.1	36.1	1.5	3.6	6.5
2002	263.62	559.04	960.49	12.0	22.4	38.4	2.2	4.7	8.0
2004	311.61	722.37	1236.84	10.9	22.2	38.0	2.0	4.5	7.7
2006	436.18	995.03	1689.81	10.8	21.6	36.7	2.1	5.2	8.0
2008	680.43	1509.85	2686.58	10.9	21.3	37.9	2.3	5.0	8.9
2010	913.06	2163.93	3827.35	10.2	21.1	37.4	2.3	5.4	9.5
2012	1258.55	3093.92	5942.64	10.0	20.9	40.1	2.4	6.0	11.4

Note Caliber I includes the expenditures related to special care and social welfare and relief, retirement payment of administrative and public institutions, and expenditures in terms of social security subsidies; Caliber II is the addition of social insurance fund expenditures other than fiscal subsidies to Caliber I, and the denominator (total fiscal expenditures) for calculating the ratio of Caliber II includes social insurance fund expenditures except for fiscal subsidies. Caliber III is the addition of education and health expenditures to the basis of Caliber II; it should be noted that the ratio of social security fiscal expenditures in 2002 was big, which was related to the substantial increase in national fiscal expenditures in terms of social insurance fund subsidies. Source of data: based on the relevant data in *China's Fiscal Statistics Yearbook*, *China's Statistics Yearbook*, and *China's Health Statistics Yearbook* in past years; the source of data for the expenditure of social insurance funds from 1998 to 2008: *China's Fiscal Yearbook 2008*; the source of data for 2010: The National Fiscal Expenditure Final Report; the source of data for 2012: Final Account Data of National Fiscal Expenditure 2012, Statistical Bulletin of National Economic and Social Development 2012, and Statistical Bulletin on Human Resources and Social Security 2012; due to different statistical calibers in different years, the data of some years deviate to some extent as prevent and avoid its negative regulatory role. On the whole, China adopts the insurance-based social security mode and generally employs the mode of "combining social pooling and personal accounts". The introduction of personal accounts and the many problems arising in the course of implementation have further weakened the overall role of social security in terms of income redistribution in China.

8.3 Evaluation of the Re-Distribution Effect of China's Social Insurance Revenues

(i) The income redistribution mechanisms of different social insurance items

The social insurance system is the most important part of the whole social security system. The mechanism for the social insurance system in regulating income distribution is complicated, and consideration should be given to such aspects as fund-raising mode, fund source, responsibility allocation, fund-raising level, benefit determination mode, and benefit adjustment mechanism. Also, different social insurance items also vary in their regulation mechanism for income distribution.

The old-age insurance system is the center of the social insurance system. The regulation of income distribution by the old-age insurance system is mainly reflected in two aspects: the fund-raising mode and the benefit determination mode. The pay-as-you-go fund-raising mode and the defined-benefit mode, through the social pooling and payment of old-age insurance funds, play a major role in income distribution; the fund accumulation mode and the contribution-defined mode are mainly income regulation systems employed within an individual's lifetime, from his/her youth (working period) to his/her old age (non-working period). It should be noted that the pay-as-you-go system and the benefit-defined system do not correspond one-to-one, while the fund accumulation system and the contribution-defined system also do not correspond exactly. The old-age insurance systems in many countries tend to be a mixture of different fund-raising modes and benefit-defining modes, and their role in determining income distribution is even more complicated.

The medical insurance system is also an important system in social insurance. It is not only is related to individuals' health, but also regulates income distribution to some extent. The measurement of the role of the medical insurance system in income distribution should be made in the light of the different types of medical insurance system, as well as that of the fund-raising mechanism and benefit compensation mechanism selected. The modes of the medical insurance system include the national (all-inclusive) medical insurance mode, the social medical insurance mode, the commercial medical insurance mode, the cooperative medical insurance mode and the savings medical insurance mode. Due to differences in the fund-raising mechanism and compensation modes, different modes of medical insurance play different roles in the regulation of income distribution.

Compared with the old-age insurance and medical insurance systems, the unemployment system, work-related injury system and maternity insurance system, though relatively small in coverage and fund scale, can regulate income distribution to some extent. Unemployment insurance mainly regulates income distribution by way of fund raising and benefit payment. Different types of unemployment insurance system (including compulsory unemployment insurance, voluntary unemployment subsidies and unemployment assistance, etc.) have different effect in regulating income distribution. Compared with other social insurance systems and social security systems, the unemployment insurance system can better help to directly or indirectly regulate primary distribution. Work-related injury insurance, which does not require personal contributions and provides relevant compensation for anyone subjected to work-related injury, especially helps those of medium and low income and poor people alleviate medical burdens and thus plays a significant role in regulating income distribution. The maternity insurance system, by providing relevant economic support and services for women before and after giving birth, also regulates income distribution to some extent.

(ii) Measurement of the effect of social insurance on income redistribution

To further analyze the effect of social security on income redistribution, this study made a detailed analysis on the social security income gap regulations by using the survey data in 2012. In terms of the basic information of interviewees, males accounted for 47.2%, and females accounted for 52.8%, with an even gender ratio; age was mainly between 18 and 60, accounting for 84.3% of the surveyed population; CPC party members accounted for 17.9%; in terms of religious beliefs, 93.8% of the interviewees had no religious belief; in terms of household register types, those with rural household registers accounted for 53%, and those with non-rural household register accounted for 47%, with a basically balanced ratio; in terms of educational background, those who without any schooling accounted for 4.8%, those with primary school education accounted for 18.1%, those with junior middle school education accounted for 30.7%, those with senior middle school education accounted for 15.1%, those with technical high school/vocational high school/technical secondary school education accounted for 6.4%, those with junior college education accounted for 11.7%, and those with a bachelor's degree and above accounted for 13.2%; in terms of occupation, white-collars accounted for 20.7%, blue-collars accounted for 53.1%, retirees accounted for 12.7%, and other people (students, people awaiting employment and unemployed people) accounted for 13.5%; in terms of employers, those employed by publicly-owned units accounted for 20.7%, those employed by privately-owned units accounted for 24.4%, farmers accounted for 39.5%, and other people accounted for 15.3%. Through comparison, samples are characteristically close to the data of the sixth national census, in which males accounted for 51.27%, and females accounted for 48.73%; the population aged 0–14 accounted for 16.60%, the population aged 15–59 accounted for 70.14%, and the population aged at and above 60 accounted for 13.26%; the urban population accounted for 49.68%; the rural population accounted for 50.32%; of the population above 6 years old (1,242,546,122 people), those without any schooling accounted for 5%, those with primary school education accounted for 28.7%, those with junior middle school education accounted for 41.7%, those with senior middle school education accounted for 15%, those with junior college education accounted for 5.5%, those with a bachelor's degree accounted for 3.7%, and those with an academic degree above the master's accounted for 0.3%. On the whole, the samples are evenly distributed and representative of China's overall conditions.

In this survey, the average annual income of families covered by subsistence security is RMB 15,690.25, and the average subsistence social security they receive is RMB 5564.16, with an average subsistence security replacement rate of 24.36%; in 2010, the subsistence demand was RMB 10,926.48, while the subsistence compensation rate reached 45.10%. In terms of the income of residents covered by social insurance, the per capita benefits from the social insurance system account for 14.5% of the annual income. The average social benefits and income ratio of the non-rural population is 18.0%, and that of the rural population is 12.1%. Therefore, we can conclude that social security income has become an important source of income for Chinese residents, especially those with low income.

As the ratio of the population samples receiving social assistance and social welfare is very small and the role of social assistance and social welfare in regulating income gap is direct and obvious, this article mainly analyzes the effect of social security on income redistribution taking social insurance as an example. In terms of measurement methods, the Gini coefficient of residents' income before and after social insurance is for reflecting the impact of the income transferred from social insurance (see Tables 8.2 and 8.3). The transferred income of social insurance here mainly refers to pure social insurance income after the deduction of various social insurance contributions and expenditures, which has a relatively good measurement value. Constrained by space, the detailed revenues and expenditures of various types of social insurance will not be repeated here, as they can be found in another book we have edited.[21]

The Gini coefficient is an international index for measuring income gap, and the changes in the Gini coefficient in 2012 survey samples before and after the transfer of annual social insurance income into total annual income can reflect the regulation of income gap by the social insurance system. The social insurance annual income in this article is the sum of = all types of social income of each sampled interviewee in 2012, that is, the sum of annual income from urban employee's basic old-age insurance, urban employee's basic medical insurance, urban resident's social old-age insurance, urban resident's basic medical insurance, new rural cooperative medical insurance, new rural social old-age insurance, unemployment insurance, work-related injury insurance, and maternity insurance.[22]

---

[21]See Wang Yanzhong ed. (2013), *A Survey of Income Redistribution by Social Security in China*, Social Science Academic Press.

[22]To be consistent with the total annual income, social income expenditures are not deducted from social insurance revenues in this article. In the survey, social insurance contribution, as part of personal expenditures, is not deducted from personal annual income.

Table 8.2 The impact of the income transferred from social insurance on the Gini coefficient in 2012

	Income before the transfer of social insurance		Income after the transfer of social insurance		Extent of Gini coefficient reduction (%)
	Mean value	Gini coefficient	Mean value	Gini coefficient	
All samples	28,761.55	0.547	30,261.19	0.512	6.40
Non-rural household register	36,648.70	0.525	39,407.54	0.462	12
Rural household register	21,160.02	0.546	21,448.43	0.536	1.80
– Farmers	12,490.17	0.461	12,706.17	0.447	3.00
– Migrant workers	38,463.44	0.570	38,608.82	0.569	0.10

Table 8.3 The impact of the transfer of various types of social insurance on the Gini coefficient

Social insurance item	After the transfer of social insurance income		Reduction of the Gini coefficient (%)
	Mean value	Gini coefficient	
Old-age insurance	30,020.45	0.515	5.88
– Urban employee's old-age insurance	29,926.68	0.518	5.30
– Urban resident's old-age insurance	28,810.56	0.545	0.24
– Rural resident's social old-age insurance	28,806.31	0.545	0.32
Medical insurance	28,984.25	0.544	0.49
– Urban employee's medical insurance	28,914.51	0.546	0.20
– Urban resident's medical insurance	28,771.65	0.547	0.02
– New rural cooperative medical insurance	28,821.19	0.545	0.27
Maternity, work-related injury and unemployment insurance	28,779.58	0.547	0.04

On the whole, before the transfer of social insurance, the Gini coefficient of the annual income of all the samples is 0.547, which turns into 0.512 after the transfer of social insurance. Therefore, the transferred income from social insurance plays an obvious role in terms of income redistribution, seeing as the Gini coefficient is reduced by 6.4% after the transfer of social insurance.

Among residents holding urban household registers, the Gini coefficient is 0.525 before the transfer of social insurance income, and turns into 0.462 after the transfer of social insurance; the social insurance income reduces urban residents' Gini coefficient by 12%. Among residents holding rural household registers, the Gini coefficient is 0.546 before the transfer of social insurance income, and turns into 0.536 after the transfer of social insurance; the social insurance income reduces rural residents' Gini coefficient by 1.8%. Thus, although social insurance plays a positive role in regulating income redistribution among urban residents and rural residents, the effect of the urban social insurance system on regulating income distribution significantly outperforms the rural social insurance system. Meanwhile, among residents holding rural household registers, the effect of social insurance on narrowing income gap is mainly reflected in the gap between farmers engaged in agricultural production and migrant workers working in cities. The Gini coefficient in terms of individual income among farmers engaged in agricultural production stands at 0.447, while that of migrant workers is 0.569. Between urban residents and rural residents, social insurance has a "reverse regulation" effect in that before the transfer of social insurance, the income of residents holding non-rural household registers is 1.7 times than that of residents holding rural household register, while after the transfer of social insurance, the income of residents holding non-rural household registers is 1.8 times that of residents holding rural household registers, meaning that the gap is not narrowed, but further expanded.

In terms of the impact of various types of social insurance on income redistribution, old-age insurance exerts the greatest impact, followed by medical insurance, while maternity insurance, work-related insurance and unemployment insurance, due to their narrow coverage, only play a limited role in redistribution. After the transfer of old-age insurance income, the Gini coefficient is reduced by 5.88%; after the transfer of medical insurance income, the Gini coefficient is reduced by 0.49%; maternity insurance, work-related insurance and unemployment insurance, together, only reduce the Gini coefficient by 0.04%. The income redistribution effect of different old-age insurance and medical insurance also differs. Urban employee's old-age insurance reduces the Gini coefficient by 5.3%, urban resident's old-age insurance reduces the Gini coefficient by 0.24%, and rural social old-age insurance reduces the Gini coefficient by 0.32%. In comparison with urban employee's old-age insurance, urban resident's old-age insurance and rural social old-age insurance were established not long ago, with low benefits, so that their role in income redistribution is limited. Meanwhile, it is the benefit gap between urban old-age insurance and rural old-age insurance that leads to the adverse old-age insurance regulation of income distribution and the whole social insurance system between urban and rural residents. New rural cooperative medical insurance reduces the Gini coefficient by 0.27%, while urban employee's medical insurance and urban resident's medical insurance reduce the Gini coefficient by 0.2 and 0.02% respectively. Though the redistribution effect of medical insurance is limited, it plays a positive regulation role between urban and rural areas, and the establishment and implementation of the new cooperative medical insurance system, to a limited extent, has narrowed the income gap between urban and rural areas.

In sum, as to the coexistence of positive and negative social insurance regulations for internal income distribution in rural and urban areas and income distribution between rural and urban areas, there is an obvious stratification. On the whole, urban residents and rural residents belong to the same or to a similar class stratum within their place of residence, but the class difference between rural and urban residents is obvious. Despite the fact that people have the same opportunity to be covered by social insurance, more urban residents belong to advantageous classes, with discourse power for social security and a stronger sense of the need to safeguard their rights to social security, thereby acquiring more social security resources; while rural residents tend to passively receive security, and due to their limited capability and other reasons, they lack the opportunity to participate in the preparation of social security policies, thus can hardly safeguard their own rights and interests. This situation tends to expand the social security benefits gap between urban and rural residents.

8.4 Subjective Comments on the Re-Distribution Effect of China's Social Insurance Revenues

We process to the evaluation on the income redistribution effect of the social insurance system mainly on the basis of two aspects: the public's satisfaction with the social insurance system and its fairness.

(i) Satisfaction evaluation

The concept of public satisfaction originates from that of customer satisfaction in the field of marketing. Tang (2012) proposes that public satisfaction is the public's recognition of the gap between their expectations of the effect before consuming any public goods or services, and their actual experiences after consumption. Social insurance in China covers old-age insurance, medical insurance, work-related injury insurance, unemployment insurance and maternity insurance. Different systems vary substantially in terms of time of establishment, sources of funds, security targets, fiscal investment, contribution level, and benefit level; it is inevitable for the public to have varying satisfaction with various systems. By analyzing the survey data, we can see that the overall satisfaction with the social insurance system is not very high, as only 3.5 and 40.5% of the interviewees are very satisfied or satisfied with the system respectively. The low satisfaction fully illustrates the substantive gap between the public's expectations of the system's effect and their actual experiences. The satisfaction with work-related injury insurance, unemployment insurance and maternity insurance is even lower. The proportions of interviewees very satisfied and satisfied with work-related injury insurance are 1.2 and 29.6% respectively; the figures for unemployment insurance are 1.7 and 23.8% respectively, and those for maternity insurance are 1.8 and 28.2% respectively. The satisfaction gap among different types of insurance in the old-age insurance and medical insurance system is wide, with rural residents being more satisfied with

Table 8.4 Evaluation of satisfaction with the social insurance system

	Evaluation of satisfaction with the system				
	Very satisfied	Satisfied	So-so	Dissatisfied	Very dissatisfied
Overall evaluation of the system	3.5	40.5	34.7	18.7	2.5
Urban employee's old-age insurance	1.7	26.1	42.9	24.2	5.1
Urban resident's old-age insurance	2.7	25.2	47.1	23.0	2.1
Rural resident's old-age insurance	7.1	52.9	26.6	12.1	1.3
Urban employee's medical insurance	1.5	26.2	44.2	23.8	4.3
Urban resident's medical insurance	2.6	26.3	47.3	21.5	2.4
Rural residents' medical insurance	8.0	56.0	22.9	11.7	1.4
Work-related injury insurance	1.2	29.6	45.3	20.7	3.2
Unemployment insurance	1.7	23.8	49.9	20.2	4.4
Maternity insurance	1.8	28.2	48.9	17.8	3.3

old-age and medical insurance. 7.1 and 52.9% of the interviewees are very satisfied and satisfied with rural resident's old-age insurance respectively, while 8.0 and 56.0% of the interviewees are very satisfied and satisfied with rural residents' medical insurance. These figures, obviously higher than other types of insurance, show that farmers are more satisfied with the insurance systems (see Table 8.4).

(ii) Fairness evaluation

Fairness is one of the objectives pursued by social policies. Fairness may be classified into objective and subjective fairness (Zou 2012). In this article, fairness refers to the public's subjective evaluation of the fairness of the social insurance system. From the survey data, it can be concluded that the fairness evaluation of the social insurance system is not high on the whole, as only 4.6 and 35.9% of the interviewees think it very fair and fair respectively, which shows that there are big problems with the design of China's social insurance system in terms of fairness and operation effect. The serious fragmentation and segmentation of the system, as well as the lack of overall consideration and top-level design, lead to the failure of the system to bring into full play its role in regulating income distribution. Rural residents have given higher fairness evaluations of old-age insurance and medical insurance. With regards to the farmers' old-age insurance system, the ratios of interviewees who consider it very fair and fair are 8.7 and 45.2% respectively; in the case of the farmers' medical insurance, the ratios of interviewees who consider it very fair and fair are 9.1 and 49.3% respectively (see Table 8.5). These results

Table 8.5 Evaluation of fairness of the social insurance system

	Evaluation of fairness of the system				
	Very fair	Fair	So-so	Unfair	Very unfair
Overall evaluation of the system	4.6	35.9	36.9	19.4	3.2
Urban employee's old-age insurance	3.1	26.9	36.2	27.4	6.4
Urban resident's old-age insurance	2.9	27.4	42.4	22.2	5.1
Rural resident's old-age insurance	8.7	45.2	31.0	13.3	1.9
Urban employee's medical insurance	2.7	26.5	41.2	24.6	5.0
Urban resident's medical insurance	2.2	27.4	46.7	20.1	3.6
Rural residents' medical insurance	9.1	49.3	28.1	11.9	1.6
Work-related injury insurance	3.4	24.6	48.1	19.4	4.6
Unemployment insurance	2.5	22.9	48.9	19.8	5.8
Maternity insurance	3.4	28.3	48.3	15.3	4.7

show that though farmers do not receive high benefits from the social insurance system, and although there is a big gap between them and urban employees, yet they do not have a strong sense of unfairness about the current system.

The existence of this phenomenon does not negate the existence of unfairness in social insurance, but only shows the different class consciousness and right awareness as well as the different expectations about social security among different classes in urban and rural areas. In practice, this point cannot be taken to conceal the fairness of social insurance. However, we cannot look at problems statically. With the change of urban and rural class structures, change in class awareness and rise of demand, disadvantaged people will change their attitude towards the fairness of social insurance.

(iii) Factors affecting the evaluation of the effect of social insurance on income redistribution

(1) Variable setup

First, the dependent variable of this study is the public's evaluation of the effect of the social insurance system in alleviating income gap. In the questionnaire, there are five options: "very big", "big", "so-so", "low" and "very low". This article studies the factors affecting the public's evaluation of income gap, and therefore it is very necessary to appropriately handle dependent variables and combine them into binary variables. In analysis, "very big", "big" and "so-so" are combined into "good effect", with a value assignment of "1"; "low" and "very low" are combined into "poor effect", with a value assignment of "0". Second, the author has selected three levels (the personal level, focusing on individual interviewees, the social level, and the system level, each level containing three variables) according to the author'sanalysis of relevant literature and understanding of this problem (see Table 8.6 for the meaning, value assignment and descriptive statistic analytic results of each variable).

Table 8.6 Variable setup and their statistical descriptions

Variable		Meaning of variable	Value assignment of variable	Mean value	Standard deviation
Individual	X1	Gender	Male = 1; female = 2	1.53	0.50
	X2	Age	15 ~ 89	47.9	13.62
	X3	Political affiliation	CPC party member = 1; Others = 0	0.18	0.39
	X4	Religious belief	Having religious belief = 1; having no religious belief = 0	0.06	0.24
	X5	Education background	No schooling = 1; primary school = 2; junior middle school = 3; senior middle school or occupational secondary school = 4; technical secondary school = 5; junior college = 6; bachelor's degree = 7; postgraduate degree = 8	3.90	1.83
Social	X6	Household register	Agricultural household register = 1; non-agricultural household register = 2	1.47	0.50
	x7	Location factor	West China = 1; Central China = 2; East China = 3	2.11	0.67
System	X8	Level of contribution	Too high = 1; high = 2; appropriate = 3; low = 4; too low = 5	2.88	0.69
	X9	Level of benefits	Too high = 1; high = 2; appropriate = 3; low = 4; too low = 5	3.43	0.72

(2) Model selection

Suppose that the probability that the public i thinks that the social insurance system has a "good effect" on alleviating the income gap is p (y = 1|X) = pi, and 1—pi means the probability that the public thinks that the social insurance system has "no good effect" on alleviating the income gap. They are both nonlinear functions formed by the dependent variable vector X:

$$p_i = \frac{1}{1 + e^{-\left(\alpha + \sum_{i=1}^{m} \beta_i x_i\right)}} = \frac{e^{\alpha + \sum_{i=1}^{m} \beta_i x_i}}{1 + e^{\alpha + \sum_{i=1}^{m} \beta_i x_i}},$$
$$1 - p_i = 1 - \frac{e^{\alpha + \sum_{i=1}^{m} \beta_i x_i}}{1 + e^{\alpha + \sum_{i=1}^{m} \beta_i x_i}} = \frac{1}{1 + e^{\alpha + \sum_{i=1}^{m} \beta_i x_i}} \tag{8.1}$$

The ratio of the probability that the public thinks that the social insurance system has a "good effect" on alleviating the income gap against the probability that the public thinks that the social insurance system has "no good effect" on alleviating income gap, pi/1—pi, is called the odds of experiencing an event (shortened as Odds) which must be of a positive value (because 0 < pi < 1) without an upper bound. Logarithmic transformation is conducted for Odds to get the linear representation of the logistic regression model:

$$\mathrm{Ln}\left(\frac{\mathrm{p_i}}{1-\mathrm{p_i}}\right) = \alpha + \sum_{i=1}^{m} \beta_i x_i \tag{8.2}$$

In formulas (8.1) and (8.2), α is a constant term, m is the number of independent variables, and βi is the coefficient of independent variables, reflecting the direction and degree of the influence of independent variables on the public's attitude towards the social insurance system.

(3) Results of examination by the regression equation

To examine how the nine independent variables of the above three levels affect the public's attitude towards the effect of the social insurance system on alleviating income gap and the degree of influence, independent variables meeting the level of significance are added to the model one by one; through three selection steps, independent variables X9, X7 and X3 are entered into the model one by one to get two logistic regression models:

$$\text{Logit P} = 4.188 + 0.437\text{X3} - 0.531\text{X7} - 0.772\text{X9}$$

In which the p value of the regression coefficient significance examination of X1, X2, X4, X5, X6 and X8 is bigger than the significance level 0.05, and thus these independent variables are removed from the model. From the significance examination by a regression equation (Table 8.7), it can be found that the probability P value corresponding to the observed value of the likelihood ratio chi-square is less than the significance level 0.05. Therefore, the linear relationship between all the

Table 8.7 Significance check of the regression equation (gradual selection strategy)

		Chi-square	Degree of freedom	Significance
Step 1	Step	64.729	1	0.000
	Module	64.729	1	0.000
	Model	64.729	1	0.000
Step 2	Step	18.936	1	0.000
	Module	83.665	2	0.000
	Model	83.665	2	0.000
Step 3	Step	5.894	1	0.015
	Module	89.559	3	0.000
	Model	89.559	3	0.000

Table 8.8 Partial regression coefficient check

		B	S.E.	Wald	df	Sig.	Exp(B)
Step 1 (a)	X9	−0.774	0.100	59.922	1	0.000	0.461
	Constant	3.147	0.345	83.196	1	0.000	23.265
Step 2 (b)	X9	−0.777	0.101	59.603	1	0.000	0.460
	X7	−0.528	0.123	18.432	1	0.000	0.590
	Constant	4.270	0.444	92.441	1	0.000	71.521
Step 3 (c)	X9	−0.772	0.101	58.556	1	0.000	0.462
	X7	−0.531	0.123	18.667	1	0.000	0.588
	X3	0.437	0.183	5.680	1	0.017	1.548
	Constant	4.188	0.445	88.598	1	0.000	65.916

explaining variables and Logit P is significant, which shows that it is reasonable to adopt this model. In light of the partial regression coefficients (Table 8.8), the partial regression coefficients of the equality have all passed the significance check. Therefore, the linear relationship between independent variables X3, X7 and X9 and dependent variables is significant.

Through the above analysis, we can get the final form of the model:

$$P = \frac{1}{1 + \exp[4.188 + 0.437X_3 - 0.531X_7 - 0.772X_9]}$$

To sum up, the factors affecting the public's evaluation of the effect of the social insurance system on alleviating the income gap mainly include: the political affiliation on the public's personal level, the location factor on the social level and the benefit level on the system level. Other variables, such as gender, age, religious belief, educational background, type of household register, type of place of residence, and level of contribution, have no significant impact.

Influence of factors on the personal level. Political affiliation, at a statistic level of 5%, has a significant positive influence on the public's evaluation of the effect of the social insurance system on alleviating the income gap; that is to say, CPC party members think that the social insurance system has an obvious effect on alleviating income gap (EXP (β) = 1.548). The results of descriptive statistics also support this conclusion. Of CPC party members, 48.5% think that the system has a good effect on alleviating the income gap, while only 34.1% of those who are not CPC party members think that the system has a good effect on alleviating the income gap. The possible explanation is that CPC party members, through their regular party member study activities, have a better understanding of the party's guidelines and policies and of the state's social insurance system, and thus have a more positive subjective evaluation of the effect of system implementation. Therefore, in future system development and improvement, we should strengthen state policies propaganda so that the masses can have a full understanding of the original intention, course of implementation and possible predicaments of policy implementation.

Then the objective performance of policy development will be fully recognized by the people.

Influence of factors on the social level. The location factor has a significant negative impact on the public's evaluation of the effect of the social insurance system on alleviating the income gap; that is, those in Central China and West China have better evaluation of the effect of the social insurance system on alleviating the income gap than those in the developed regions in East China. The statistic results of the survey show that 41% of those surveyed in Central China and West China think that the social insurance system has a good effect on alleviating the income gap, while this ratio is 36.6% in East China. A possible explanation is that Central China and West China are less developed regions; the public's overall income is lower than that in East China, and therefore social insurance income accounts for a higher ratio in citizens' personal income, with a better effect on narrowing the income gap than in East China. The location difference in system evaluation fully illustrates the imbalance in the development of the social security system in China, which, closely related to the regional imbalance of economic development in China, obviously fails to conform to the value of "fairness, justice and sharing" in the development of the social security system in China. In the future, we should pay more attention to the fairness of basic security projects and gradually strike a basic balance between the regional allocations of government public investments.

Influence of factors on the system level. The statistical level with a 1% benefit level has a significant negative impact on the public's evaluation of the effect of the social insurance system on alleviating the income gap; with higher benefits from the social insurance system, the system has better effect on alleviating the income gap. The public's subjective evaluation also verifies the effect of the social insurance system on regulating income distribution, and the effect of regulation has positive correlation with the level of benefits. Therefore, to improve the benefits level of the system has obvious effect on alleviating the income gap. With the stable increase of government fiscal investments, the effect of the social insurance system on alleviating the income gap will become more and more obvious, and meanwhile, the principle of moderation of fiscal investments should also be reasonably grasped to avoid any fiscal problem resulting from "welfare rigidity" in the future.

8.5 Survey Conclusion and Policy Suggestions

Since the initiation of reform and opening-up, major progress has been achieved in the development of the social security system in China, and the system has promoted the reform of the economic system, maintained social stability and safeguarded people's basic livelihood, thus alleviating the expansion of the income gap and regulating income distribution to some extent. The interviewees do not have a high evaluation of the role of the social security system in narrowing residents' income gap, and their negative evaluation even exceeds their positive evaluation with regard to some social security items, which, from one perspective, illustrates that there is still a certain discrepancy between the social security system in China and the public's psychological expectations.

The effect of China's social security system on income distribution is not satisfactory for many reasons. First, policy propaganda and coverage is inadequate. The understanding of social security is an important factor affecting urban and rural residents' participation in social security (mainly social insurance). Some people do not quite understand the social insurance system, especially those with medium and low incomes and lower educational backgrounds, as well as rural residents. For various reasons, quite a number of people do not participate in social insurance. Some poor people have not been included into subsistence security, and a large amount of people have not enjoyed their due social welfare. Second, the development of social security is out of balance. Social assistance and social welfare for poor and under-privileged people are not adequately developed, while the limited fiscal investments are inclined towards social insurance, resulting in inadequate investments in social welfare and social assistance, which naturally affects the overall effect of social security on income redistribution. Over a long period of time, China's social security system mainly addressed urban residents, without mentioning the backward development of rural social security, which all in all are not ideal conditions for social security to effect its role in narrowing the income gap between urban and rural residents. Due to occupational advantages, public employees acquire higher social security benefits, while people of low income, no regular employment or flexible employment do not have satisfactory social security. Third, the design of the social security system is not good enough. Many current social security items are specifically "tailored" for some people, thus segmented and unable to be shared by all, thereinafter affecting the fairness of the social security system. In terms of fund raising, the unreasonable responsibility sharing mechanism is not conducive to the regulation of income distribution, and the inadequate government fiscal investment mechanism is also not good for income redistribution. In terms of benefits, the benefits of current social security are mainly based on the contribution-defined mode, and benefits are largely correlated with contributions, which is not ideal for improving the income of poor people.

Therefore, in the future course of deepening reform, promoting reasonable income distribution among residents, and improving the social security system in China, we must attach greater importance to and conscientiously resolve the problems above. First, we should strengthen propaganda and guidance related to social security policies, and actively expand the coverage of social security. In particular, we should allow the under-privileged people, the low-income people and the poor people to gain better access to social security and make social security the risk resolving mechanism and subsistence security mechanism for these people. The expansion of social security coverage has entered a key stage, and the targets for key support include rural residents, migrant workers, residents in former revolutionary bases, and people with flexible employment. Quite a number of such people do not have a very clear understanding of social insurance, and relevant government departments should strengthen propaganda and guidance to reduce their concerns about participating in insurance. Second, we should break down the barriers of household registries as well as promote urban-rural social pooling and the system integration of social security. We should take the urban-rural social pooling of residents' old-age insurance system as a breakthrough point, and promote the development of urban-rural social pooling for the medical insurance system, the subsistence security system and the social assistance system. In the future, we should improve the unity of basic social security; strengthen system integration, and narrow gaps among different groups of people. Third, we should strengthen the fairness of the basic social security system. People have low overall satisfaction with the social insurance system and low overall evaluation of the effect of the system for alleviating the income gap, which fully illustrates that the unfair benefits of China's social insurance system have been challenging people's critical tolerance. People attach more importance to the fairness and justice of the basic social security system, and the fairness of basic social security should be further strengthened in the future. Fourth, we should improve fiscal investments in social security as well as the transfer payment mechanism. While maintaining a balanced aggregate of social security fiscal funds, we should improve the fiscal investment mechanism, define the key directions and fields of fiscal investment, strengthen the development of social assistance and of the social welfare system, and strengthen rural social security and fiscal transfer payments for Central China and West China. Fifth, we should improve the design of the social insurance system. In terms of fund raising, we should give particular support to people of medium and low incomes and poor people, and appropriately lower the contribution rate of their basic social insurance. We should increase the ratio of social pooling and appropriately reduce the contribution ratio of personal accounts. We should explore a "progressive" contribution method. Those with higher incomes should have a higher contribution rate. We should establish an effective interactive mechanism for the fund-raising mechanism and the benefit compensation mechanism, and bring into better play their role in regulating income distribution. For example, with old-age insurance, we may establish a "regressive" benefit sharing mechanism related to benefit sharing and benefit balance, and explore the establishment of a balanced minimum benefit guarantee mechanism.

In terms of specific social security items, we should focus on promoting the development of old-age security, medical security and the social assistance system in the future, so as to further effect the role of social security in income redistribution in China. In terms of old-age security, we should follow the principle of "everybody participates, everybody contributes and everybody shares" in order to promote the development of an equitable and sustainable old-age security system; we should establish a reasonable responsibility sharing mechanism, realize national pooling of the basic old-age insurance system and establish a scientific benefit adjustment mechanism; we should continue to improve the modes of the old-age insurance system, and optimize the design of the old-age insurance system; we should strengthen and improve investments in old-age insurance funds, and improve the risk-resistance capability of social insurance funds; we should improve the multi-level old-age insurance system, and gradually establish a basic old-age service and care system for old people of advanced age. In terms of medical security, we should accelerate the integration of urban-rural residents' medical insurance policies and management; we should improve the personal account system, gradually incorporate the funds in personal accounts into outpatient pooling, and improve the scope and ratio of reimbursement for outpatient services of insured people; we should improve the negotiation mechanism for the terms of payment of health care costs, and strengthen the whole-process supervision and the internal constraints of medical services; we should comprehensively implement the urban-rural residents' serious disease insurance system, and develop a diversified medical security system. In terms of social assistance, we should better effect its poverty alleviation and income regulation functions, and coordinate the development of the social assistance system; we should coordinate the development of subsistence social assistance and development social assistance; we should coordinate fund assistance, material assistance and service assistance, and bring into play the role of the social assistance system for comprehensive support; we should realize the organic connection of social assistance with social insurance and poverty-relief and development policies, and bring into play the function of social assistance as general support.

Of course, we do not advocate the "equalization" of social security, and try to prevent hyper-correction. We should appropriately reflect the "appropriate" differences of benefits and contributions in fields that stress the personal responsibilities of workers and social members. Due to long-term interest accumulation and the complexity of influential factors, the role of social security in income redistribution cannot be fulfilled in one single step. We should absolutely not pursue the "overnight accomplishment" of such a task, but rather should closely refer to and adapt to the current economic and social backgrounds in China, actively and properly promote the reform of the social security system, properly handle the interest relationship of different groups, and stimulate economic and social vitality while promoting the equitable development of the social security system.[23]

[23]This article, written in collaboration with Long Yuqi, Jiang Cuiping and Xuqiang, is published in *Economic Research Journal*, 2016 (2).

Chapter 9
Establishing a More Equitable and Sustainable Social Security System

The "Suggestions on Preparing the Thirteenth Five-Year Plan for National Economic and Social Development" of the CPC Central Committee clearly points out that a more equitable and sustainable social security system should be established during the Period of the thirteenth Five-Year Plan. The Suggestions not only directly reflects the new outlook on development—that is: innovation, coordination, green, opening-up and sharing—but also will surely guide the healthy development of the social security system with clear targets in the new period.

9.1 Social Security Lays an Important Institutional Foundation for All People to Share the Results of Reform and Development

Social security, a social policy handling social risks and resolving social problems in order to protect and improve the basic living standard of social members, is an important equalizer of basic public services. The nature of social security is to maintain social equity and thus promote a stable social development. The social security system not only helps workers and social members guard against personal risks but also helps distribute and re-distribute national revenues, and is thus a very important guarantee that all people may share the results of development. Since reform and opening-up, especially during the period of the twelfth Five-Year Plan, rapid development has been achieved in terms of China's social security system, which has not only realized full coverage but also has been playing an increasingly important role in the coordinated development of economy and society.

Y. Wang, *Social Security in China: On the Possibility of Equitable Distribution*, Research Series on the Chinese Dream and China's Development Path,
DOI 10.1007/978-981-10-5643-7_9

(i) The social security system keeps improving and has basically realized full coverage

During the period of the twelfth Five-Year Plan, China gradually established and improved various social security systems on the basis of the original reform on social security. In terms of old-age insurance, in June 2011, the State Council issued the "Guiding Opinions on Conducting Pilot Projects in Urban Residents' Social Old-age Insurance" to explore the establishment of an urban residents' old-age insurance system; in February 2014, the State Council issued the "Opinions on Establishing a Uniform Urban-Rural Residents' Basic Old-age Insurance System", covering all eligible urban and rural residents; meanwhile, the Ministry of Human Resources and Social Security also improved the "Interim Measures for Linking-up the Urban-Rural Old-age Insurance System" to actively promote the connection, integration and integrative development of urban and rural residents' old-age insurance systems, clarify policies on enterprise annuities, occupational annuities and personal income tax, as well as accelerate the construction of supplementary old-age insurance systems. In terms of medical security, outpatient pooling for urban residents' basic medical insurance has been basically established. In August 2012, six ministries and commissions including the NDRC jointly issued the "Guiding Opinions on Developing 'Serious Disease Insurance' for Urban and Rural Residents" to explore the establishment of an insurance system for serious, special and major diseases. Important steps have also been taken in the establishment of unemployment, work-related injury and maternity insurance systems. Explorations are being made to use unemployment insurance funds to prevent unemployment and promote employment; active efforts are being made in terms of work-related injury rehabilitation and work-related injury prevention, as well as to expand pilot projects on work-related injury prevention. The coverage and expenditure scope of maternity insurance have been constantly expanding, and residents' maternity medical expenses are being gradually included into the urban residents' medical insurance and the new rural cooperative medical system's scope of reimbursement. In terms of subsistence security, in March and May 2011, ministries and commissions such as the NDRC, the MOCA and the MOF issued the "Circular on Establishing a Linkage Mechanism Connecting Social Assistance and Security Standard with Price Rise" and the "Guiding Opinions on Further Regulating the Preparation and Adjustment of Subsistence Security for Urban and Rural Residents", which marked the official establishment of a dynamic adjustment mechanism for urban and rural subsistence security standards; in September 2012, the State Council issued the "Opinions on Further Strengthening and Improving Subsistence Security", which further standardize the urban and rural subsistence security. In terms of old-age services, in 2011, the General Office of the State Council issued the "Plan for the Construction of a Social Old-age Service System (2011–2015)"; in 2013, the State Council issued "Several Opinions on Accelerating the Development of the Old-age Service Industry" to promote the rapid development of the old-age service industry. In terms of charity services, in 2011, the MOCA issued the "Guidelines on the Development of the Charity Services in

China (2011–2015)"; in 2014, the State Council issued the "Guiding Opinions on Promoting the Healthy Development of Charity Services", which put forward objectives and policy measures for promoting the healthy development of charity services. In terms of supplementary security, in 2014, the State Council issued "Several Opinions on Accelerating the Development of the Modern Insurance Service Industry", which clearly mention that "commercial insurance should be developed into an important pillar for the social security system", which especially mentioned that the supplementary role of commercial insurance for basic old-age and medical insurance should be brought into full play. In 2014, the Office of the Ministry of Human Resources and Social Security issued the "Opinions on the Further Filing of Enterprise Annuity Schemes", to actively promote the development of the enterprise annuity system. Active development has also been achieved in terms of the construction of other types of social security systems. The revised "Regulations on Work-related Insurance" took effect on January 1, 2011. The revised "Regulations on Pension and Preferential Treatment on Servicemen" officially took effect on August 1, 2011. By 2015, all provincial governments nationwide had issued new opinions on the implementation of urban and rural residents' insurance, whereas urban and rural residents' basic old-age insurance systems had been basically unified. Meanwhile, the central government decided to reform the old-age insurance system for government departments and public institutions, which should be implemented simultaneously nationwide in line with the principle of "one unity (the basic old-age insurance system integrating social pooling and personal accounts is implemented for urban employees in government departments, public institutions and enterprises etc.), and five simultaneous measures". This reform, which has integrated the old-age insurance system for government departments, public institutions and enterprises, is conducive to alleviating the "benefit gap", promoting social equity and harmony, promoting the reform of government departments and public institutions as well as the development of a mechanism of reasonable personnel mobility, and has been widely recognized by all social circles.

(ii) The gradual increase of social insurance coverage and the constant expansion of social insurance funds

The later period of the Twelfth Five-Year Plan saw rapid expansion of social security coverage in China. With the establishment and improvement of various social systems, a social security system covering urban and rural residents has been basically developed, and full coverage had been realized. With the establishment and improvement of the urban employees' basic medical insurance system, the new rural cooperative medical system, and the urban residents' medical insurance system, the medical insurance system has taken the lead to cover all people in China by developing the largest medical security network in the world. In light of the number of people covered by the five items of social insurance, the number of people covered by basic old-age insurance increased from 235 million in 2009 to 820 million in 2013; the number of people covered by urban basic medical insurance increased from 401 million in 2009 to 571 million in 2013; the number of people

Table 9.1 Status of social assistance. *Unit* million people

Index	2009	2010	2011	2012	2013	2014	August 2015
Urban residents covered by subsistence security	23.456	23.105	22.768	21.435	20.642	18.770	17.685
Rural residents covered by subsistence security	47.600	52.140	53.057	53.445	53.880	52.072	50.056
Rural residents supported by "Five Guarantees"	5.534	5.563	5.51	5.456	5.372	5.291	5.209

Source of data Statistical Bulletin on the Development of Social Services in 2014, and statistical data on the website of the MOCA

covered by unemployment insurance increased from 127 million in 2009 to 164 million in 2013; the number of people covered by work-related injury insurance increased from 149 million in 2009 to 199 million in 2013; and the number of people covered by maternity insurance increased from 109 million in 2009 to 164 million in 2013. By the end of 2013, 2489 counties (cities and districts) nationwide had developed new rural cooperative medical care, covering 802 million people at a coverage rate of 98.7%.[1] In terms of social assistance, the number of urban residents covered by subsistence security has been maintained around 20 million, the number of rural residents covered by subsistence security around 53 million, and the number of old people supported by the "Five Guarantees" around 5 million (see Table 9.1). By June 2014, the number of people covered by basic old-age insurance nationwide had reached 824 million, and the coverage of the three basic medical insurance systems, namely employees' medical insurance, urban residents' medical insurance and new rural cooperative medical care, exceeded 95%, accomplishing the Twelfth Five-Year Plan's objective in advance. By September 2015, the number of people covered by basic old-age insurance, basic medical insurance, unemployment insurance, work-related injury insurance and maternity insurance nationwide was respectively 852 million, 658 million, 171 million, 211 million, and 178 million, having increased by 9.39 million, 60.17 million, 0.86 million, 4.27 million and 7.42 million respectively from the end of 2014. In light of the number of people covered, China has established the largest social insurance and social security network in the world.

With the development of the social security system, especially with the constant improvement and expanding coverage of the contribution-based social insurance

[1]Source of data: *Statistical Bulletin on the Development of Health and Family Planning Services in 2013*, and the website of the Commission of Health and Family Planning.

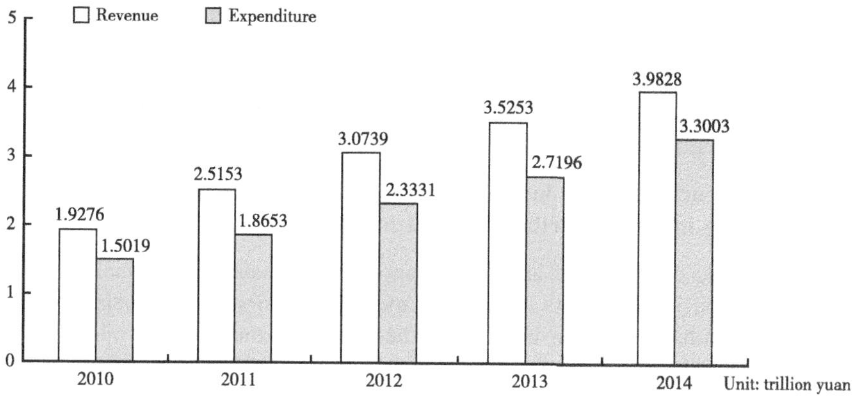

Fig. 9.1 Social insurance fund revenues and expenditures of in the recent five years. *Unit* trillion yuan

system, the scale of revenues and expenditures of social insurance funds has also been expanding. The fund revenues of the five types of social insurance (excluding new rural social old-age insurance) rose from RMB 1.6116 trillion in 2009 to RMB 3.5253 trillion in 2013; and fund expenditures rose from RMB 1.2303 trillion in 2009 to RMB 2.7916 trillion in 2013. Specifically, the fund revenues of basic old-age insurance in 2013 were RMB 2.4733 trillion, having increased by 13.3% from the previous year; fund expenditures of basic old-age insurance in 2013 were RMB 1.9819 trillion, having increased by 18.6% from 2012. The total revenues of urban basic medical insurance funds in 2013 were RMB 824.8 billion, and total expenditures were RMB 680.1 billion, having increased by 18.9 and 22.7% respectively from 2012. In 2013, the fund revenues of unemployment insurance were RMB 128.9 billion, having increased by 13.2% from 2012; the expenditures were RMB 53.2 billion, having increased by 18.0% from 2012. In 2013, the fund revenues of work-related injury insurance funds were RMB 61.5 billion, and fund expenditures were RMB 48.2 billion, having increased by 16.7 and 18.7% respectively from 2012. In 2013, the fund revenues of maternity insurance were RMB 36.8 billion, and fund expenditures were RMB 28.3 billion, having increased by 21.1 and 28.9% respectively from 2012.[2] By 2014, the annual surplus of urban employees' basic old-age insurance, basic medical insurance, work-related injury insurance and maternity insurance was RMB 587.5 billion, and the accumulated surplus was RMB 4.3765 trillion. By the end of 2014, the total fund revenues of the five types of social insurance (including urban and rural residents' basic old-age insurance) amounted to RMB 3.9828 trillion, having increased by RMB 457.5 billion from 2013 at an increase rate of 13.0%. Fund expenditures amounted to RMB 3.3003 trillion, having increased by RMB 508.6 billion from 2013 at an

[2]Source of data: *Statistical Bulletin on the Development of Human Resources and Social Security Services in 2013.*

increase rate of 18.2% (see the following Fig. 9.1). By the end of September 2015, the fund revenues of five types of social insurance were RMB 3.31866 trillion and the expenditures RMB 2.81905 trillion, with a 10–20% surplus after break-even; in addition to the accumulated surplus of RMB 5.7366 trillion, the operation of the social insurance funds was safe on the whole, capable of resisting risks.[3]

(iii) Social security benefits keep increasing and the function of social security for regulating income is further brought into play

With economic development and the enhancement of national financial strength, China has been increasing its fiscal investment in social security. Social security benefits have obviously been improved. The state has consecutively raised enterprise retirees' old-age pension 11 times; on January 1st 2015 the basic old-age pension of enterprise retirees was raised by 10%. By the end of 2014, 230 million people received old-age pensions, including 85.93 million retirees and 143 million urban and rural senior citizens. After 11 years of consecutive adjustments, the basic old-age pension of enterprise retirees has increased twofold from a monthly pay of RMB 647 in 2004 to over RMB 2000 now. The consecutive large-scale adjustments of basic old-age pension have been playing an active role in improving enterprise retirees' life and promoting social equity. The standard minimum basic old-age insurance benefits for all urban and rural residents nationwide has risen to RMB 70 each month for each person; that is a 15-yuan increase from the original base of RMB 55 per person each month, increased benefits being counted from July 1st 2014.[4] In terms of medical insurance, in 2014, urban employees received 1.52 billion person-times of medical insurance benefits, urban residents received 420 million person-times of medical insurance benefits, and the reimbursement ratio of inpatient medical expenses covered by the policies of employees' basic medical insurance and urban residents' basic medical insurance reached over 80% and about 70% respectively; the maximum amount of payment from funds was raised to 6 times that of the annual average salary of local employees and that of the per capita annual disposable income of local residents respectively, which, to some extent, alleviated the problem of expensive medical treatment. In terms of unemployment, work-related injury and maternity insurance, the number of people entitled to benefits and the level of benefits were substantially improved. The level of subsistence security has been stably rising. The average standard for subsistence security of urban residents rose from RMB 251.2/person/month in 2010 to RMB 373/person/month in 2013; the monthly per capita subsidy for urban residents covered by subsistence security nationwide rose from RMB 189 in 2010 to RMB 293 in August 2015. The average standard for rural subsistence security rose from RMB 117.0/person/month in 2010 to RMB 202.8/person/month in 2013; the per

[3]Website of the Ministry of Human Resources and Social Security, *The Development of Human Resources and Social Security Work in Q3 of 2015 and Arrangements of Work for the Next Step*, October 27, 2015.

[4]Source of data: "Another 100% Rise in Enterprise Retirees' Basic Old-age Pension after 11 Consecutive Rises", http://finance.people.com.cn/GB/n/2015/0116/c1004-26396343.html.

capita subsidy for rural residents with subsistence security rose from RMB 74/person/month in 2010 to RMB 135/person/month in August 2015. In terms of poverty relief in rural areas, in 2011, the state determined that the new rural poverty relief standard should be RMB 2300, equivalent to farmers' per capita net income, as well as on par with the international standard absolute poverty line, so that more and more poor people are included into the scope of poverty relief to share the results of reform and development in China.

With the constant improvement of the social security system and the rise of the ratio of the revenues and expenditures of social security funds in the national economy, the social security system including subsistence security, old-age security, medical security, unemployment security and education security has been playing an active role in income distribution in China. In 2012, social security revenues accounted for 14.5% of urban and rural residents' income, and over half (the biggest portion) of senior urban residents' income came from social old-age pension. The transferred income from social security reduced the Gini coefficient of urban and rural residents' income by 4.53%, including a 22.76% drop of the Gini coefficient between urban residents, and a 1.82% drop between rural residents'. The old-age pension property has a significant property redistribution effect in the families of urban enterprise employees, as it reduces the Gini coefficient of family property distribution by 8% points, and also reduces the inequality of family property distribution by 20%. The compensation of new rural cooperative medical care is more inclined towards the sick, and people with lower income receive higher compensations than those with higher income. The subsistence security policy can improve the living conditions of some low-income people and help relieve urban poverty. In Gansu and Yunnan, the effect of subsistence security policies is more obvious in that the Gini coefficient in these regions was reduced by 1.23 and 1% after the adoption of subsistence security, and the average income ratio of the 10% people with the highest income as well as that of the 10% people with the lowest income was reduced by 3.2% after the adoption of subsistence security. The subsistence security system indeed restrains the income gap within urban areas and within rural areas.

(iv) The lawful governance of social security has been obviously improved as more attention is paid to the development of legislation and management capability

The Fourth Plenary Session of the 18th CPC Central Committee gave more attention to the strategy of "rule-of-law" as well as to the development of the executive power of systems, which provides an important basis for the law-based development of social security. The development of a legal system is an important guarantee for the scientific and sustainable development of social security. During the period of the twelfth Five-Year Plan, China attached great importance to the construction of a legal system for social security and positive progress has been achieved. The most outstanding achievement was the NPC Standing Committee's adoption of the Social Insurance Law of the People's Republic of China in October 2010, which took effect on July 2011. This is an important mark for the legal system of the social security system in China, laying a legal basis for the development of social insurance services in China. The "Social Insurance Law" provides norms for basic old-age insurance, basic medical insurance, work-related injury insurance, unemployment insurance, maternity insurance, collection and contribution of social insurance premiums, social insurance funds, and social insurance handling. The "Military Service Insurance Law" adopted at the 26th meeting of the 11th NPC Standing Committee on April 27th 2012 provides for military injury and death insurance, decommissioning old-age insurance, decommissioning medical insurance and the establishment, payment and transfer of insurance for servicemen's spouses in the army who are not employed. In February 2014, the "Interim Measures on Social Assistance" promulgated by the State Council defined the management system, fund guarantee and content system of social assistance, promoted the integration and improvement of social assistance systems, and rendered the social assistance systems scientific and normal. Moreover, positive progress has been made in the "Regulations on Urban Housing Security" and the "Measures on Maternity Insurance". In 2014, the State Council promulgated the "Regulations on the Personnel Management of Public Institutions", and the Ministry of Human Resources and Social Security along with the Commission of Health and Family Planning promulgated a number of laws and regulations, such as the "Administrative Measures on the Appraisal of Work Capacity of Employees Injured in Work", which provide a better defined legal basis and operational norms for the regulation of personnel management in public institutions, guaranteeing the legal rights and interests of personnel working in public institutions, and strengthening social security in fields such as work capacity appraisal management. By holding various types of law popularization and business backbone training activities, the degree of lawful governance in the field of social security has been constantly improving.

To sum up, in terms of the developments of social security in China during the period of the twelfth Five-Year Plan, we have observed the following outstanding characteristics. First, more stress is laid on the top-level design and coordinated promotion of social security, with efforts focused on strengthening theoretical study and policy design of social security development strategies, overcoming the deficiencies resulting from earlier emergency coping reforms, and the constant optimizing of various social security systems. Second, the objectives of the development of social security are more defined, striving for the equitable and sustainable development of social security, conducting policy improvement for social security problems issues related to equity and sustainability, striving to enhance the equity and sustainability of social security, while stressing the role of social security in the promotion of income redistribution and maintenance of social equality and justice. Third, we've been actively promoting the urban-rural coordinated development of social security, the integration of social security systems, realize the integration of urban and rural residents' old-age insurance, and strive to realize the coordinated development of urban and rural residents' medical insurance and subsistence security. Fourth, we've been actively promoting the development of the lawful governance of social security; with the promulgation and implementation of social security laws such as the "Social Insurance Law" and the "Military Service Insurance Law", important steps have been taken in the legal system for social security in China, which will surely promote the scientific development of social security in China. Fifth, more importance is being attached to the coordinated development of social security systems; while stressing economic security, more and more importance is given to service security; while stressing basic security, more and more importance is given to the development of supplementary security; while the social insurance system has been improved, more and more importance is given to the development of social welfare and the social assistance system. Sixth, more and more importance is gradually being given to the effective combination of government and market. The government is always the dominant player in terms of social security, as well as an important bearer of responsibilities; while stressing the government's role, the reform of social security attaches more and more importance to market and social forces, in attempts to jointly improve social security equity and efficiency.

9.2 The Social Security System Is Still Confronted with Tremendous Equity and Sustainability Challenges

The Third Plenary Session of the 18th CPC Central Committee decided to establish a more equitable and sustainable social security system. The "Proposal on Preparing the thirteenth Five-Year Plan for National Economic and Social Development" of the Fifth Plenary Session of the 18th CPC Central Committee reiterated this objective, which means that in the development of the social security system in the period of the thirteenth Five-Year Plan, we should not only attach importance to extensive developments, such as the expansion of coverage and the expansion of fund scale, but also give priority to the equity and sustainability issues of the social security system.

The social security system is intended to be a social system promoting social equality, preventing social risks and maintaining social stability. However, the realization of the above objectives depends on the constant improvement of this system. For example, as one function of social security is to regulate income distribution, social security may not only promote income redistribution and narrow the income gap, but may as well induce negative regulation and widen the income gap. The negative or positive role of social security in income redistribution depends on the relevant factors of influence such as system mode, coverage, system design, system transition and management services. We should give full play the positive regulation role of social security for income redistribution and prevent negative regulation. Meanwhile, the development of the social security system is conducted against the macro background of drastic economic and social transformation in China. The change of the social stratification structure and the reform of the social security system are conducted almost simultaneously in China, with the two related to and influencing each other. Different social classes' economic and social status as well as group awareness varies greatly, and the standards for judging social equity are even more varied. It is very difficult to reach a consensus in terms of the reform and development of the social security system, which makes it more difficult to reform the social security system. During the reform and construction of the social security system in the new period, we face the following formidable challenges in terms of the further establishing a more equitable social security system: ensure that each class and each group (such as farmers and migrant workers) can equitably and conveniently acquire reasonable social security resources; ensure that more and more people enjoy increasing benefits; narrow the gap of social security benefits among different groups; and improve the sense of acquisition of an increasing number of people, if not that of all residents.

Another major challenge related to the above challenges is improving China's security system, especially in terms of the sustainability issue of social insurance systems such as basic old-age insurance. On the one hand, with the tendency of the Chinese population to age at a very rapid speed, to resolve the basic security problems of a huge number of old-age people who fail to become rich before they become old is the huge responsibility of each family, as well as that of the whole society and various levels of governments. In 2015, the population over 60 exceeded 200 million in China (accounting for 15% of the total population in China), and 230 million people were receiving old-age pensions (accounting for 17% of the total population). Old people above 60 will double in the future two decades, and at their peak they will account for about 1/3 of the total population. Currently, only employee's basic old-age pensions can secure basic life needs after retirement, while the role of basic old-age pensions for urban and rural residents is very limited. If basic old-age pensions of urban and rural senior residents were raised to 50% of the current retired employees' basic old-age pensions, old-age pension expenditures alone would double, far exceeding the payment capacity of current old-age security and even of the whole social security system. Keeping the growth of old-age pensions basically abreast with the growth of the national economy and urban and rural residents' income while providing basic security for the basic life and service of old people at their population peak has presented very urgent and formidable pressure and challenges to the construction of the social security system in China. To further stress the sustainability of the social security system at this moment is of very great strategic significance in terms of guiding the construction of the social security system in the future five years or more. On the other hand, effectively strengthening the management capability of the social security system, improving the efficient and reasonable use of social security funds, improving the value preservation and increase of accumulated funds, and strengthening social security funds risk control and monitoring are all important tasks for the construction of the current social security system. Since the start of the 21st century, there has been some small surplus after the balance of revenues and expenditures in the funds for the five types of social insurance (including urban and rural residents' basic old-age insurance) nationwide, which amounted to RMB 5.23

trillion as of 2014. If the national social security funds and each year's fiscal social security allocations are taken into account, the social security funds are of a tremendous scale and have increasing management chains and links. Managing such funds, especially accumulated surplus funds, is an enormous challenge for China's social security management team. As social security funds are the "survival money" of the people, we must ensure their security and must not allow even the smallest error, let alone any unwarranted diversion. A stricter fund management system and information disclosure system should be established to further effectively strengthen the preventive mechanism against the evasion of social security funds. However, strict regulation does not mean that the accumulated surplus funds should be allowed to "fall asleep". To address the depreciation risks imposed by inflation and falling interest rates, we must deepen the reform of the fund investment system and mechanism, and conduct diversified investments with a more flexible mechanism (provided that the security of funds is ensured) so as to realize the preservation and increase of accumulated funds value. In 2005, the central government introduced Regulations on Investment Operations for the Basic Old-age Insurance Fund. The new reform measures are good for expanding fund sources and enhancing the supporting capacity of old-age security funds, thus rendering social security funds less vulnerable to risks, which is of great significance in terms of the sustainable development of the old-age insurance system and the stability of the social security system. The crux is how to implement the above conceptions and reform measures and achieve good results. This is not only a challenge in terms of professional fund management for the social security department, but even more so in regards to the construction of relevant departments as well as that of the whole national security system.

9.3 Vigorously Constructing an Equitable and Sustainable Old-Age Security System

Old-age security, as the center of the social security system, is the basic security that must be established for an aging society as well as the foundation for the basic public service system. During the period of the thirteenth Five-Year Plan, the reform and development of the old-age insurance system in China remains a formidable task. We should continue to deepen reform by actively adapting to the rapidly aging population and the new economic and social development norms. In line with the principle of "everybody participates, everybody contributes and everybody shares", we should render the basically established basic old-age insurance system more fixed and mature, and at the same time, in light of the further rise of demands for old-age services, we should integrate various forces, such as government, society, market and family, in order to take new steps in terms of old-age life services security. As per the suggestions in the third Five-Year Plan, we should focus on work in the following aspects:

(i) Deepen the reform of the basic old-age insurance system and improve the employees' old-age insurance personal account system

The combination of social pooling and personal accounts constitute the institutional mode of basic old-age insurance in China, which is a product of international experiences and Chinese national conditions. To introduce personal accounts is an important measure in the reform of China's old-age insurance system. In practice, this mode is constantly being reformed and improved. Personal accounts are an important part of China's basic old-age insurance system, playing an important role in balancing equity and efficiency, securing the interests of those covered by old-age insurance, and enhancing the incentives of the old-age insurance system. Currently, personal accounts still present several practical problems to solve, such as orientation, the "empty accounts", management, scale, as well as pension granting method, which affect the interests of insurants. In the future, we should rationally understand the significance and orientation of personal accounts, and continue to reform and improve the personal account system. Provided that the equity of the system is not influenced, we may appropriately adjust the scale of personal accounts, and improve the pension granting method of personal accounts by adjusting the number of months according to per capita life expectancy. We should enhance the flexibility of personal account accumulation, improve the mechanism allowing for more benefits based on contributions, mobilize individual contributions, and enhance the incentive, efficiency and sustainability of the old-age insurance system. The establishment of the personal account system is good for defining individuals' contribution obligations; in the future, we should establish and improve the contribution-related benefit granting mechanism in line with the principle of combining rights and obligations. We should strengthen the management and investment of personal accounts, improve the of personal account management and investment system, promote the value preservation and increase of personal accounts of old-age insurance, and effectively maintain the rights and interest of insurants to their personal accounts.

(ii) Realize national pooling and establish a reasonable adjustment mechanism for employees' basic old-age pensions

China's basic old-age insurance benefits include two parts, basic pension and personal account pension, of which the pay-as-you-go system relates to basic pension. Social pooling for basic old-age insurance in China is of low level, and has been mostly practiced at the prefecture and municipal pooling for a long period; currently, provincial pooling has been basically realized. Nevertheless, social pooling levels for old-age insurance in China are still very low, while the management of the old-age insurance system is subject to local segmentation; this situation is not conducive to the integration of old-age insurance resources nor the improvement of the management services of old-age insurance, nor that of personnel trans-regional migration, nor that of the management and investment of old-age insurance funds, nor to that of the equity and efficiency of the old-age insurance system. Therefore, it is imperative that we further improve the social pooling level of the basic old-age insurance system; in particular, we should realize national pooling for basic old-age pensions sooner rather than later. To realize national pooling for employees' basic old-age pensions, we should have all-round considerations and arrangements for the nation as a whole, strengthen the mutual assistance of the basic old-age insurance system, and consider the financing, payment, management and supervision activities related to basic old-age pensions. National pooling for employees' basic old-age pensions requires the establishment of an old-age insurance financing mechanism commensurate with said pensions as well as the establishment and improvement of basic old-age insurance budgeting. We should regulate old-age insurance revenues and expenditures, and centralize the base, contribution rate and collection for basic old-age insurance. We should unify the expenditures of basic old-age pensions and balance old-age burden differences across different regions. We should establish a reasonable responsibility sharing mechanism and define the relationship between the central government and local governments as well as the relationship between local governments. In the future, we should continue to promote the realization of the national pooling of the whole basic old-age insurance system on the basis of national pooling for employees' basic old-age pensions.

Reasonable benefits are inevitably required for insurants to be able to share the results of development as well as for the sustainable development of the system. We should establish a basic old-age insurance benefit regulation mechanism in line with the principles of equity, sharing and sustainability. In recent years, China has raised old-age pension benefits for several years in a row so as to secure the basic life of retirees and enable them to enjoy the results of reform and development. However, there are still has many issues with the adjustment of old-age pension benefits in China, as the basis for adjustment is not clearly defined, the adjustment actions are not standardized in that mainly temporary policy documents are relied upon to promote benefit adjustment, and no scientific old-age pension benefit adjustment mechanism has been developed, which is not conducive to maintaining retirees' old-age rights and interests. In the future, we should establish and improve a basic old-age pension benefit adjustment mechanism on the basis of regulating and improving the old-age pension benefit granting method. In light of international experiences, we have observed that there are mainly three practices in the adjustment of overseas old-age pension benefits: adjustment according to the salary increase of in-service personnel, adjustment according to price level, and adjustment in light of salary increase and price level. The adjustment of basic old-age pension benefits in China should not be based on salary increase or price increase alone, but should take into account equity and efficiency by comprehensively considering factors such as financial sustainability, life expectancy, regional economic development, salary level, and price level, in order to establish a scientific benefit adjustment index and realize index-based, normalized and scientific benefit adjustments.

(iii) Strengthen and improve investment of old-age insurance funds and reduce the vulnerability of social insurance funds

To strengthen the scientific management and investment of old-age insurance funds and to realize the value preservation and increase of old-age insurance funds are the important tasks of the reform and development of the old-age insurance system in the future. We should establish a scientific and highly effective old-age insurance fund investment system and make investment in old-age insurance funds more professional, independent, diversified, social and law-based. We should further improve the management system of old-age insurance and realize the independent financing, management and investment for old-age insurance funds. We should develop a number of professional fund investment institutions, as well as realize moderate and orderly competition, reduce investment cost and improve return on investment. We should strictly regulate the old-age insurance funds access threshold for investment institutions. We should attempt to establish a minimum income guarantee mechanism for old-age insurance investment funds. The diversification of old-age insurance fund investment requires further expansion of investment channels, the improvement of investment portfolio strategies, the active and steady promotion of the entry of old-age insurance funds into the capital market, and the strengthening of old-age insurance funds' investments in major domestic public projects. We should strengthen investment in old-age insurance funds, improve returns on investment, and require the improvement of supervision over investment in old-age insurance funds and the establishment of a risk control mechanism. We should establish an information disclosure mechanism for the investment of old-age insurance funds, realize supervision over various stakeholders' whole participation course in old-age insurance fund investment, prevent old-age insurance funds investment risks and timely settle problems in the course of fund investment.

With the constant acceleration of population aging, China will face tremendous pressure in terms of old-age care; when the aging population peaks, in particular, the old-age insurance system will have to face the pressure of revenues falling short of expenditures. Also, in the course of the transition of the old-age insurance system, system transition debts are forming due to improper treatment of the rights and interest of some "in-service persons", and this issue should be resolved by raising funds through effective channels to cope with the payment demands when said "in-service persons" retire. Therefore, improving the old-age insurance funding mechanism and expanding the funding channels for old-age insurance are inevitable requirements for the reform of the old-age insurance system against the backdrops of the aging population. To transfer state-owned capital to substantiate old-age insurance funds and social insurance funds is an important measure for strengthening old-age insurance funding and deal with old-age insurance debts. Due to the public nature of state-owned capital, income should belong to the state and benefit all the people as it is property shared by all. In the future, the reform of the old-age insurance system, the reform of state-owned enterprises and the reform of the financial and taxation system should be taken into consideration as a whole, in order to gradually improve the ratio of state-owned capital gains to be submitted to public finance, and thus substantiate old-age insurance funds in the form of fiscal expenditures, or support old-age insurance funds by selling state-owned shares. Since reform and opening-up, China's state-owned enterprises have been constantly developing and expanding, and a tremendous amount of state-owned capital has been developed, which creates conditions for substantiating old-age insurance funds and social insurance. In the future, we should prepare specific measures for state-owned capital to substantiate old-age insurance funds and define the procedure, amount and proportion of state-owned capital transfer, as well as specific management issues and relevant supporting work after such transfer.

(iv) Progressively postpone the retirement age and improve the basic old-age pension pickup incentive and constraint mechanism

The definition of the retirement age is an important consideration of China's retirement system, which is also an important parameter for China's old-age insurance system. With the rapidly accelerating aging of the population and the obvious prolongation of life expectancy in China, the problem of retirement age has become an important concern in the various social circles in recent years. Currently, the retirement age in China basically copies the practices of the early days of the People's Republic of China, and thus is seriously out of balance in consideration with current life expectancy. The connection between the definition of retirement age and the old-age care system is not flexible, and the retirement age has become an important condition for receiving old-age pensions, which exerts pressure on the payment of old-age insurance funds against the backdrops of an aging population. To postpone the retirement age is inevitable in terms of the future economic and social development in China, so as to help cope with the disappearance of the "population bonus", make full use of human resources, and improve the old-age insurance system. To postpone the retirement age is an important task related to the interests of various stakeholders, so it should be actively and steadily promoted with the correct strategies and measures while considering all parties' interests and the overall situation of economic and social development. We should postpone the retirement age gradually, instead of suddenly. There are different approaches and methods for postponing the retirement age, and one feasible method is to "advance gradually with women preceding men". In the near future, the retirement age of both men and women should be set at 60 years old. On this basis, the retirement age of men and women will be postponed jointly and gradually. The method of "being slow at first and accelerating later" or "postponing at an even pace" may be adopted to postpone the retirement age in 20–30 years. We should fully consider the interests of different groups against the overall interest framework of national economy and society, taking into accounts the employment wishes and development demands of some people as well as the retirement wishes, health rights and interests, and social security rights and interests of some other people.

As the reform of the retirement age and old-age pension covers a wide range, relevant schemes should be publicized as early as possible in order to enhance the rights of relevant personnel to know and participate. The determination of the scheme will require quite a long period if we are to realize a steady transition. With the postponement of the statutory retirement age, detailed schemes may be prepared according to different industries, different types of work and different labors, so as to establish a flexible retirement system to some extent, and integrate the compulsory retirement system and the voluntary retirement system. While defining minimum retirement age, standard retirement age and latest retirement age, some people should be allowed to choose early retirement, but may receive old-age pensions only after they reach the standard retirement age. People with qualifications and such an intention should be encouraged to voluntarily postpone their retirement age. Besides, a dynamic adjustment mechanism connecting retirement age and life expectancy may be established through explorations. An old-age pension claim system connecting pension benefits with length of service and payment years should be established to strengthen incentives and constraints of pensions over the retirement system.

(v) Improve the multi-level old-age insurance system, and gradually establish a system of basic services and care for people of advanced age

The old-age security system is significantly diversified, including not only the basic old-age insurance system but also the supplementary old-age insurance system and the personal savings old-age insurance system, in addition to family old-age security, social charity and community services, etc. This kind of diversification may reduce the government's fiscal pressure in the old-age security system, and also help improve different people's diversified old-age insurance demands as well as their old-age security benefits, while ensuring the equity and efficiency of the old-age insurance system. The establishment and improvement of a diversified old-age insurance system is an important objective for the reform and development of China's old-age insurance system, which has been mentioned in many important documents. However, constrained by various factors, China's basic old-age insurance system has not been finalized; the contribution rate stipulated in the basic old-age insurance system is too high, affecting the development of old-age insurance system of other levels. Therefore, many important tasks have to be undertaken to improve a diversified old-age insurance system. We should properly handle the relationship between basic old-age insurance and supplementary old-age insurance, define the functional orientation of the two types of insurance, actively develop occupational annuities, enterprise annuities and commercial old-age insurance, so as to develop a multi-level old-age insurance system in which basic security and supplementary security support and complement each other. We should properly handle the relationship between the government and the market. The government should encourage and often use the market mechanism to develop the supplementary old-age insurance system and further improve the tax policy support of supplementary insurance in order to create a fine environment for the development of a multi-level old-age insurance system.

In light of the objective reality of population aging, and particularly the objective reality of an aging population with too few children, we should establish a basic care system for people of advanced age. We should vigorously develop a home-based community old-age care and service system and provide necessary basic care and services to incapacitated old people by developing social work teams. The method of government purchasing family care service experimented in some regions of Jiangsu merits our attention; regions with fitting conditions may try the old-age care insurance system to better combine basic old-age insurance benefits with old-age care and overcome the lack of care caused by family downsizing. We should establish the social service index system as soon as possible so as to promote the healthy development of old-age care and basic public services.

9.4 The Deepened Reform of Medical Insurance Promotes the Construction of "Healthy China"

Remarkable achievements have been made in the new round of medical care and health system reform implemented since 2009 in China. However, in face of the tremendous pressure on the health system exerted by the aging population, maladjustment still exists in many aspects of the current medical care and health system. The steady and rapid rise of health costs imposes a tremendous burden on national public finances, social insurance funds and residents' income. Leveraging the medical insurance system plays a fundamental guiding role in deepening the reform of the medical care and health system during the period of the thirteenth Five-Year Plan and promoting the construction of a healthy China.

(i) Integrate urban and rural residents' medical insurance policies and gradually implement the policy for retired employees to pay medical insurance premiums

Rural residents and urban residents in most regions of China are covered by the new rural cooperative medical care system and the urban residents' basic medical insurance system respectively. The new rural cooperative medical system is often managed by the health and family planning department, while the urban residents' basic medical insurance is managed by the human resources and social security department. In fact, the two systems are similar in many aspects, such as payers, funding method, reimbursement method, financial balance method, and management method. With the acceleration of urbanization in various regions of China, the current separate participation of urban and rural residents' in insurance and their compartmentalized handling and management will further constrain the orderly movement of rural laborers and the urbanization process. This results in over expensive handling and management costs for local governments and affects the sharing of information about insurance coverage. Against the backdrops of accelerating urbanization and the deepening of the reform of the government's administrative system, we must: accelerate the integration of urban and rural residents' medical insurance policies, handling and management; actively explore the connection and integration of the urban and rural residents' medical insurance policies and urban employees' basic medical insurance system; improve the management efficiency of medical insurance funds; eliminate repeated insurance coverage by systems and promote the free movement of laborers across rural and urban areas and across regions.

In the course of integrating the urban residents' basic medical insurance system with the new rural cooperative medical care system, the medical insurance system covering urban and rural old-age residents should extend to the employees' basic medical insurance system. Currently, urban employees whose payment years have reached the standard defined by the state when they reach statutory retirement age do not have to pay premiums for their basic medical insurance after retirement, while they enjoy basic medical insurance benefits as per state regulations.[5] However, rural residents and urban residents have to go on paying for medical insurance. The difference of this contribution mechanism tends to exert a negative impact on the fairness of the medical insurance system and the sustainability of system fund operations. From 2010 to 2014, the ratio of retired urban employees covered by insurance in the total number of urban employees covered by insurance was respectively 25, 24.9, 25, 25.3 and 25.6%, presenting a gradually increasing trend year by year; however, the ratio of retired urban employees covered by basic medical insurance in the total number of urban employees insurance was respectively 13.7, 13.3, 12.3, 12.2 and 12.1%, presenting a gradually decreasing trend year by year.[6] The two data groups show that with the constant increase of urban retirees, the shares of medical resources that retirees have to occupy in the entire urban employees' medical insurance will also keep increasing. The ratio of old people's medical expenses in their living expenses is far higher than that of middle-aged laborers. Therefore, to study the policy for retired employees to pay medical insurance premiums is not only an internal requirement for the finalization and optimization of medical insurance, but also an important measure for the horizontal fairness among insurants, the safety of the system, and financial sustainability. We may revise the relevant articles in the "Social Insurance Law" and gradually explore the measures for retired employees to pay premiums for basic medical insurance on the basis of pilot projects. During the transition period, special government fiscal subsidies may be stepped up so as to guide individuals' participation in insurance, and resolve the issue of individuals unable to pay premium and

[5]Note: according to the provisions in the "Social Insurance Law of the People's Republic of China", individuals participating in basic medical insurance for employees whose cumulative premium payment period reaches the period stipulated by the State at the time they reach the statutory retirement age will no longer pay basic medical insurance premiums after they retire and may then enjoy basic medical insurance benefits in accordance with the provisions of the State; if cumulative premium payment has not reached the period stipulated by the State, he/she may continue to pay premiums until reaching the period stipulated by the State.

[6]Note: Arranged and calculated on the basis of the data in *China Statistics Yearbook 2011–2014* and the *Statistical Bulletin of the Development of Human Resource and Social Security Services in 2014*.

allow them to participate in the basic medical system by allocating state-owned assets gains as well as employing other methods.

(ii) Improve personal accounts in basic medical insurance and deepen the reform of medical insurance payment method

In the early period after the establishment of the social security system, the personal account system was set up in the basic medical insurance system in China. However, with the passage of time, the functions of the personal medical account system have been gradually adjusted. No personal account have been set up in urban residents' basic medical insurance; since 2008, pilot projects of outpatient social pooling have been carried out in most regions' new rural cooperative medical care system. Currently, personal accounts have been set up only in the initial period urban employees' basic medical insurance system, and a large amount of fund deposit has been accumulated, which, to some extent, constrains patients' afflicted by chronic diseases and serious illnesses in terms of the amount to be reimbursed for outpatient services, and leads to poor use and efficiency of medical insurance funds. The thirteenth Five-Year Plan clearly promotes the improvement of the personal account system, and the gradual inclusion of personal account fund into outpatient service pooling, which will not only improve the reimbursement scope and ratio of insurants who receive outpatient services but also enhance the financial sustainability of medical insurance.

The medical insurance handling institutions of most countries and regions in the world are confronted with the problem of inadequate financial sustainability, with much appeal to the control of medical insurance costs. As the population keeps on aging, this problem has been receiving even more attention from various social circles. In face of the rapid increase of medical costs, the cost control function of medical security should be brought into better play. Traditional medical security is mainly to bring into play the function of compensation (reimbursement) after the administration of medical services, while there is a lack of will to get involved in the reform of medical organization, medical mode and medical cost. Currently, the payment of medical expenses is directly settled by medical insurance handling institutions and medical service provision institutions, and consists in a medical cost post-payment system paid mainly according to items, with cost control limited effect.[7] As the main sources of total medical cost and an organized group purchase mechanism, medical insurance funds should function better as a guide for controlling the excessive increase of medical cost. The post-payment system based on items should be reformed, diversified and compound medical insurance payment methods (such as payment according to persons, types of disease and total pre-payments) should be actively promoted, and the negotiation mechanism for the terms of payment of medical insurance costs should be improved to strengthen the

[7]Note: The post-payment system means that a patient, after the occurrence of expenses, goes to a handling institution for reimbursement or applies for reduction in a medical institution, and the amount of reimbursement or reduction is calculated according to the actual amount incurred.

whole-course supervision and internal constraints of medical service behaviors. We should deepen the reform of the medical service system focusing on the reform of public hospitals and constrain the profit-seeking trend in public hospitals.

(iii) Comprehensively implement the urban and rural residents' serious illness insurance system and develop a diversified medical security system

The serious illness insurance system consists in the development and extension of the combined functions of the new rural cooperative medical care system and the urban residents' medical insurance system. Serious illnesses are one of the important reasons reducing and reverting urban and rural families to poverty. Due to poor production and living environment and low basic public health services, the very low ratio of actual reimbursement of various basic medical insurance systems, and the very limited coverage of the medical assistance system,rural farmers' families and West China's urban and rural families, in particular, are unlikely to be able to resist being impoverished by serious and major diseases. Therefore, there is a very strong realistic need for the construction of a diversified medical security system to address these expensive medical expenses. In August 2015, the State Council issued the "Opinions on Establishing the Urban and Rural Residents' Serious Illness Medical Insurance System", which suggested that a sound serious illness insurance system be established in 2–3 years, and should be closely connected with such systems as medical assistance so as to jointly play the role of basic security, effectively prevent catastrophic medical expenses and significantly improve the fairness of urban and rural residents' medical insurances.[8] Currently, the framework of the serious illness insurance system has been established in most Chinese provinces, but with narrow coverage, small funding scale and limited functions. We should grasp the opportunity to implement the thirteenth Five-Year Plan to further improve the operation mechanism and management mechanism of the serious illness medical insurance system, and better leverage the active role of commercial insurance institutions in providing more management support for the operations of the serious illness insurance system.

The basic medical insurance and serious illness medical insurance system, to some extent, are still within the scope of basic medical security guided by the government. Though the policy-based compensation ratio of basic social medical insurance stands 70% or even higher, yet the actual compensation ratio is only reaches about 50%, which means that the absolute majority of insurants have to bear a large proportion of medical care cost. While improving the current medical insurance system, we should further improve measures such as taxation preference to encourage enterprises to establish supplementary security, support individuals' purchase of supplementary medical insurance and commercial health insurance, create a social atmosphere and legal environment in which commercial insurance

---

[8]General Office of the State Council, "Opinions on Establishing the Urban and Rural Residents' Serious Illness Medical Insurance System", official website of the State Council, at http://www.gov.cn/zhengce/content/2015-08/02/content_10041.htm, accessed on November 4, 2015.

institutions actively underwrite residents' health insurance in an orderly manner, and actively use the advantages of the market in addressing risks to resolve urban and rural residents' risks of being impoverished by illness. The development of commercial medical insurance is not only a useful supplement to basic medical security but can also reduce governmental costs in terms of handling and providing relevant management technologies and experiences. An important task in the period of the thirteenth Five-Year Plan is to improve the management and operation efficiency of the basic medical insurance system and provide better services to people covered by insurance. On one hand, we should further develop grassroots medical insurance handling teams at county and township levels; on the other hand, we may expand the method of government purchase of social services and fully leverage the advantages of commercial insurance institutions with good qualification in medical insurance handling. In recent years, rapid development has been achieved in both state-owned commercial insurance institutions and non-public-owned commercial insurance institutions, which has laid a solid foundation for their participation in the handling of basic social medical insurance. We should further improve the mechanism and method for government purchase of services from commercial insurance institutions to make them play a larger role.

(iv) Deepen the reform of the medical insurance management mechanism and strengthen the management and handling capability of medical insurance

Currently, the five social insurance systems for urban employees are managed in a scattered manner; the internal relationship between basic medical insurance and maternity insurance is artificially cut apart, and further exploration should be made to establish a new system for integrating the two. Maternity insurance benefits include maternity medical expenses and maternity subsidies, etc. By the end of 2014, altogether 170.39 million people were covered by maternity insurance nationwide; and 6.13 million person-times enjoyed maternity insurance benefits that year. Different from urban employees, whose maternity medical expenses have to be compensated through the maternity insurance system, women covered by the new rural cooperative medical system and the urban residents' basic medical insurance system may directly get reimbursement from the medical insurance system. By drawing on the management experience of urban and rural residents' maternity insurance, we should explore a new system combining urban employees' maternity insurance and basic medical insurance during the period of the thirteenth Five-Year Plan. The combination of the two systems may reduce the workload of social insurance handling institutions in terms of the collection of maternity insurance premiums and the supervision of fund revenues and expenditures, reduce the operating cost of handling institutions, improve social insurance handling management, and reduce application costs for urban employees' compensation of maternity medical expenses. Currently, China's maternity insurance funds comprise a big surplus. The combination of the two funds may enhance financial sustainability and improve the equity of urban employees and urban and rural residents in terms of maternity security.

Currently, the urban and rural residents' basic medical insurance system follows the principle of localized management, with a relatively low level of social pooling.

The level of pooling and the size of a region directly decide the amount of reimbursement and the cost of medical expense reimbursement for the hospitalization of insurants. We should explore the gradual raise of the level of medical insurance pooling, gradually transit to prefecture-level (municipal) pooling in places with mature conditions, strengthen the interconnection of information systems, realize IT-based management for the long-distance settlement of medical expenses within a province, and gradually promote the exploration of long-distance medical treatment across provinces; in particular, for retired employees inpatient medical expenses, direct settlement will be gradually adopted for convenient and high-efficient services. The main reform measures are: the basic medical system should be gradually raised to provincial pooling; the medical insurance information management systems of various provinces should be integrated and a national medical insurance information sharing platform should be set up to provide powerful technical guarantee for the direct settlement of long-distance medical expenses across regions. We should strengthen supervision over medical insurance funds, and increase penalties for institutions and personnel who commit any insurance fraud so as to ensure fund security.

9.5 Bring into Better Play the Anti-poverty Function of the Social Relief System

Social assistance is an important part of China's social security system, and plays a critical role in terms of subsistence security for poor people and those subject to any accident. The period of the thirteenth Five-Year Plan is a decisive period for China to complete the process of building a comprehensive moderately well-off society. To channel efforts in poverty alleviation, and help poor people and regions throw off poverty, are strategic objectives defined for the thirteenth Five-Year Plan, while relieving rural poor people from poverty is also the most difficult task in the comprehensive construction of a moderately well-off society. On one hand, we should vigorously find ways to alleviate poverty, accurately support the poor and relieve them from poverty, take measures addressing individual and local needs, and improve the effect of poverty relief. On the other hand, we should implement the subsistence security policy and connect such policy with poverty relief policies for residents without labor capacity, and ensure all poor people are covered to better bring into play the functions of social security, especially that of social assistance systems such as subsistence security.

(i) Do a good job in social assistance for survival, and promote social assistance for development

To secure basic survival is the core objective of traditional social assistance. For a long period of time, social assistance in China consisted in providing subsistence security for urban and rural residents to help them overcome difficulties and maintain subsistence. The function of social assistance in securing subsistence cannot be negated, rather it should be especially stressed and improved at the initial stage of development of social assistance; however, with the improvement of economic and social development and the increasing demand of urban and rural residents, the effect of subsistence assistance is limited, even subject to vicious circles and causing an "assistance trap", which makes it difficult to realize the true objective of social assistance. Therefore, while improving the "subsistence security" function of social assistance, we should also improve its assistance methods and adjust its assistance benefits levels so that the function of "promoting development" comes to be highlighted as it secures subsistence. Personal development will raise income levels, thus realizing a virtuous circle. With the gradual improvement of the social security system, urban and rural residents' living standards keep improving, the absolutely poverty-stricken population has been substantially reduced; however, the problem of relative poverty is becoming more and more serious. Social assistance cannot stop at survival assistance in the traditional sense; the scope and level of social assistance should be gradually improved. To upgrade survival assistance to development assistance is also required in the period of economic transition in China to improve human capital and expand domestic demands. With economic development shifting to a new normal, we should transform the traditional mode of economic growth and drive economic growth by improving human capital and expanding domestic consumption. The investment in human capital in a country should not rely on ordinary education and training alone, but should focus on developing special groups of people including the poor.[9] Against the backdrops of new Chinese economic development norms, we should actively promote investment in human capital and foster the sources of power promoting economic growth. Developing social assistance can help improve the poorer population's human capital, cut down the inter-generational cycle of poverty, and help improve the consumption capacity of poor families, thus expanding domestic demands.

Besides developing traditional survival assistance and improving social assistance benefits, we should attach more importance to employment assistance, education assistance and medical assistance, and thus improve the health conditions and labor capacity of assistance recipients, enhance their human capital, and upgrade their life quality. Development assistance not only involves the upgrading and improvement of the contents of assistance but also the reform of assistance measures. We should improve the past traditional assistance target identification measures, exit mechanism and benefit payment mechanism. In the identification of assistance targets, we should change the passive practices of the past and establish a pro-active identification mechanism to "assist all those that should be assisted in an

[9]Guan Xinping (2014), Towards a More Proactive Social Assistance System: On the Direction of Reform of China's Social Assistance System in the New Situation, *China Public Administration*, 2014 (7), pp. 16–20.

accurate manner". We should not only "assist all those that should be assisted" but also "should withdraw assistance from all those for whom assistance is unnecessary" to prevent assistance dependencies and traps. The assistance benefits should be paid according to demands, instead of being fixed payments. For assistance targets that are marginal and can easily overcome poverty, in particular, we should enable them to actively withdraw from the team of assistance recipients by enhancing the incentive of the social assistance system.

(ii) Promote fund assistance, material assistance and service assistance coordinately and leverage the role of the social assistance system as comprehensive support

Based on different demands of social assistance targets, social assistance includes such items as fund assistance, material assistance and service assistance. With the improvement of the social assistance system and the level of assistance, we should actively promote the development of service assistance. The targets of social assistance are often poor and weak people, such as old people and the disabled, who not only need fund support and material provision but also are in urgent need of services. To promote service assistance on the basis of fund assistance and material assistance is an effective way to improve the effect of social assistance. The development of service assistance can help improve the health conditions and living standards of assistance targets. Poverty is often related to illness and poor health, which lead to a vicious circle. Service assistance can help strengthen disease prevention and treatment for poor people and help the disabled to recover as much as possible of their health and labor capacity. Service assistance can also provide convenience for the life of assistance recipients and improve their living standards. The specific contents and methods of service assistance should be decided according to the recipients' different needs. Social assistance services mainly include diversified and individualized services such as life assistance, psychological counseling, emotional aid, resource connection, ability enhancement and social integration; all of these may be classified into three types: daily care services, ability development services and support and integration services.[10] Due to the special and professional nature of social assistance services, we should train a large amount of social assistance service professionals, improve the professionalism of social assistance services and improve the effect of social assistance services. We should integrate the service resources of social assistance, and vigorously develop social work, volunteer services and community services, so as to provide different people with different types of social assistance services. We may make full use of private social assistance service resources through government purchases. Assistance services may be purchased from social organizations. The mechanism for government purchase of social assistance services should be improved.

[10]Lin Mingang (2015), Reflection on Government Purchase of Social Assistance Services, *Administration Reform*, 2015 (8), pp. 24–27.

(iii) Coordinately consider the life assistance and employment development of targets of subsistence security with labor capacity, and realize the organic connection of social assistance with social insurance, poverty relief and development policies

The coordinated development of life assistance and employment assistance is an important reflection of the coordinated development of survival assistance and development assistance. Social assistance implementation, especially in regards to demand evaluation and method adoption, should fully consider the actual conditions of families and individual recipients, while integrating the two based on the former. The life difficulties and labor capability of assistance recipients should be accurately evaluated. While actively securing the survival needs of poverty-stricken families, various measures should be taken to encourage and constrain assistance recipients with labor capacity to take an active part in work and acquire income and means of subsistence through work. On one hand, such measures can help prevent assistance recipients from becoming assistance-dependent, improve the use efficiency of subsistence security and social assistance resources, reduce the institutional burden, and enhance the equity and efficiency of the social assistance system. On the other hand, these measures can help assistance recipients gain self-respect, self-reliance and self-improvement as well as improve their living standards. We should appropriately classify them in classes such as: no labor capacity and conditions, partial labor capacity and conditions and full labor capacity and conditions; moreover we should adopt a differentiated subsistence security system, and maximize the effect of the subsistence assistance system. As for people with full labor capacity, we should not let them sit back and wait for assistance, but should help them dismiss their dependence on assistance and maintain their subsistence and that of their families through work and employment, and help them get jobs by job introduction, training and education. Even if they fail to get a job, they should fulfill their work obligations through voluntary work or earn their assistance through work. For those with partial labor capacity, we should comprehensively use life assistance and employment assistance to help them work properly. To promote assistance recipients with labor capacity to take an active part in work, we should adjust the current subsistence security system, and should particularly reform the current benefit examination and approval mechanism to enhance benefit grant incentives. The level of subsistence security should be appropriately improved to create conditions for assistance recipients to get employment. The connection between subsistence security benefits and employment income may be appropriately relaxed to improve the incentive for people receiving subsistence security to work.

Social assistance should be reformed and developed on the basis of the overall framework of social security and improvement of people's livelihood, so as to realize the coordinated development of social assistance, social insurance, social welfare and poverty relief, and bring into full play the comprehensive functions of the social security system. Social assistance and other items of social security all play an important role in fighting poverty. Social assistance should focus on poverty governance and poverty reduction. Traditional social assistance mainly consists in post-event assistance and passive assistance, mainly for securing the recipients' subsistence. Social assistance focuses on the prevention of poverty. Various measures should be taken for fighting poverty, with equal attention being given to prevention and governance. While securing the subsistence of poor families, we should actively support families receiving assistance to participate in social insurance such as old-age insurance and medical insurance to strengthen the defense against poverty. The continuous progress of social assistance entails its shift from subsistence-oriented to development-oriented for people's higher enthusiasm and proactivity in it. The government should introduce proper institutional and policy support to facilitate social insurance participation for able-bodied social assistance recipients through employment or by fiscal subsidies so that they can better overcome poverty and improve their life quality.

Social assistance and poverty relief are direct measures fighting poverty, and the coordinated development of the two can help improve their effectiveness. With regard to the connection of subsistence security and poverty relief, in particular, we should follow the idea of accurate security and realize accurate assistance and poverty relief. We should follow the idea of development-based assistance and development-based poverty relief and improve the "hematopoietic" role of subsistence security and poverty relief. In the course of poverty relief, we should actively strengthen occupational skills training for poor people with labor capacity, enhance the labor skills and employment competitiveness of assistance recipients, and fully tap in the human capital and labor capacity of targets of subsistence security to relieve poor people from poverty.

(iv) Explore the regional coordinated development mechanism for the social assistance system and help diversified recipients of social assistance overcome poverty

For a long period of time, China's social assistance system has had a low level of coordination and been subject to such problems as urban and rural segmentation and regional segmentation, which, to some extent, impedes population mobility, goes against the equitable development of social assistance, and is liable to widen urban and rural gap and regional gap with regard to social assistance. The need for coordinated urban and rural development has become a consensus for the future development of the social security system in China, and progress has been made in the coordinated urban and rural development of social assistance. With the deepening of the reform of the household registry system, in particular, the coordinated urban and rural development of social assistance will be further promoted. In contrast, the regional segmentation and regional gap of social assistance have not received adequate attention, which is not ideal for population cross-regional migration and integrated regional development. Therefore, while actively promoting the coordinated urban and rural development of social assistance, we should also promote the regional coordinated development of social assistance to cope with population migration and promote social equity. We should stick to the idea of coordinated and shared development, and improve the practice of localized management, so as to meet the social assistance needs of relevant local people. We suggest that a national uniform social assistance system and basically uniform classified security standards be established with provinces as units according to the actual conditions of income and living expenditures as well as the assistance needs of urban and rural residents; moreover, we suggest that the implementation mechanism and actions of social assistance be regulated, a social assistance standard system be established, and the diversified social assistance needs of various groups of people in a region be secured in line with the principle of equity. We should establish a regional pooling and coordination mechanism for social assistance and strengthen inter-regional cooperation on social assistance, so as to ensure the seamless full coverage of social assistance when population mobility is realized, to promote the social assistance targets within a region to acquire roughly equal security benefits, and enhance the unity and equity of social assistance. The practice of enjoying social assistance benefits based on household registry should be reformed; the household registry factor should be weakened, a residents' residence permit system should be established, and actual living and residential needs should be taken as important basis for enjoying social assistance benefits.

(v) The basic role of different social assistance entities such as government, market and society should be well leveraged

The government is always the most important entity of responsibility for social assistance. The leading role of the government in social assistance is mainly reflected in coordinated planning, system development, fiscal investment, talent training, organization and coordination. We should establish a uniform and sound social assistance system under the leadership of the government, while actively promoting the legislation of social assistance, stepping up the training of professionals for social assistance management and services, and coordinating the relief efforts of different assistance entities. Special stress should be laid on the government's responsibility for social assistance fiscal expenditures, the power of office and the financial power should be reasonably divided, and a social assistance responsibility sharing system between the central government and local governments should be established to allow governments at different levels to better play their respective role in the social assistance system. We should define the responsibility of provincial governments for fiscal expenditures, establish an inter-regional coordination mechanism for local governments, and prevent expenditure loopholes and repeated expenditures. We should further strengthen the responsibility of the central government for social assistance expenditures, establish and improve a scientific central fiscal transfer expenditure mechanism, and integrate the use of various types of social assistance funds. The government's leading role does not mean that the government should take care of everything; we should actively cultivate market and social resources and realize social assistance through government service purchases. Social assistance should not entirely depend on the state and the government, but the market mechanism and social resources should be made full use of in terms of resource collection and service purchase. The "Interim Measures on Social Assistance" have clearly provided that the state should encourage social forces such as employers and individuals to participate in social assistance by donation, establishing sponsorship projects, creating service organizations and providing volunteer services. In the future, we should vigorously cultivate private resources for social assistance, strengthen the "socialization" of social assistance, professionalize social assistance and thereby realize a "strong government" and "strong society" in terms of social assistance. In light of international experiences, the gradual transition from state responsibility to "state + market" responsibility and "state + market + society" responsibility is an important trend in the social welfare reform of developed countries.[11] In the future development of social assistance in China, while stressing the leading role and basic responsibility of the government, we should establish a responsibility sharing mechanism, actively employ market and social forces, and fully mobilize individuals' initiative.[12]

[11]Han Keqing (2015), The Reform and Development of China's Social Assistance System, *Teaching and Research*, 2015 (2), 29–35.

[12]This article was published in *The Journal of Liaoning University*, 2016 (1).

Postscript

This book is a collection of special topic articles arranged upon the invitation of Ms. Song Yuehua of the Social Sciences Academic Press. Due to press limitations, this collection only includes ten articles, most of which detail the representative results of my researches, as well as record my reflections and main viewpoints in the field of social security and medical security. It should be noted that all these articles have been published either in newspapers or periodicals. Content or viewpoints have not been alterated in any way, except for the abridgment of some chapters and the adjustment of some titles. As the articles collected in this book span over nearly two decades, the overlap of some content is inevitable. Some articles co-authored in collaboration with my doctoral students are also collected here as required by the theme. Here, I would like to express my sincere gratitude to the Social Sciences Academic Press for its invitation, the newspapers and journals that allowed me to re-publish these articles, and the students who have joined me in the writing of these articles, Long Yuqi, Jiang Cuiping, XuQiang, etc.

January 22, 2016 Wang Yanzhong

Y. Wang, *Social Security in China: On the Possibility of Equitable Distribution*,
Research Series on the Chinese Dream and China's Development Path,
DOI 10.1007/978-981-10-5643-7

References

Chen, Jiagui, and Wang, Yanzhong. 2004. *The Development of Social Security in China: a Report* (2001–2004) [M]. Beijing: Social Sciences Academic Press.

Chen, Jiagui, and Yanzhong Wang. 2007. *The Development of Social Security in China: a Report (2007) [R]*. Beijing: Social Sciences Academic Press.

Chen, Jiagui, and Wang, Yanzhong. 2010. *Green Book on Social Security in China 2010*. Social Sciences Academic Press.

Chen, Jiandong, Yang, Wen and Feng, Ying. 2011. The Income Distribution Effect of Subsistence Security and Individual Income Tax: An Empirical Study. *Reform of the Economic System* (1).

China Development Research Foundation. 2009. *Establish a Development-Based Social Welfare System Shared by All People*. Beijing: China Development Press.

CPC Central Committee. 2015. The Suggestions of the CPC Central Committee on Preparing the Thirteenth Five-Year Plan for National Economic and Social Development

Dong, Yiren, and Tao, Pengde. 2005. Statistical Analysis of Factors Affecting Patients' Satisfaction. *Journal of Applied Statistics and Management* (1).

Fan, Liming, E., Xie, and Yin, Lin. 2009. Farmers' Participation in New Rural Cooperative Medical Care and Analysis of Their Satisfaction. *The Journal of Shandong University* (1).

Feldstein, Paul J. 1998. *Health Care Economics*. Beijing: Economic Science Press.

Gao, Wenshu. 2012. The Effect of Social Security on Regulating Income Distribution Gap: An Empirical Study Based on the Data of a Survey over Residents in Baoji, Shaanxi. *Social Security Studies* (4).

Gao, Linyu. 2011. The Relationship between Social Security and Income Distribution Gap in Developed Countries and Its Implication for China. *Local Public Finance* (7).

Gruat, J.V. 1998. Trends in Social Security System Development, Presentation Paper on Social Security Funds Management at International Seminar, Beijing.

Gu, Cheng, and Li, Junyi. 2004. Expansion of the Gap between Urban and Rural Income Distribution and the Integration of China's Social Security System. *The Journal of the Dongbei University of Finance and Economics* (4).

Guan, Xinping. 2014. Towards a More Proactive Social Assistance System: On the Direction of Reform of China's Social Assistance System in the New Situation. *China Public Administration* (7).

Guo, Yang. 2008. A Study of the Old-age Benefit Gap between Enterprises and Government Departments and Public Institutions in China. *Gansu Social Sciences* (6).

Han, Dawei, Fang Li, and Jiaheng Wu. 2000. *The Old-age Pension System: International Comparison*. Reform Approach and Development Measures: Economic Science Press.

Han, Keqing. 2015. The Social Assistance System in China: Reform and Development. *Teaching and Research* (2).

He, Lixin. 2007. The Effect of Income Distribution by the Reform of the Urban Old-age Insurance System in China. *Economic Research Journal* (3).

Y. Wang, *Social Security in China: On the Possibility of Equitable Distribution*,
Research Series on the Chinese Dream and China's Development Path,
DOI 10.1007/978-981-10-5643-7

He, Ping, Li, Shi and Wang, Yanzhong. 2009. Study of Public Financial Support of the Development-Based Social Welfare System in China. *Public Finance Research* (6).

James, E. 1998. New System for Old-Age Security: Theory, Practice, and Empirical Evidence, Presentation Paper on Social Security Funds Management at International Seminar, Beijing.

Jin, Caihong. 2005. A Study of the Income Redistribution Mechanism of China's Medical Security System. *Reform of Economic System* (6).

Kou, Tiejun, and Zhou, Bo. 2007. International Experience and Implication with Regard to Responsibility Division of Government Expenditure: A Comparative Analysis Based on the Government Expenditure Structure of Developed Countries and Developing Countries. *Public Finance Research* (4).

Li, Lianyou. 2000. *Theory on the Operation of Social Insurance Funds.* Southwestern University of Finance and Economics Press.

Li, Shaoguang. 2000. *The Old-age Pension System and the Capital Market.* China Development Press.

Li, Shi, and Yang, Sui. 2009. The Impact of China's Urban Subsistence Security Policy on Income Distribution and Poverty. *Chinese Journal of Population Science* (5).

Lin, Mingang, 2015. Reflection on Government Purchase of Social Assistance Services. *Administration Reform* (8).

Lin, Yuming. 2007. Government Performance in Social Security and the Evaluation Index System. *The Journal of the South-Central University for Nationalities (Humanities and Social Sciences)* (1).

Liu, Jin'an, Sun, Hui, Xu, Lingzhong, Tang, Cheng, Yang, Zhenhui, Cao, Xiuling, and Song, Xiaofei. 2008. Satisfaction with New Rural Cooperative Medical Care and Analysis of Influencing Factors. *Chinese Journal of Public Health* (2).

Liu, Leshan. 2008. Overseas Fiscal Measures for Regulating Income Gap and Their Implications, paper delivered at the 18th Annual Conference of the Chinese Society of Laws of Economics.

Long, Yuqi. 2013. Theoretical Speculation on the Role of Social Security in Income Redistribution. *Theory Monthly* (11).

Ma, Junsheng et al. 2005. Reflection on Improving China's Medical Insurance Fund Supervision System. *Chinese Health Economics* (10).

Martin, Feldstein. 2009. Reflection on Social Insurance. *Comparative Economic & Social Systems* (4).

Mu, Huaizhong. 2003. *National Wealth and Redistribution of Social Security.* China Labor and Social Security Publishing House.

Peng, Haoran, and Shen, Shuguang. 2007. A Comparative Study of the Income Redistribution Effect of China's Old-age Insurance System before and after the Reform. *Statistical Research* (2).

Qing, Lianbin. 2009. Four Distributions of National Wealth. *People's Forum* (19).

Ren, Ran, and Jin, Feng. 2007. A Study on the Health Service Accessibility and Medical Service Burdens after the Implementation of New Rural Cooperative Medical Care. *China Health Economics* (1).

Shen, Yan. 2012. On the Realization Mechanism of Social Security for Regulating Income Distribution. *The Journal of Hubei Normal College* (5).

Shi, Jianxiang. 2003. *On the Development Mode of Medical Insurance in China.* Beijing: China Price Press.

Statistical Bulletin on the Development of Labor and Social Security Services. 2002–2008. Co-issued by Ministry of Human Resources and Social Security of the People's Republic of China and National Bureau of Statistics of the People's Republic of China

Stiglitz, J.E. 1989. Financial Marker & Development. *Oxford Economic Policy Review* (4).

Tan, Xiaoting, and Zhong, Funing. 2010. The Effect of Income Distribution of Different Modes of Compensation in New Rural Cooperative Medical Care: Empirical Analysis Based on 1500 Rural Households of 30 Counties in Jiangsu and Anhui. *Chinese Rural Economics* (3).

Tang, Xingzhi. 2012. Analysis and Reflection on Public Satisfaction with Community Health Services: Empirical Analysis of Research Data of An Area in Beijing. *Dongyue Tribune* (8).

Tao, Jikun. 2008. Social Security System and Urban-Rural Income Gap. *Lanzhou Academic Journal* (12).

Tao, Jikun. 2010. A Comparative Analysis of the Regulation of Distribution Gap by Social Security System in Western Countries. *Contemporary Economic Research* (9).

The Beijing Cairncross Economic Research Foundation. 2004. China's Social Security Report [R]. Internal document.

The General Office of the State Council. 2015. *The Opinions of the General Office of the State Council on Comprehensively Implementing Serious Disease Insurance for Urban and Rural Residents.*

The Information Office of the State Council of the People's Republic of China. 2004. China's Social Security Status and Policies (White Paper) [R].

The Ministry of Finance and the American Lincoln International Group. 1998. *The Reform of the Social Security System and Its Fund Management: A Global Common Topic*. Modern Publishing House.

The Ministry of Labor and Social Security and the National Bureau of Statistics. 1998–2000. *Statistical Bulletin on the Development of Labor and Social Security Services* (1997, 1998 and 1999).

The Social Insurance Administration of the Ministry of Labor ed. 1997. *China Social Insurance Yearbook 1997*. China Personnel Publishing House.

Wang, Hong et al. 2005. The Benefit Equity of Rural Cooperative Medical Care in China. *Chinese Health Economics* (2).

Wang, Hongman, Gu, Danan, Du, Yuanju, Deng, Xixian, and Wang, Hongyan. 2006. Analysis of Factors Affecting the Participation in, Satisfaction with and Sustainability of New Rural Cooperative Medical Care. *Chinese Journal of Population Science* (5).

Wang, Jiangang. 1999. *Balance of Social Old-age Insurance*. Economic Management Press.

Wang, Maofu, and Xie, Yongcai. 2012. A Study about Negative Regulation of Income Distribution by Social Security. *Studies on Mao Zedong and Deng Xiaoping's Theories* (6).

Wang, Shaoguang. 2003. Public Health in China: Crisis and Turning Point [A], Wu Jinglian, *Comparison Vol. 7* [C]. Beijing: CITIC Publishing House.

Wang, Xiaojun, and Kang, Bowei. 2009. Analysis of the Effect of China's Social Old-age Insurance System on Income Redistribution. *Statistical Research* (11).

Wang, Xiaolu, and Fan, Gang. 2005. The Trend of Income Gap in China and Analysis of Influence Factors. *Economic Research Journal* (10).

Wang, Yanzhong. 2001. A Tentative Discussion of the State's Role in Rural Health Care. *Strategy and Management* (3).

Wang, Yanzhong. 2004. *Labor and Social Security Problems in China*. Economic Management Press.

Wang, Yanzhong. 2012. *The Development of Social Security in China: a Report*. Beijing: Social Sciences Academic Press.

Wang, Yanzhong. 2013. *A Survey of Income Redistribution by Social Security in China*. Social Science Academic Press.

Wang, Yanzhong, and Long, Yuqi. 2010. The Role of People's Livelihood Improvement in Coping with the Financial Crisis, *Studies of the History of the Communist Party of China*. (6).

Wang, Yanzhong, and Long, Yuqi. 2013. Social Security and Income Redistribution: Problems, Experience and Improvement Mechanism. *Academic Research* (4).

Wang, Yanzhong (ed.). 2015. *The Report on the Development of Social Security in China: Social Security during the Period of the Thirteenth Five-Year Plan*. Beijing: Social Sciences Academic Press.

WHO Macroeconomics and Health Committee. 2002. *Macroeconomics and Health*. Beijing: People's Health Press, World Health Organization.

Wolinsky, 1999. *Health Sociology*. Beijing: Social Science Academic Press.

World Bank. 1994. *Averting the Old Crisis: Policies to Protect the Old and Promote Growth.* Washington D.C: Oxford University Press.

World Bank. 1998. *Old-age Security: Reform of China's Old-age Pension System.* China Financial & Economic Publishing House.

Wu, Min and Zhong, Jingjing. 2009. Special Report: State-owned Shares Transferred to Social Insurance Funds [N]. *Beijing News,* June 20, 2009, at http://news.163.com/09/0620/01/5C7CCBGH001124J.html .

Xiang, Ling. 2007. Several Problems Concerning the Redistribution Regression Effect in the Old-age Insurance System. *Fujian Forum* (Humanities and Social Sciences Edition) (1).

Yang, Jun. 2011. Analysis of the Effect of Income Redistribution of Social Pooling Old-age Insurance System. *Social Security Studies* (1).

Yang, Zhenlin, and Wang, Yake. 2007. An Empirical Analysis of the Redistribution Effect of China's Enterprise Old-age Insurance System. *China Soft Science* (4).

Yu, Dezhi. 2005. Analysis of Health Expenditure Growth. *China Health Economics* (3).

Zhao, Man. 1997. *The Analysis of the Structure and Operation of the Social Security System.* China Planning Press.

Zheng, Gongcheng. 2008. *China's Social Security: Reform and Development Strategies.* Beijing: People's Press.

Zheng, Gongcheng. 2010. On Income Distribution and Social Security. *Heilongjiang Social Sciences* (5); Zheng, Gongcheng. 2010. Social Security: Basic Institutional Guarantee for Regulating Income Distribution. *Chinese Cadres Tribune* (6); Zheng, Gongcheng. 2008. *Three Decades of Social Security in China.* Beijing: People's Press.

Zhou, Xuliang, and Shi, Shaobin. 2009. Analysis of Satisfaction with the Reimbursement System of New Rural Cooperative Medical Care. *Collected Essays on Finance and Economics* (6).

Zhu, Qing. 2008. Focus on People's Livelihood: Direction and Approach of the Adjustment of Fiscal Expenditure Structure. *Finance & Trade Economics* (7).

Zou, Xiang. 2012. Improving the Equity of the Old-age Insurance System in China. *China Social Security* (7).